A
TERRIBLE
ANGE

A TERRIBLE ANGER

The 1934
Waterfront
and
General Strikes
in San Francisco

DAVID F. SELVIN

WAYNE STATE UNIVERSITY PRESS   DETROIT

Copyright © 1996 by Wayne State University Press,
Detroit, Michigan 48201. All rights are reserved.
No part of this book may be reproduced without formal permission.
Manufactured in the United States of America.
99 98 97 96   5 4 3 2 1

Library of Congress Cataloging-in-Publication Data

Selvin, David F.
    A terrible anger : the 1934 waterfront and general strikes in San
Francisco / David F. Selvin.
        p.   cm.
    Includes bibliographical references and index.
    ISBN 0-8143-2610-2 (pbk. : alk. paper)
    1. Longshoremen's Strike, San Francisco, Calif., 1934.   2. General
Strike, San Francisco, Calif., 1934.   I. Title.
    HD5325.L62   1934.S35   1996
    331.89′281387164′097946—dc20   96-11397

Designer: Joanne Elkin Kinney

Cover art:

Chapter 1 appeared in a somewhat different version in the *San Francisco Chronicle*,
July 3, 1988. An edited version of Chapter 17 appeared in the *Pacific Historical Review*,
vol. LVIII, no. 3 (August 1989), © 1989 by the Regents of the University of
California. For use of oral histories, grateful acknowledgement is due the Regional
Oral History Office, the Bancroft Library, and the Institute of Industrial Relations,
University of California, Berkeley, and the California Historical Society, San
Francisco; for the use of collected papers, the Bancroft Library, University of
California, Berkeley. The author is indebted to Prof. Robert Cherny, San Francisco
State University, for sharing notes on his research for his biography of Harry Bridges;
and to Prof. Philip P. Mason for his continuing interest and support.

FOR LIZ AND ADAM,
ALEXANDER, AND CARLA,
WITH LOVE

CONTENTS

Introduction   9

1. The Funeral   11
2. Roots of Conflict   20
3. To the Victor . . .   34
4. Fourteen Years of Peace   44
5. Turnaround   53
6. The Big Guns   69
7. Deadlines   77
8. The April 3 Disagreement   83
9. Strike   88
10. The Strike Spreads   98
11. The Third Disagreement   113
12. Ready! Aim!   127
13. Bloody Thursday   141
14. Prologue   154
15. General Strike   166
16. The First Day   182
17. The Second Day (Part 1)   192
18. The Second Day (Part 2)   204

19. The Third Day   212
20. The Fourth Day   221
21. And Then . . .   236
Afterword   241
Notes   246
Bibliography   259
Index   266

Introduction

I WAS THERE, that angry, discordant summer of 1934, not as a participant, but as a young, deeply engaged observer. If I could not claim a first-row seat, my vantage point was a seat on the aisle, close-up. It stemmed largely from my meeting Sam Kagel, a graduate student in economics at the time. He served briefly as acting head of labor statistics for the state of California, then joined Henry P. Melnikow in the Pacific Coast Labor Bureau, which acted as economic counsel—a resource and advocate in negotiations and arbitration—for labor unions. Through Kagel I met and observed in action many of the men who played key roles in the events of the summer of 1934, among them Mike Casey, George Kidwell, and Harry Bridges. I spent a good many Friday nights, too, at the weekly sessions of the San Francisco Labor Council. That connection was especially useful, I am sure, in the last days of June, when Louis Bloch—whose seat in the State building Kagel had briefly filled—started to put together a research staff for the National Longshoremen's Board, only days after its appointment by President Franklin Delano Roosevelt. On July 1, I went to work for the board. As it turned out, the board became so deeply involved in its mediation efforts that it had little use for any staff except a secretary to keep its seeming twenty-four hour calendar straight. But the activities of the board—its public hearings and its endless sessions with union representatives, waterfront employers, shipowners, and

9

government officials amid the shock and anger of Bloody Thursday and the turmoil of the general strike—echoed through its quiet office. On July 31, the day of the return to work, the board began preparations to arbitrate the longshoremen's and, later, the seamen's disputes. By then, it had even less use for a staff.

As a result, early the next morning I found myself in a cubbyhole of an office in the Ferry Building, as an employee of the Pacific Coast Labor Bureau, assigned to interview prospective longshore union witnesses for the upcoming arbitration. I recall exploring with Harry Bridges, Henry Schmidt, "Dutch" Dietrich, and dozens more, over several eighteen-hour days, their experiences on the docks: job opportunities, earnings, hours of work, gang bosses, job rackets, unions, and strikes—the full sweep of the longshoreman's work life. Much of their experiences turned up in the longshoremen's case before the board and, of course, in the voluminous record of the hearings. Later, too, I had a hand in preparing the case that the seamen's unions put before the board.

In the some six decades that have since gone by, the view of the waterfront and general strikes of that summer has been blotted, revised, obscured, transformed, edited, and polished. Years of day-to-day industrial relations have extended and revised, elaborated and refined the meaning and consequences of the strikes. Economic, political, and social developments, in the economy, on the docks, and in the maritime industry itself, have moved in unanticipated directions at unexpected speeds and with unimagined results, putting new and constantly changing pressures on the views of participants, observers, and students of the time and of the generations who followed.

In these pages, I have tried to identify the changes in the views of the strikes, to put aside the ease and certainties of half a century of hindsight and reconstruct them whole and uncluttered. I no longer extend full faith and credit to my memory, except perhaps to recall cautiously the ambience, the mood, and the feel of the time. Instead, I have revisited as much of the available record and commentary as lay within my reach. I have sought to record the impulses that led to organization and conflict, to see those developments in relations to their roots in the labor movement, and to review whole the tactics and strategies, the policies and programs that undergirded the real and enduring significance of the strikes.

1.

THE FUNERAL

TWO BLACK-DRAPED TRUCKS, each bearing a coffin, headed the funeral procession on July 9, 1934, as it emerged from Steuart Street and turned west on Market Street: the scrape and shuffle of feet, the muffled dirge of a band, the thousands marching in an almost palpable silence, more thousands lining the sidewalks. Above the clamor of that strike-turbulent summer of 1934, the silence was a wrenching cry of pain and anger.

The year 1934 was marked across the country with protest against the suffering, the degradation, and the oppression of the Great Depression. Millions of workers clutched at hopes raised by Franklin Delano Roosevelt's New Deal. Some million and a half workers gave up nineteen million days of work in the nationwide industrial battle. Almost half of the disputes were fought mainly over the simple right to organize and bargain collectively. For two months, in San Francisco and along the entire Pacific Coast, the longshoremen and the seamen had been locked in one struggle in this nationwide battle.[1]

And now, this somber procession bore the coffins of two men killed in a battle with police on July 5—the day imprinted as Bloody Thursday in the legends of San Francisco's storied waterfront. The first truck, escorted by a veterans' honor guard, carried the flag-draped casket of Howard S. Sperry, a longshoreman; the second, decorated by a simple spray of flowers, the casket of Nick Counde-

11

rakis, a cook, known in the Communist Party as Nick Bordoise. They were followed by trucks banked high with flowers, a string of funeral cars carrying the mourning families, the lone band droning a death march, and a dozen men carrying a giant American flag.

Slowly the procession flowed into Market Street. A company of uniformed veterans, under an American flag and the banner of the International Longshoremen's Association, wore brassards on the sleeves of their ill-fitting World War I uniforms which identified them as ILA War Vets. The strike committee and its controversial chairman, the thin, sharp-faced Harry Bridges, walked in the procession's front ranks. Striking longshoremen, marched eight abreast, in black Frisco jeans, hickory shirts, white caps. Striking deckhands, firemen and other "black gang" workers out of the engine rooms, stewards, mates, and engineers from the hundreds of ships lying idle in the Bay were represented, along with uptown union members.

On they came, a dark surge of humanity, under a cloudless blue sky. Their dark clothes and grim silence were in stark contrast to the bright flags and pennants under which the brass bands and black uniforms, shining swords and white plumes of the Knights of Pythias had paraded the day before. On they came, in an unending stream, rank after roughly formed rank: strikers, sympathizers, supporters, the Women's Auxiliary of the ILA, and wives and children.

No one agreed on the number. Ten thousand, fifteen thousand, were frequently used counts. "At least 15,000," said the *San Francisco Chronicle*, but still "uncountable." "Fifty thousand is more like the correct figure," remembered Henry Schmidt, a longshoreman and a strike leader.[2] Whatever the number, more thousands rounded the Steuart Street corner, making their way between silent ranks of onlookers lining the sidewalks on Market Street for blocks. No talk. No strike signs. No banners. No police.

The strikers pointedly had asked to police their own procession. His customary antagonism subdued for the moment, Chief of Police William J. Quinn acquiesced. Before the strike, waterfront workers and cops had enjoyed a camaraderie of the streets. They were often relatives, neighbors, friends, and schoolmates. Now, after two months of conflict, whatever remained of that camaraderie had been shattered in the bloody violence of two July days. Now the strikers wanted nothing of the police except to be allowed to bury their dead in their own way. Chief Quinn laid down two conditions: no "Communist" contingents and no signs or banners that might inflame spectators and lead to conflict. Police worked unseen in adjoining streets to divert traffic from Market Street. The longshoremen's own marshals, wearing blue armbands, quietly and effectively guided the procession. An effort to peddle the Communist publication, the *Western Worker* (it published the official ILA daily strike bulletin), was quickly squelched; so, too, was a political candidate handing out campaign literature. Out of sight, along the docks on the Embarcadero, National Guardsmen, who had occupied the waterfront after the stunning violence of Bloody Thursday, quietly patrolled their posts.

A mile or more in length, the solemn cortege made its way to a mortuary at 17th and Valencia Streets. From there, Sperry was buried as a war veteran in the National Cemetery at the Presidio; Bordoise was buried at Cypress Lawn in a "Red funeral" with officials of the local Communist Party presiding.

Sperry and Bordoise had been killed on July 5 in a confrontation of police and strikers at the intersection of Steuart and Mission Streets, just shouting distance from the ILA's strike headquarters. The clash exploded out of the determined efforts of the Industrial Association of San Francisco—the employers' anti-union, open-shop high command—to open the strikebound port and break the strike by naked force. In its second day, the violent conflict raged all morning, up and down the hills and streets fronting the Embarcadero. It was an uneven battle, angry and bloody—riot guns, tear gas, and revolvers in the hands of the organized and disciplined forces of the law against the bricks and rocks and fists of disorganized and weaponless protesters. The fighting paused for the lunch hour, then, almost as if on signal, promptly resumed.

In mid-afternoon, police pushed the strikers back from the Embarcadero, away from the strikebreaking trucks operating from Pier 38, compressing them into a dense knot near the intersection of Mission and Steuart. Like a sword cleaving a Gordian knot, a car penetrated the intersection. A man, wearing a dark gray suit, black felt hat, and shell-rimmed glasses, got out of the car. He opened fire toward the northwest corner, then the northeast and south-east—like a man shooting birds, an observer remembered. Two men dropped: Howard Sperry and Charles Olsen. A third—Nick Bordoise—was also hit, but he managed somehow to drag himself from the scene; he was found dying a block away in front of 124 Spear Street. Olsen, listed for a time as dead or dying, disappeared but turned up some weeks later to testify at the coroner's inquest.

The police report called it a "general riot." Two inspectors, the police report said, found themselves surrounded by a mob, shouting "kill them!" Strikers showered the officers with rocks and bricks and threatened to overturn their car. "Feeling that their lives were in danger, the officers fired two shots from a shotgun and several shots from their revolvers at the men who were attempting to over-turn the car," the report said. "The two men who were struck with the bullets from the inspectors' guns later died." Strike leader Harry Bridges told the coroner's inquest that, emerging from the strike kitchen a block away, he had seen no bricks being thrown until after the shots were fired. A second witness saw no bricks thrown, either. He testified that, in response to threats to overturn the car, the officer had shouted, "If any of you sons-of-bitches want to start something, come on."[3]

Olsen testified that he had been talking to Sperry when a po-liceman started shooting at the crowd across the street. "I started to run and he must have turned the gun our way. Sperry went down. Then something hit me. I fell and remember trying to crawl away," said Olsen. Sperry had finished his duty at the strike kitchen and was headed for ILA headquarters to have his duty card punched. Bordoise, a member of the uptown Cooks' Union, Local 44, recu-perating from an appendicitis operation, had also just finished a voluntary shift in the strike relief kitchen and was apparently headed toward his apartment on Fifth Street. Said another witness: A brick hit the policeman in the leg and he fired without raising the shotgun from his hip. "Two men went down. One of them lay still. The other tried to crawl away. He was lying in a pool of blood."[4]

That afternoon steel-helmeted National Guardsmen deployed, rifles bayoneted and machines guns emplaced, across the full length of the city's docks. Strikers marked the spot where the men fell with a chalked square on the sidewalk, surrounded by flowers. In it they printed: "2 ILA men killed—shot in the back" and on two borders: "Police murder." Police scattered the crowd, scuffed out the inscription, and kicked the bouquets into the gutter. When they left, the strikers restored the memorial. Mayor Angelo Rossi gave orders to have it removed within twenty-four hours. ILA members, however, renewed their guard over the restored memorial. They asked passers-by to move on. "If we get a crowd here the cops will tear it up again," they said.[5]

The naked violence stunned the city, though almost everyone— the mayor, the employers, and the pickets on the docks—had understood its inevitability. The funeral left people astounded. Rewrite men in the newspapers' city rooms struggled to match words to the spectacle. Observers and participants alike strove to understand the emotions generated in and by that strange and awesome procession.

Propaganda, the employers said; a profound upheaval of protest, others said—against the shootings, police violence, and employer obstinacy; a stirring demonstration, some said, of union strength and confidence in the righteousness of the strikers' cause.

"A stupendous and reverent procession," said the *San Francisco Chronicle*'s Royce Brier. "While the entire city gasped in amazement yesterday these two men . . . were given the most amazing funeral San Francisco has ever seen. . . . Here they came as far as you could see in a silent, orderly line of march, a mass demonstration of protest which transcended anything of the like San Francisco has ever seen. . . . a mighty show of strength that amazed the citizens who packed the sidewalks and pressed out into the street."[6]

The *Labor Clarion*, the San Francisco Labor Council's newspaper, said the public and press "universally" agreed the spectacle was "the most striking and impressive funeral procession ever seen in San Francisco." The crowds that had lined the streets hours before the procession "were immediately awed into silence . . . and amazement was written upon faces as the magnitude of the demonstration of respect dawned upon them."[7] A summer minister at Stanford, George P. Hedley, who had spent more than a week on the waterfront, had witnessed the violent clashes that accompanied the opening of the port. The funeral procession, he reported to a church audience, "contributed to a surprising shift in the city's attitude. The newspaper accounts of the funeral were much more adequate than had been those of the killings. . . . Not to be ignored, however, is the moral influence upon the city's population of that strange, silent march—an influence which continues potent, and with which the employers and authorities must reckon far more largely than hitherto seems to have been their disposition."[8]

Paul Eliel was at the time a top-ranking staff member of the Industrial Association, the employers' premier anti-union force and, at that moment, the shipowners' strikebreaking agency. In his detailed account of that summer's strikes, he called the funeral "the most theatrically ominous and significant event in the history of the entire longshore and general strike." He insisted—with only partial accuracy—that it was largely the creation of the strike leaders—"a brilliant and theatric piece of propaganda." It was not the first time, or the last, that the employers (whose views were effectively mirrored in Eliel's account) refused to credit the simpler, and less calculated, more basic responses of the strikers. His appraisal, too, ignored the enormous content of sheer emotion—anger, protest, sympathy—that welled up in that march, in its numbers and its awesome silence. Nevertheless, he grasped the stunning impact of what he called "one of the strangest and most dramatic spectacles that had ever moved along Market Street."

> Its dramatic qualities moved the entire community without regard to individual points of view as to the justice and righteousness of the strikers' cause. It created a temporary but tremendous wave of sympathy for the workers. . . . It provided the impetus that made events which followed as inevitable as though the human beings involved in the subsequent drama had been moved by vast physical forces over which they had no control. As the last marcher broke ranks, the certainty of a general strike, which up to this time had appeared to many to be the visionary dream of a small group of the most radical workers, became for the first time a practical and realizable objective.[9]

It was as if, for the first time, the people of the city had come face to face with the strikers—the "radicals and Communists," who the newspapers, heads of state and local government, and employers had warned, were fomenting a revolution. It was as if, for the first time, the people of the city saw them, literally saw them, not as bloody-minded, bomb-throwing revolutionaries but as ordinary, everyday workers, protesting exploitation, seeking redress of their grievances.

A week later, the general strike was a reality. By that astonishing day, the strike was no longer a surprise but its dimensions as well as its substance, especially in the light of the newspapers' doomsday predictions, amazed the watching Western world. Workers by the thousands, in San Francisco and the East Bay, union and non-union, left their jobs. Hundreds of businesses, factories, and warehouses closed, many when their employees failed to show up, some out of sympathy, some from uncertainty and fear. Public services halted, then slowly, piecemeal, resumed. The newspapers had warned of hunger and riot but there was neither. By the end of the fourth day, it was over.

But the general strike opened the way, finally, after eighty-two bitter days, to end the longshoremen's and the maritime workers' strikes. They ended under an agreement to arbitrate the issues in dispute; the resulting changes encompassed more than the revised wage scales and changed working conditions handed down by the arbiters. The real settlement, as it turned out, produced radical, fundamental, and permanent changes in the economic relations between employer and employee in the then-massive and powerful Pacific Coast maritime industry. The settlement raised the curtain on a vigorous and aggressive drive by longshoremen and seamen to take charge of their jobs. The movement went beyond the black-and-white of new contracts to exert decisive control over the distribution of jobs, the pace of the work, the conditions on the job, safety—the very job control that employers had exercised unilaterally, without consultation or conscience. The settlement also produced a long-desired but short-lived coastwide federation of maritime workers.

To these tasks, longshoremen and seamen brought the class-consciousness, newly tempered in eighty-two days of strike, that, so many times over the better part of the preceding century, had brought them together in their own unions and in waterfront alliance. To serve these ends, they enlisted job action, quickie strikes, and respect for the other guys' picket lines—born-again tactics of militant unionists of another time, notably the Industrial Workers of the World. Initially they stripped the Wobblies' action at the "point of production" of its political trimmings, but before the "syndicalist mood" ran its course, the maritime workers added their own radical political concerns. This was what historian Bruce Nelson labeled a " 'Pentecostal' era of insurgent unionism and expanding consciousness" on West Coast docks and ships. And this was the "rise" in what historian Charles P. Larrowe called, in his biography of Harry Bridges, *The Rise and Fall of Radical Labor*.[10]

The sheer energy of the maritime unions' militancy helped powerfully to inspire thousands of workers in nearly every kind of industry and business to make no less sweeping changes on their own jobs and in their relations with their employers, not only in the San Francisco Bay area and in the port cities of the Pacific Coast, but also across the land.

With astonishing vigor, workers grasped the hope and, increasingly, the reality of a new day. They left behind the dilapidated, impoverished state to which the 1920s and the Great Depression had brought them and acted from a new awareness of common grievances and common purpose, a newly recognized class identity. They reached toward a revived and revised pattern of industrial relations that stretched across the land, serving major sectors of the nation's economy until it was frustrated and nearly dismantled half a century later under the administrations of Ronald Reagan. Over that half-century, millions of workers won new economic status. They powered the astonishing wave of labor organization and collective bargaining in the mid-1930s that brought down the high citadels of anti-unionism. In countless ways, workers responded vigorously to the hope, the encouragement, and the dream of dignity and self-worth—to the promise of ending dictatorship in the workplace and the job market and of achieving equality at the bargaining table—to win a just place in the American society.

The West Coast longshoremen's and maritime strikes and the dramatic San Francisco general strike were plainly not alone, were not even among the largest, of the bitterly fought industrial disputes in this decade of conflict, but they provided a stunning and, had we been able to read it, a revealing prologue to the battle. They became increasingly significant and enduring milestones on the road American workers traveled.

2.

ROOTS OF CONFLICT

THE CONFLICT DATED almost from San Francisco's flush and fabled beginnings. "A lot of stevedores and longshore sailors struck for wages . . . raising the banner of '$6.00 a day' and paraded the streets during the morning," the *Alta California* reported on May 26, 1851. But the Gold Rush had waned and San Francisco was facing hard times; its labor supply, for the moment, was in surplus. Two years later, with business activity on the rise, dock workers again hoisted the banner of $6 a day, a nine-hour day, and $1 an hour overtime. Some four hundred men paraded the length of the waterfront, recruiting the support of their fellow longshoremen. By afternoon, with the strike in full sway, the employers yielded.[1]

On the heels of their successful strike, the skilled men who rigged the gear and stowed the cargo for sailing ships organized the Riggers' and Stevedores' Association. That summer, too, hundreds of other San Francisco workers organized (or reorganized) unions of their own.

Unionism had arrived in San Francisco hard on the heels of the forty-niners—one historian suggested that workers might have met en route and agreed to organize. Some of the early arrivals carried the idea in their baggage, certainly, but it seems more likely that they united simply to deal more effectively with grievances they shared: living costs inordinately inflated by Gold Rush shortages, which overwhelmed constantly lagging wages. These elemental

20

pressures effectively bound the burgeoning city's work force—lawyers and preachers, school teachers and farmers, frustrated gold-hunters and countless others—in a kind of elementary class-consciousness and a crudely cohesive union movement.

Down the years, the city's unions and, no less, the Riggers' and Stevedores' Association, fought against the inexorable deflation of Gold Rush-inflated wages, then to raise their living standards. They confronted overloaded labor markets, iron-fisted shipowners, and open-shop alliances that linked employers, bankers, merchants, and industrialists in a vigorous and formidable anti-union front.[2] Over some eighty years, workers and employers alike raised the issues, created the alliances, and developed the tactics and strategies that were born again, almost as if newly discovered, in the heat of the battle in the summer of 1934.

Long before the plane, the truck, or the train, ships moved people and things. Nations were founded and cities built where seas or rivers linked them to the known world. Overseas or across the bay, up a nearby river or to a distant coast, ships transported the labor and materials on which the world depended—people, necessities and luxuries, raw materials, and finished products. Shipowners commanded a strategic and powerful place in the nation's economy.

Astride this flow of commerce, stood the longshoremen on the docks, flanked by the seamen on the ships. They loaded and un-loaded the cargo and sailed the ships; they linked shipper and recipient, origin and destination into the flow of commerce. But the interests of the longshoremen and the seamen did not always or necessarily coincide with those of the shipowners. The shipowner provided the job. He decided how often, how long, when, and where the men would work. He chose the men for the job, set the wage, fixed the pace, and laid down the conditions. The men could, and often did, dispute any or all of these vital decisions. In a free labor market, of course, the longshoreman or seaman was free to accept the shipowner's offer or leave it; in practical terms, standing alone, without resources, living on the edge of subsistence, the longshoreman or seaman was powerless to resist. Common experience and common grievances forged strong class ties among the workers. They plainly learned early—or grasped intuitively—that only by joining with their fellows on the job could they achieve any substantial voice in these vital decisions.

When San Francisco unions in the mid-1860s paraded to celebrate winning the eight-hour day, the Riggers were prominent marchers, but the celebration was premature. A sharp depression and tough employers wiped out their gains and undermined union organization. In the remaining years of the century, the struggling frontier economy pressed down on workers' wages. The new transcontinental railroad opened the San Francisco market to the lower-wage competition of midwestern, eastern, and foreign producers. An unending flow of immigrants, foreign-born and domestic, intensified the competition for jobs and made stable union organizations difficult to achieve. Employers, singly and in alliance, vigorously combated workers' attempts to organize unions and resisted their efforts to improve their conditions.

The impulse to organize persisted—in defense against wage cuts and in pursuit of improvement. The Riggers tried to fight off job competition by demanding high initiation fees and restricting membership. Longshore lumberhandlers, shunned by the more skilled riggers, formed their own union. The sailors organized the Coast Seamen's Union, which soon became the Sailors' Union of the Pacific. Marine firemen united. Steamship stevedores formed a third union of longshore workers. The struggling unions sought to strengthen their hands through alliances—the Council of Wharf and Wave Unions and the City Front Labor Council were among short-lived but persistently recurring efforts. Employers, too, found advantages in organization. In many industries and often citywide, employers joined forces, not to deal with unions, but to evade or destroy them.

As the nineteenth century ended, returning prosperity renewed the growth of the union movement. The three longshore unions joined the International Longshoremen's Association (ILA), organized in 1892 and chartered by the American Federation of Labor in 1896. In 1901, capping a half century of conflict, the ILA joined the city's teamsters in fighting off a major attack by a new, well-heeled, and secretive Employers' Association of San Francisco. It was—until 1934—the most decisive test of the city's union movement. It put in place union tradition and union leadership that figured prominently in the conflict of 1934.

Michael Casey, who helped to organize the teamsters' union in 1900 and served as its leader for more than a third of a century, often claimed that the battle in 1901 was provoked by a teamsters' picnic. Henry P. Melnikow, a longtime associate and later economic counsel for the longshoremen in their 1934 arbitration, remembered Casey saying that the city's business came to a virtual standstill when the teamsters took a day off for a union picnic. "This so shocked the Chamber of Commerce and the powers that be in the economic world," Melnikow recalled Casey saying, "that they determined that this was a dangerous thing and that the teamsters' union ought to be destroyed."[3]

The opportunity developed from a dispute over a non-union firm hired to handle the luggage for an Epworth League convention. Employers fired the union men who refused to work the "hot" convention luggage. The union retaliated with a citywide strike. It quickly boiled up into an angry, violent battle.

The draymen under the whip of the Employers' Association recruited strikebreakers from every possible source: farm hands from the valleys, black workers, college students, and discharged Army teamsters just back from the Philippines. Mayor James D. Phelan assigned extra police to ride guard on the wagons, guide the inexperienced drivers up and down the city's hills, even help handle the freight. Strikers attacked the scabs; police attacked the strikers. Violence rode the city's streets.

Union leaders were convinced that the real target of new employers was not the teamsters alone, but the city's unions as well. Talk welled up of a general walkout to back the teamsters, but the city's union leadership turned instead to the City Front Federation, made up of the older, more experienced—and richer—dockside and seafaring unions. It turned out its 13,000 members in a sympathy strike. "There is no way of having peace except by fighting for it," said Andrew Furuseth, secretary of the Sailors' Union of the Pacific and chairman of the strike committee.

The employers turned aside every petition for peace or even for negotiations. It refused to deal with representatives or members of the unions, though it claimed to respect workers' right to organize. "Organize what?" asked Casey. "A smoker?" Complaints of police brutality were rejected. "If they don't want to be clubbed, let them go back to work," the mayor reportedly (though probably inaccurately) told a union spokesman.

On October 2, after some eleven weeks of stalemate, Governor Henry T. Gage moved into the dispute. Apparently threatening to impose martial law on both employers and unions—nobody said it publicly—he forced an end to the strike. Details were never published. To the teamsters, though, survival was victory; to the employers, the union's survival was clearly defeat.

Teamsters returned to work alongside scabs, though most of the strikebreakers disappeared from the drays within weeks. For a time, the union lost its closed shop. The other unions were badly mauled. From the turmoil and the resentment, the newly formed, largely union-based Union Labor Party captured the mayoralty and, soon after, complete control of city government. In the aftermath, too, came an upsurge of union organization that swept across the city and in a short time established San Francisco's reputation as a "union town." The Employers' Association disbanded soon after the strike ended.[4]

At 6:00 A.M., June 1, 1916, some 10,000 longshoremen up and down the Pacific Coast struck to enforce the new wage scale and working conditions established by the recently concluded convention of the ILA's Pacific Coast District. If employers resisted the demands, put up a fight, or sought a local settlement or local negotiations, the port unions were instructed to refer them to the district executive board. It alone was empowered to settle the strike.

This, the first coastwide strike of longshoremen, had been building almost from the turn of the century. Unionism had come early to the other Pacific Coast ports: Longshoremen in Portland formed a "Protective Union" in 1868. In the 1880s, Tacoma longshoremen organized a cooperative in an effort to restrict the labor force and limit the competition for jobs. In the last years of the old century, San Pedro began developing a spacious inner harbor and, soon after, longshoremen in San Pedro organized a union. In 1901 Seattle longshoremen joined the ILA. Local unions in the dozen or more ports in Oregon and Washington in 1908 formed the Longshoremen's Union of the Pacific in an unsuccessful effort to rescue a desperate strike. In 1909, recuperating from its disastrous loss, the coastwide union became District 38 of the ILA, with a sweeping grant of autonomy that played a key role in the strike twenty-five years later. Of the twenty-six unions on the coast, only the Riggers' and Stevedores' in San Francisco held out. Finally, in 1914, it, too, affiliated.

That year, too, a small group of shipmasters and boss stevedores moved to unite. C. W. Cook, Pacific Coast manager for the American-Hawaiian Steamship Company, was a moving spirit in forming the Waterfront Employers Union (WEU), along with "Old Captain [William] Matson," Captain Robert Dollar, R. P. Schwerin of the "old Pacific Mail," remembered Thomas G. Plant, who headed the WEU in the 1934 strike. Most of its thirteen members "were sole owners of their businesses, and they had come up from the beginnings to their positions of wealth and eminence through their own efforts," Plant recalled. Plant insisted that the WEU dealt only with longshore labor relations; it was never authorized to deal—nor did it ever—with other maritime workers.[5] Plant returned repeatedly in 1934 to that careful distinction, a major strongpoint in the shipowners' defenses.

Attention in the 1916 strike quickly focused on San Francisco, where a major part of coast shipping made its headquarters. Decisions made there were quickly echoed in the other ports. Longshore employers charged the strike was a clear violation of the Riggers' contract. Sixty days' notice was required; the union had given just two weeks. The nation's first Secretary of Labor, William B. Wilson (a former official of the United Mine Workers), scolded the longshoremen, labeling their walkout a deliberate violation. The longshoremen's allies in the Waterfront Workers Federation, a renewal of the City Front Federation of 1901, already suspected the

Riggers' union was strongly influenced by the radical program of the Industrial Workers of the World (Wobblies). Now, its repudiation of its contract gave the federation reason to back away. The Teamsters' Union offered no help. The WEU denied any intent to impose an open shop. Pending further negotiations, it offered to return the men to work under the wage scale they had demanded; with a final settlement it would discharge all strikebreakers. The Riggers called off their strike and returned to work June 9.

The strikebreakers, however, remained over the ILA's vigorous objections. Strikebreakers were beaten and strikers slugged; two union men were shot. The ILA warned it would renew the strike unless strikebreakers were immediately removed. The employers refused. On June 22, the Bay Area longshoremen walked out for the second time and on the same day, the directors of the San Francisco Chamber of Commerce laid down their own ultimatum: it would commit its resources and influence to maintain the open shop and to defeat any effort to enforce a closed union shop.

Labor called it a "declaration of war." The chamber moved promptly to the attack. On July 5 it asked then Mayor James Rolph to put five hundred policemen on the waterfront to protect the movement of goods. The mayor refused; instead, he ordered police to intensify its search of strikebreakers for concealed weapons. Chamber President Frederick J. Koster responded by calling a meeting of some two thousand of the city's businessmen. He warned them: unless they were "in the frame of mind" to do their "full duty," they would "best quietly and promptly leave." He called on them to provide funds and authority to a committee of five—the Law and Order Committee, chaired by Koster—to open the waterfront to an unimpeded flow of goods and take action against "any other intolerable harassments of local business." Koster was reinforced by speakers from the Bank of California and Southern Pacific, and by Captain Robert Dollar. In his experience, Captain Dollar said, "quietness had been secured in a few days when union men went to the hospital in ambulances. . . . If a peaceful working man is beaten up by strikers, then beat up two strikers in turn."[6] Within minutes, the meeting pledged $200,000 to the newly created committee; within a week, the committee reported it had raised more than $600,000. It acquired the support of the city's leading business firms, among them Standard Oil of California, Pacific Gas & Electric Co., London Paris National Bank, and Crocker National Bank. The Law and Order Committee set a course that led to the Industrial Association, keeper of the city's deep-rooted open shop tradition and principal strikebreaker in the strikes of 1934.

Days after that fateful session, the Waterfront Employers' Union put its affairs in the hands of the Law and Order Committee. At almost the same time, though, the employers proposed a return to work—under pre-strike conditions—while negotiations continued. On July 17, 1916, the Riggers accepted.

The lumber handlers who had been out since June 1 remained on strike but their strike faded. It ended formally November 22. The steamboatmen's strike, which had also been launched June 1, was broken. Along the coast, the unity of June 1 was in shambles. San Pedro longshoremen returned to work in mid-July pending negotiation of a compromise wage scale as of August 1. Parity between ship and dock workers—"that, of course, could not be conceded," an employer said—was put off until another time. Seattle and Tacoma rejected the return-to-work formula. Except at one dock, the union in Tacoma was broken. In Portland, the Chamber of Commerce launched a drive for a state law making the open shop mandatory. The longshoremen returned to work July 22 under pre-strike conditions.[7]

On July 22, five days after the longshoremen returned to work in San Francisco, a thinly disguised front for the Chamber of Commerce staged a Preparedness Day parade, ostensibly in support of efforts to gird the national defense in the face of European war. Labor held back, convinced that it was, at best, a flag-wrapped demonstration in the chamber's vendetta against the unions. At 2:06 that afternoon, the parade barely a half hour old, a bomb exploded at the corner of Steuart and Market Streets. It killed ten persons and wounded forty-four. Four days later, in memory of those who died in the explosion, the chamber convened a meeting in the Civic Auditorium. These "brooding shades" of the vigilantes of 1856, a chamber-paid reporter wrote, "would vindicate the city's honor."

The target of these "vigilantes," labor was convinced, was the city's unions. That conviction was strengthened as the frameup that trapped Tom Mooney and Warren Billings unfolded. With the help of perjured, sometimes fraudulent, even psychopathic testimony, the two men were ultimately convicted of placing the bomb at Steuart and Market Streets. Not until 1939, after more than twenty years of protest, was a measure of justice accorded them.[8]

With the turbulence of the strikes and the Preparedness Day bombing heavy in the air, the Law and Order Committee launched an intensive and successful initiative to outlaw picketing. "There is no such thing as PEACEFUL picketing," said Frederick Koster, chairman of the committee. "Picketing is an instrument of violence. It is un-American. It hurts the city . . . leads to crime, and does labor no good." Every voter with a telephone was asked to back the chamber's stand. Most of them did.

Alex Walthers, an old-time longshoreman who spoke at the funeral services for the victims of Bloody Thursday in 1934, recalled the 1919 longshoremen's strike. "I took part in the 1919 strike, and we were holding out very well, and then our strike committee prevailed upon the membership to make an additional demand. That is to demand that the union be given representation on the employer board. Trying to get union men on their board. That helped to break us up,"[9] he said. Twenty-one years later, Thomas Plant remembered, horror underlying his words, two of the demands made in 1919: "25 percent stock ownership in each of the steamship companies, together with a number of seats on the boards of directors."[10]

These startling demands emerged from a background of turbulence that marked the end of both World War I and the wartime truce between workers and their employers. Talk of nationalization flourished, with the railroads and coal mines prime candidates. Attacks on radicals, real and imagined, spread. Prices climbed, unrest mounted, strikes broke out. Union-open shop feuds stilled by wartime conditions were revived.

In San Francisco, longshoremen balked at an agreement with the employers and on September 15 walked out. Turmoil swept the docks. Seafaring unions continued to sail the ships; teamsters dropped their cargoes at, but not on, the docks. The employers recruited strikebreakers—$10 a day for the "independent" employee, $20 reward for his recruiter. A suspected strikebreaker was killed; two days later, a union man. Employers demanded vigorous prosecution of the strikers. Captain Dollar later told the National Association of Manufacturers how they had forced one judge into line.

> We told him that because of his reluctance to prosecute we had found it necessary to form a vigilance committee and if the serious conditions along the waterfront did not stop at once, our first official act would be to take him and string him up to a telephone pole. . . . I can see that official yet. He could not believe we really meant it, so he said to me, "Mr. Dollar, do you mean that?" I answered, "I was never more earnest in my life." My reply brought him to task and he at once promised to cooperate with us and he did.[11]

The Waterfront Employers' Union refused to meet either a negotiations committee elected by the rank and file or the union's executive officers. Instead it directed an intensive propaganda campaign against the union leadership: "Radicalism has no place here!" The union, they said, was "dominated by a radical element . . . no faith could be taken in any agreement they might enter into."[12]

In mid-December, a group of foremen organized the Harmony Club, sometimes called the "Bosses' Club," ostensibly to encourage a brotherly feeling and end rivalry among themselves. From it, came a new union, shorn of its "radical element" and called the Longshoremen's Association of San Francisco and the Bay District. The Waterfront Employers Union promptly entered into a five-year closed-shop contract. No man, the shipowners announced, could work without the blue dues book of the new union. For fourteen years, the Blue Book union dominated the San Francisco docks and the lives of the longshoremen. Paul Eliel, the Industrial Association's industrial relations director, thought it was "probably inspired by the employers," but was neither "company-dominated" nor "completely independent."[13] To Plant twenty years later, "It so happened that a large number of the longshoremen had gotten sick and tired of their radical leadership and it was overthrown." He added, "I think we can refer to the fourteen years that followed as fourteen years of peace."[14]

To most longshoremen, however, the Blue Book union was an unqualified company union, employer-dominated, employer-controlled. The Harmony Club had been formed under the employers' prodding, they said. Its president had "collaborated with the employers to set up a company union." The employers had provided headquarters for the new organization, the *Waterfront Worker* reported later. In the end, two unarguable results emerged: The Riggers' and Stevedores' of the ILA were smashed; the Blue Book union dominated the waterfront.[15]

The voluble Captain Dollar told the National Association of Manufacturers: "Up to the time of the strike San Francisco had been known as the tightest 'closed shop' city in the world. When the last rumble of the dock strike had died away, the labor aspects in San Francisco had undergone a complete change. It became known as the most wide 'open shop' community in America. How shipping men brought this about has lots of thrills."[16]

Employment on the waterfront was, and had always been, casual, intermittent, short-term—"by the hour, not by the day, and never steadily," a longshore personnel expert said.[17] Longshoremen historically had been hired off the docks, later formalized in daily "shape-ups" at appointed times and places—on a waterfront street or indoors in a variety of halls operated variously by the employers, the union, and, later, jointly. Hiring under these conditions, even more than wages, determined the longshoreman's earnings and thus became a key issue, not only in his worklife but in his relations with the longshore employers. Unequal opportunity for jobs and "feast-or-famine" distribution of work ranked high on the longshoreman's bill of grievances. The strategic role of hiring nowhere became clearer—until the 1934 strike—than in the years immediately following World War I when waterfront employers in Seattle, Portland, and San Pedro defeated the ILA local unions and instituted hiring systems ostensibly aimed at distributing work more equally among the men retained on newly restricted lists. In each instance these so-called decasualization plans called for employee participation, but the employers carefully stage-managed the actual role of longshoremen.

In Seattle the ILA was eliminated in 1920 in a renewal of a running dispute over hiring. During the war years, the union had managed to forestall the employer-sponsored "rustling" card as a condition for obtaining work. In 1920, it struck for hiring from a union list. The employers responded by setting up a hiring hall in a barge at the Grand Trunk Dock where, longshoremen complained, union men were bluntly denied work. Soon after, several Seattle employers came back from President Wilson's industrial conference imbued with the notion that industrial relations should be a joint employer-employee concern, though they ignored any suggestion that an independent union might act effectively as the men's representative. Out of it came the nation's first serious attempt to regularize ("decasualize") longshore employment.

When the ILA agreement in Portland expired in 1922, the waterfront employers announced jobs henceforth would be handed out through the employers' hiring hall. The employers insisted the new hall would be neutral, under joint direction. Recruiting eligible longshoremen would begin April 23. The longshoremen chose instead to go on strike. Clashes with strikebreakers, housed in an old steamship and taken to work by launch, were frequent until injunctions sharply curtailed picketing. The decision of the U.S. Shipping Board to use the ILA hall, rather than the employers' hall, helped bring a temporary end to the strike. But in a dispute over dispatching nonunion men, the employers locked out the union men. By the end of 1923, the union had lost any part in the scheme and ceased to function.

In San Pedro, the employers successfully extended the open shop in the face of strikes by the ILA and the IWW. Efforts to settle an IWW-led strike in 1923 ruptured over the demand for a union hiring hall and elimination of the Sea Service Bureau, the employers' hiring hall. The strikers rallied substantial support, but police roundups swept up seventy-one IWW strike leaders; radical writer Upton Sinclair, a socialist who was to run for governor in 1934 as a Democrat, was arrested for publicly reading the Declaration of Independence. The employers built up their force of strikebreakers until they claimed they had a large enough force to handle the port's work and declared the strike over. The remaining strikers voted to move the strike on to the job.[18]

Like the longshoremen, seagoing workers had turned to unions of their own in the latter years of the nineteenth century to seek redress of their greivances. On a fogbound wharf on San Francisco's waterfront in 1885, with the help of a small group of uptown radical unionists, sailors launched the Coast Seamen's Union. Almost immediately, it fell into—and lost—a battle with the shipowners over their newly instituted "grade book," which recorded sailor's experience, rating, and job performance—predecessor of the later and hated "fink book." It served effectively, too, to keep union-minded seamen off their ships. In 1891, the Coast Seamen's Union merged with the Steamship Sailors' Protective Union to form the Sailors' Union of the Pacific. Over some seventeen years the new union had fought bitter and usually violent battles for a voice in pay, job conditions, and hiring until it gained its first contract early in the new century. Two decades of relative quiet freed the seamen to concentrate on rewriting the barbaric laws that made seamen virtual slaves on shipboard.[19]

In 1921, shipowners served demands on their ship crews for a 15 to 25 percent cut in pay, the elimination of overtime, and a return to the two-watch system (an increase in weekly hours from 56 to 84). The wartime Shipping Board, still operating a major portion of the nation's merchant marine, backed their demands. When the board and the operators unilaterally imposed a wage cut, six unions of licensed and unlicensed seamen struck. The operators retaliated by declaring an open shop on their ships. War-trained sailors, jobless workers, and strikers drifting back to their jobs broke the strike and it was called off in mid-summer. Andy Furuseth, the Sailors' Union chief who had seen his union membership crumble from 115,000 in 1919 to 16,000 in 1923, commented: "We have lost many battles before and this is only one more battle lost. . . . We can and shall win again, if you can see the way and have the courage to walk it."[20]

Thus, in the half-decade following the war, the shipowners and waterfront employers swept the docks and ships clear of unions, taking total, unilateral control of employee relations and job conditions. In the decade or more ahead, they exercised that dominance through employment systems stripped of employee input, pressed by unending mechanization, and driven by an insatiable demand for production and profit. From these years, the employers reaped the "terrible anger" that honed the issues, the tactics, and the goals that would surface explosively in the summer of 1934.

3.

To the Victor . . .

> We have been hired off the streets like a bunch of sheep, standing
> there from 6 o'clock in the morning, in all kinds of weather; at the
> moment of 8 o'clock, we were herded along the street by the police
> to allow the commuters to go across the street from the Ferry Build-
> ing, more or less like a slave market in some of the Old World coun-
> tries of Europe.[1]

That, as Harry Bridges knew it, was the shape-up that took place
daily, rain or shine, on the sidewalk across the street from the Ferry
Building on San Francisco's waterfront. For hundreds of longshoremen, newcomers and old-timers, star gangs and casuals, the shape-
up was the historic core of waterfront work—an intermittent, tenu-
ous link with their industry and their worklife identity. It had become a basic element in the system of labor relations maintained
and intensified since the employers had driven independent unions
from the docks and took total control of the jobs. The format of
the systems in the major ports of the Pacific Coast differed nomi-
nally, but they shared the inequity, the insecurity, and the indignity
that led to the explosive summer of 1934.

The summer before, a San Francisco longshoreman had written
to the *Waterfront Worker:* "Cushion Foot Olsen at Pier 40 McCormick S.S.Co., was out the other day to hire two men. There were
some sixty stevedores there and he milled through them for some
time before he could make a choice. He would remind you of a

stock buyer. The only difference was he didn't feel the muscles or look at the teeth."[2] When the employer needed extra men, Thomas Plant said,

> your port captain went down in front of this saloon or this clothing store or this lodging house; there would be groups of men standing on the pier side of the waterfront. And he knew them all. He'd go up and say, "I want you and I want you and I want you." . . . And sometimes they were organized in gang units, and he'd pick out a gang boss and say, "Bring the gang along, Johnny; got a ship starting at eight o'clock." So Johnny would go down and bring sixteen men or eighteen men or whatever number it was.

Inevitably, on some days men outnumbered jobs. Many, after standing around for hours, would be told simply, "No work today."[3]

"The occupation is casual and fluctuates widely," Plant explained to the National Longshoremen's Board. "Men, therefore, are hired as jobs are available." Frank P. Foisie, architect of Seattle's decasualization plan, spelled out what that meant:

> It suffers the full brunt of a depression, the slack of seasons, and in addition must deal with fluctuations daily and hourly peculiar to itself. Discharging and loading vessels is subject to the variables of uncertain arrival of ships, diverse cargoes, good, bad, and ordinary equipment, regrouping of men and different employers; and is at the mercy of the elements of time, tide, and weather.
>
> As a consequence, "casual work makes casual workers" never had truer meaning. Hiring is by the hour, not by the day, and never steadily. "That's all" when the hatch is finished means the end of that job with an uncertain wait for the next one. Labor turnover may be said to be 100% a day. Competition by longshore labor for the job, and by the [employing] stevedore for labor is keen and continuous. To further complicate matters, a waterfront is the "the scapegoat of competitive industry"—the dumping ground of human surplusage from all other industries and the last refuge of the down-and-outer.
>
> The contrasts in work opportunities vary all the way from the extremes of "Not a ship in port, not a man at work" to "A harbor full of ships and every man working," sometimes on consecutive days. It means a feast or a famine, for men who feel "steaky" one day but may find themselves asking, "when do we eat," the next. Even star gang

men regularly and frequently go from "big money" by working a ship straight through, sometimes even twice round the clock, to a stretch of several days' idleness.

In a port where men get their jobs and the ship its men by lining-up or shaping-up at the dock gate, it frequently results in a surplus of men at one point and a scarcity at another. An unregulated waterfront is a graphic example of a "glutted labor market" with inevitable hiring abuses.[4]

Foisie labeled it a "wasteful and demoralizing" practice— calling men, day after day, to a hiring place with little or no chance of work. The benefits of leisure time, he said, could be reaped with no cost to the employer "except personal consideration for its men, coupled with a little planning."[5]

The power of selection vested in the walking boss or gang boss under the shape-up system led inevitably to corruption. "It is largely left to him," a Department of Labor study noted, "to decide who shall be employed and who shall be left behind. He is seldom hampered in his choice, especially in regard to the more casual men. He can take them or reject them. He can call them today and ignore them tomorrow."[6] "A Stevedore" wrote to the *Waterfront Worker*: "How would you like to get a job from Einar? Of course, you all know him. . . . All you got to do is to supply him with two or three gallons of wine with a gallon of good moonshine thrown in for good measure, and you are sure of a job."[7]

The man who somehow snagged a job had cleared only the first barrier but his course was still pitted with boobytraps. His payday might be anywhere from a day to a week away; different companies paid on different days and at different hours. He might be working when the company for which he worked last week paid, or the time between jobs simply stretched beyond the pay in hand. "A lot of the guys were living from hand to mouth," Germain Bulcke, later a union official, recalled. To bridge the pay gap, men used the brass check, issued to identify them on the payroll, as security for loans until payday.[8] The going rate was usually 5 or 10 percent. In addition to the 5 percent men, Bridges recalled how, before Prohibition was repealed, bootleggers would cash a man's brass check for the price of several drinks. The lender would then use brass checks to collect the men's paychecks, deduct their loans with interest, and return the balance, if any, to the men.[9]

Waterfront employers emphatically disclaimed responsibility for the loan sharks, job-buying, or the gang bosses' favoritism. They sometimes mailed paychecks, refused delivery to any but the man or his wife, or demanded identification or a written order if a paycheck was claimed by a third party. Herman Phleger, the ship-owners' lawyer, explained the abuses in part by noting that "long-shoremen are notorious for being 'hot after their pay.' "[10]

Longshore work, because of its casual nature, commanded a somewhat higher rate of pay than common labor. But even a higher rate did not compensate when a man worked only a few hours a week or suffered long periods of inactivity. Irregular job distribu-tion—feast and famine, side by side—was inherent in longshore employment. In some cases, shipping companies with large and steady operations offered their preferred gangs what the WEU's Plant described as "almost steady employment." These, the star gangs, got most of the work, the best jobs, the best hatches, and the longest shifts. Bridges, himself a member of a star gang, said the star gang got the "big hatch," a full day's work or more, while the extra gang had to make do with a two-hour hatch. They were "highly efficient," Bridges said, but they paid a high price for their star status. Fear of losing that status—other longshoremen were always waiting just outside the dock gate—led to "more abuses, indignities, bad working conditions."[11] They often worked short-handed and were held over to clean up the ship's hatches (while short-hour gangs were knocked off), ordered down at all hours, and less likely to claim overtime or to complain of long stretches of stand-by. Under the threat of being displaced, they throttled their protest against speed-up and undue risks on the job. They put up with round-the-clock shifts, cut short rest periods between jobs, and missed meal periods.

The star or steady gang system produced a sharp disparity in earnings that condemned to poverty, if not sheer want, a substantial number of men who looked to the industry for a livelihood. Boris Stern, who made a comprehensive study of longshore labor condi-tions for the U.S. Bureau of Labor Statistics in 1933, concluded:

perhaps one-fourth of the longshoremen [in the U.S.], those who received preference in the distribution of jobs, earned $40 a week or
more. The remaining three-fourths averaged only $10 to $12 a week,
even less. In normal times, only a small part of this supply [of longshore labor] is earning what may be considered a decent wage. Probably a larger proportion is earning a subsistence wage, i.e., just about
enough to make ends meet on a comparatively low standard of living.
The balance is always on the brink of starvation and depends largely
on outside support, chiefly charity. At the present time a very conservative estimate would probably place more than 50 percent of all longshoremen on the relief rolls.[12]

Union representatives and employer spokesmen quarreled
sharply over how the work force in Pacific Coast ports divided between the "haves" and "have nots." Granting that the star gang
system created "a considerable disparity in earnings," Plant contended some 900 men on the San Francisco waterfront (of an average daily workforce of 1,300, and a maximum of 2,500) had
"practically steady employment." (Plant threw in the low-earning
group that he called "foofoo" gangs—men who did not want to
work steady. "They wanted to make a few dollars and then knock
off and blow it in and when they got hungry go back to work again.
So it was no hardship on them."[13]) A. H. Petersen, a San Pedro
union official, challenged the employers' figures. He estimated that
one-third to one-half of the men "have no regular channel [of earn-
ings] open to them, they just pick up their work wherever and however they can." Some individual companies, as well as the
decasualization schemes at Seattle, Portland, and San Pedro, attempted to equalize the earnings of their steady gangs. The less
steadily employed gangs, the casuals and extras, and longshoremen
working for employers outside the main hiring hall fared nowhere
near as well. In Portland's "big hall," the union objected to a differ-
ential of more than 40 percent in earnings between the top gang
and the lowest as "too much difference."[14]

Pressures generated by the "feast or famine" distribution of
work, with its "considerable" disparity in earnings permeated the
entire work force. So long as more men shaped-up than there were
jobs, so long as job-hungry men "prospected" the individual docks,

hanging on with hope that ran beyond reason, so long as jobs could be bought by fee or favor, the more fiercely the man who had the job clung to it and paid the price.

One longshoreman remembered reporting to Oakland at 8:00 in the morning three mornings in a row, being held until noon, held again in San Francisco until 5:00, and finally told to report next morning. For each of the three days he was paid his ferry fare—42¢—and a half hour traveling time. On the other hand, Bridges said his longest shift was twenty-eight hours, though he knew of many longer. In Portland, a longshoreman said, men worked twenty-four hours or more, while others were idle; six to eight hours without a meal period was not unusual. In San Pedro, A. H. Petersen said that over a period of five years he had worked at least forty Sundays a year—"from noon Sunday to noon Monday or later. We might go on another boat Monday." Either you worked the twenty-four-hour shifts—"always another man willing to work them"—and made good money or "you dropped away from that gang . . . and [you were] thrown into the 'alley' (where casuals shaped-up in San Pedro)." Bill Lewis, later president of the Pacific Coast District, said he had worked anywhere from two hours to thirty hours at a stretch but had never objected: "If you would say anything of that kind you would just simply be fired." Henry Schmidt remembered leaving San Francisco at 7:00 in the morning, working at Port Costa through the day and past midnight, falling into bed at 3:30 the next morning, under orders to report to Alameda again at 7:00. "So I never showed up. It was just too much. . . . you work up a terrific anger against the employers."[15]

Continuing mechanization accelerated the shipowners' drive to boost output. The first slingboard was used to protect shipments of plaster and cement destined for San Francisco after the 1906 earthquake and fire. The single board, though, was too narrow and had a tendency to spill its load; it was widened to stabilize the loads, at the same time increasing the loads still further. Man-hauled, four-wheel trucks moved larger loads to (or from) the ship's hook. Motorized jitneys took over hauling the trucks to or from the hook, enormously lengthening the distance of the haul. Without them, an employer asserted, an "army of men" would have been needed.

Soon jitneys fitted with "arms"—the forklift—hoisted loads that had been built on pallets. Jitneys saved hand hauling, but they also eliminated men on the dock and speeded up the gang in the hold. In the hold, rollers, four-wheel trucks, and hold winches decreased the work—and, one longshoremen added, the men, too. "There is hardly a wrinkle in the development of the speed-up that the shipowners have overlooked," a longshoreman asserted in the *Waterfront Worker:*

> They have introduced the fast jitney. The double board is the rule. The size of the gang has been cut. The loads have increased and are still increasing. Finally, the shipowners have carefully picked bosses that know how to speed-up. And how well the shipowners have found what they wanted.
>
> The increase of the size of loads is the main method in the speed-up. Four bales of cotton make a load in place of two or three. A ton and a half of lead makes a load instead of the former 1800 pounds. Twenty bags of rice now make a load instead of twelve or fifteen. . . . Forty cases of canned goods is common in place of the previous eighteen. The lads are climbing higher and higher. "Pile them up boys," say the shipowners. "Pile them up; higher and higher, one tier, two tiers, three tiers, and faster, boys, faster. The hook is hanging. Pile 'em up, boys; the Blue Book says it's OK."[16]

During his years on the waterfront, Bridges watched the loads get bigger, the winches faster, and the work tempo speed up. They used to sling nine to eleven bundles of gas and water pipe to a load; now the loads were limited only by what the winch could lift—as much as three tons, about thirty bundles. Nail kegs ran twelve to fifteen to the load; with a new board, twenty-five to thirty. Steel was formerly handled in the piece, about 1,500 pounds to the load. Then steel was loaded in bundles weighing about 2,500 pounds. Formerly eight men had worked steel in the hold; with the bundled steel, only two men were needed to guide and steady the loads as they were landed.[17]

Once a pair of one-man winches, directed by a hatchtender, hauled the loads between the dock and hatch. They were replaced by the double winch, operated by one man looking directly into the hatch. Then they began using laggings to speed up the winches—

and the work—by increasing the diameter of the winch drums and winding up more fall with each turn of the drum.[18]

"The rawhide system," one longshoreman explained, helped to make the work harder. "It means a boss standing over you telling you if you don't kick into it, you can get off the boat." Or the boss incited competition to speed the work. "You better get with it—you're ten tons behind," he would tell one gang. Then he would tell another: "You're ten tons behind that other gang."[19]

Longshore employers contended the newer methods of work required less physical energy. The work, one said, "would be terrible if a man had to do it by hand." Another employer interviewed his men on the job. They told him, he said, they preferred the double board and the jitney. "The natural inference seems to me to be that the work now cannot be more burdensome than it used to be," the employer said.[20]

Longshoremen were no less concerned with the impact of the effort to boost output on the already substantial hazards of longshoring. "Anyone who knows anything about the waterfront," one longshoreman said, "knows well that the work is very hazardous, because of neglect and the very large loads, the unsafe loads, and the unsafe gear." Another wrote in the *Waterfront Worker:* "The winchdriver is not supposed to hang a load over the men working in the square of the hatch, well, just listen to that man, Tanglefoot Gus, holler, 'COME IN WITH IT' while there are two loads landed in one section and the men are flooring off."[21] Schmidt led a gang in protesting a boss who ordered a sling load dropped on the round top of a shaft alley. Schmidt saw it start to roll off and led the gang out of the hold. The gang did not get back on the dock for two weeks and when it did, the boss told Schmidt, "you're not going in."[22] Bridges charged the speed-up resulting from competition between gangs was responsible for killing at least one man and cutting off the leg of another.

Petersen told the National Longshoremen's Board that "one out of every four men working on the Pacific Coast was off because of injury last year [1933]. One out of every eight was off for a period of at least a week."[23] The union cited a study by the Metropolitan Life Insurance Company, covering the years 1920 to 1926. Though the sample was small, it showed a much higher death rate for long-shoremen than the average for all occupied males and 37 percent more accidental deaths than for all occupational groups.[24]

In 1927—coincidental with the enactment of the federal long-shore workers' compensation system, though some employers denied any connection—the shipowners established their Accident Prevention Bureau and for the first time began to accumulate figures on what was happening on longshore jobs. Its founder and director, Byron O. Pickard, contended that job accidents fell from about 400 disabling injuries per million hours worked in 1927 to about 100 in 1933.[25] But the bureau's information yielded no measure of the severity of job accidents. Nor did it investigate the cost of injuries. The union claimed that about half of the average of 1,750 men working on the San Francisco waterfront were injured in 1933; in San Pedro and Portland, though the work forces were smaller, 914 men had been injured. More than half of the reportable injuries resulted in disablement.[26]

To these disordered practices were added still other job complaints. New men—sheepherders, one longshoreman called them; somebody's brother-in-law or a just-graduated nephew—were shoved into longshore gangs by the dockside officers or by one of the bosses.[27] Seniority was little heeded in this haphazard system. One hiring agent refused to hire a longshoreman because "we could not have men on the job who were continually getting hurt." Another, who had been a witness in a job injury lawsuit, was refused work; he was "nothing but a stool pigeon for the lawyers," he was told.[28]

In some ports, employers cut wages by assigning men who had worked as longshoremen to dock work at a lower rate. Waiting without pay was a condition of employment. "Well, sorry, the ship is late," a longshoreman remembered a boss saying, after ordering the gang down that morning. "You can hang around if you want or come back at two o'clock this afternoon."[29] And always implicit in this misshapen pattern of employment was the almost certain knowledge that protest would result in loss of the job or of the opportunity to compete, however unfavorably, for work of any kind.

Bridges and Plant described the results of the industry's labor practices in similar terms, though their implications were worlds apart. "Without a question of doubt," Bridges said, "the output per man and per gang in San Francisco during those years or on the Pacific Coast during those years was higher than any other country in the world." Plant retroactively voiced a similar conclusion: "It is faint praise to say that we got a fair day's work for a fair day's pay. The longshoremen on the Pacific Coast became known as the best and most efficient in the world. . . . During the greater part of this period we paid a premium over the Atlantic Coast, usually of ten cents an hour, and the men certainly deserved it because of the excellence of their work."[30]

4.

FOURTEEN YEARS OF PEACE

> Jack Bryan was a very well-known longshoreman on the waterfront.
> And he had unusual ability, and he talked to the employers to see if
> they would recognize a union if he could get one together, and they
> said they would. So Jack went to work and formed a union, and the
> recognition was on the basis of that understanding with Bryan. . . .
> and he ran it with an iron hand. And it was good for the men. You
> never saw such a good lot of workers as we had on the front during
> the Blue Book union days.[1]

This is how the employers' spokesman, Thomas Plant, remembered the founding of the Longshoremen's Association of San
Francisco in the waning months of the 1919 longshoremen's strike.
Roger Lapham concurred in Plant's fond recollection. Lapham,
scion of a wealthy family, was Plant's boss at the American-Hawaiian Steamship Company and a major player among the shipowners
in the 1934 strikes. Later, he served as mayor of San Francisco during World War II and formation of the United Nations, and as
administrator of United States aid to Greece and China. Bryan, he
said, "was a very fine man. He had gone to sea in his early days as a
sailor, knew the waterfront from A to Z, and knew his men. He was
a fine citizen."[2]

Henry Schmidt remembered Bryan this way: "He had been a
longshoreman in his time . . . a 'Red Book' man. When the 1919
strike smashed the union he collaborated with the employers to
set up a company union, which got the name of San Francisco's

Longshoremen's Association, but everybody knew that it was controlled by the shipowners. . . . and, incidentally, he was an Aussie, too; he talked like an American though."[3] (Bridges, the other Aussie, talked like one.)

Blue Book dominance from 1919 to 1933 provided an effective tool for stifling the men's complaints, wiping out any traces of independent collective bargaining, and maintaining the employers' unchallenged control of the job. In other ports—principally Seattle and San Pedro—employers used their decasualization schemes to the same ends. No small part of the bitterness that erupted in the summer of 1934 flowed from the employers' almost total denial of the longshoremen's claim to be heard.

The Waterfront Employers Union signed three five-year agreements with the Blue Book union and met once a year with Bryan to fix wage rates for the following year. The employers gave him a "complete closed shop," Plant said. "If Bryan didn't have the men, he'd go out and rustle them up. . . . And his contract was inviolate; he had an incipient strike [in 1923] among the barley handlers [at Port Costa] and he hired strikebreakers and broke it himself. . . . [He] fired the men who went out on the wildcat strike and they never worked on the front again." Looking back later, Plant summed up: "I think we can refer to the fourteen years that followed as fourteen years of peace."[4]

Bill Lewis remembered the Blue Book differently: "Everything was done under the sun, putting a lot of men on this waterfront, to break down every condition that existed previous to 1919." Employers brought men from everywhere, he said—no questions where a man came from or whether he could do longshore work, only whether he could pay $10 to join the union.[5]

Six months after Harry Bridges went to work on the front, the Blue Book delegate, Ed Roth, generally known as "Sharkey," told him he would have to join. Bridges refused and was promptly fired. After that, Bridges said, he stuck to short-run jobs for six or seven months in an effort to dodge the dues collector. But it soon became impossible to work for more than a day or so before Roth would catch up with him and have him fired. "Since it was imperative that I make a living," Bridges said, "I found it necessary to join the

Blue Book union." Even then, when Bridges fell behind in his dues payments—which was often—he "invariably" lost his job.[6]

Not long after Germain Bulcke came to the waterfront, when he was working at the Admiral Line, he found himself on "standby"—without pay. His gang filled in for an hour or two at lunchtime. "You hung around all day and you might get four hours' work," he said. When he complained to the older men, they suggested he take it up with the union. The young and innocent Bulcke turned up for the next union meeting. After the small group in attendance heard the minutes of the previous meeting, the presiding officer asked if there were any questions. Bulcke arose and asked about standby pay. "The business agent got up—he was a big, husky man," Bulcke remembered. "He grabbed me by the back of the neck and the seat of my pants and said, 'You haven't been here long enough to be dry behind your ears, and you're going to tell us how to run our business?' And he shoved me down the steps."[7]

Longshoremen commonly looked on the Blue Book union as a company union, dominated if not directly controlled by the employers. It played no part in the hiring process, nor did it ever seek, in any way, to equalize earnings or modify the "feast-and-famine" distribution of work. Its neglect of the complaints that welled up from the men on the docks was taken for granted. The Blue Book came to be seen mainly as a device to extort money from the men and to protect the employers against independent organization.

For a time, though, its stature was enhanced when it affiliated in 1927 with the San Francisco Labor Council and the California State Federation of Labor. John A. O'Connell, the feisty teamster who was secretary-treasurer of the council, later argued that, by then, older hands and traditional unionists had gained control of the union that had been set up by the employers—"transforming a company union," he called it in the *American Federationist*. The invitations to join, however, were extended with at least an implicit understanding that, in due course, the Blue Book union would affiliate with the AFL International Longshoremen's Association. After four years had gone by, though, without affiliation, the ILA reminded the labor council and the state federation that the presence of an unaffiliated union in their ranks was a violation of the

AFL constitution. Rather than affiliate, the Blue Book union withdrew. The employers later cited its short-lived affiliation with the council to ward off accusations of employer domination.[8]

In the struggle surrounding the reorganization of the ILA on the waterfront in 1933, it became clear that the Blue Book union was the employer's chosen instrument. But even in the face of Blue Book dominance, longshoremen repeatedly attempted to revive their union. The 1924 report of the Employment Service Bureau—set up originally by the shipowners as a hiring hall for seamen—charged that the strike of barley handlers at Port Costa in the summer of 1923 was due to "the Red Element in the stevedores who, because of the great volume of work had secured positions along the waterfront." The Blue Book union quickly replaced (and blacklisted) the men who struck, with practically no delay in ship operations.

The report also noted the mysterious rise of an organization calling itself the Longshoremen's Council of California, "who are composed of certain radical members of the old Riggers' and Stevedores' Association." A San Francisco unit, the report said, voted to strike after employers rejected its demands for recognition and higher wages and if a strike were voted in Seattle. "At Seattle," the employers' report mysteriously noted, "the strike vote was called, and after the ballot was closed the ballots were burned without counting them. That ended this effort to make trouble."[9]

In the fall of 1924, a leaflet in the name of Riggers' and Stevedores' Union, Local 38-33, ILA (made up then mainly of lumber loaders) spoke to the general longshore workers on the waterfront. "As the month of November approaches," it said, "the so-called 'Blue Book' will try to sweeten the bitter pill of selling out the longshoremen of this harbor with the promise that at least you will be guaranteed the continuation of the present wage scale." Under the "blessings" of the Blue Book, the leaflet argued, "longshoremen are compelled to tramp miles looking for work, losing valuable time, and often losing jobs by being somewhere else at the time. We not only suffer from irregular employment and lose hundreds of dollars a year in wages but there also exists in this harbor 'favoritism,' 'slave-driving,' accidents and sickness, with no protection from unscrupulous employers."

The union committee from Local 38-33 had asked him to help draw up its program, Henry P. Melnikow remembered. Melnikow was a longtime economic consultant to unions, later deeply involved in hearings on the proposed shipping code under the National Recovery Administration and in many aspects of both the waterfront and general strikes. He also argued the cases for the longshoremen and seamen before the National Longshoremen's Board in 1934–1935. In 1924, he said, the attempt to reorganize was aborted by employer support of the entrenched Blue Book union. But, Melnikow added, "there was considerable doubt, to say the least, on the part of the leadership of the labor movement whether they wanted to go back to a Red Book union, with all the troubles it had caused them, all the way from 1916 to 1919." Men like Paul Scharrenberg of the seamen's union, and the teamsters, he thought, felt it "had put the entire labor movement in jeopardy for either silly or political reasons and they didn't want that type of problem again."[10]

A small group of longshoremen in 1928 got together during lunch hours or after work, Bulcke remembered, to "see whether or not we could get a union started." The group included Bridges, Henry Schmidt, and Bill Lewis—the latter "a fellow that later on became president of the district whose nickname was 'Burglar Bill' " (a comment on his dark-stubbled chin).[11]

Between 1929 and 1931, organizing revived in the northwest ports, where employer-dominated decasualization plans had kept the men in line. The Tacoma local, the only functioning ILA local on the coast, provided the leadership with W. T. Morris, later secretary of the Pacific Coast District. As the depression made inroads on work, however, men in Everett quit paying dues to the Tacoma local. In Gray's Harbor, the employers replaced union men as rapidly as they identified them. Reorganization got underway in Seattle and Portland but "then the depression came on stronger. Men were not making very much money and did not seem to be doing much, and we did not make much headway."[12]

In San Francisco, an organizing campaign initiated by the Marine Workers Industrial Union (MWIU) failed. "They didn't catch on," Bridges said, "because, although their program was pretty revolutionary, pretty idealistic, and . . . despite the fact that people felt pretty desperate, they didn't cotton too much to . . . their political views."[13] The MWIU's attempt apparently did spur Lee Holman in that same year to take the first, tentative steps toward reestablishing an ILA local on the San Francisco waterfront. Holman hailed from a pioneer family in the San Joaquin Valley and prided himself on being an old-time longshoreman and Red Book unionist. Though he had been expelled by the Blue Book union, he hung on, working when he could. He warned the ILA's president, Joseph P. Ryan, that unless they got busy, San Francisco could be lost to the communists. Soon after, Holman reported to Ryan that he and eight others had met and agreed to "continue with a small membership until further orders from the International." They had decided "not to establish ourselves as a full-fledged organization at present," and to lay over fees and dues "until further notice," and had elected him temporary president and business manager.

E. A. Quigle, a contracting stevedore at Seattle, remembered that they used a "barge" as a hiring hall for employing their longshoremen after the 1920 strike. Soon after, though, several local employers returned from President Woodrow Wilson's industrial conference imbued with the notion that industrial relations ought to be managed jointly by employer and employee. As Quigle remembered it, the employers first "sold . . . thirty or forty" leading men on the merit of a jointly-directed hiring scheme. They then presented it to a meeting of longshoremen who voted, about 3 to 2, to accept the plan.[14] In a survey of waterfront conditions that followed, they found twice too many men with new men constantly cutting in. Men left and returned at will. Earnings were concentrated among a few. The proposed cure called for stopping the intake of new men, preventing men from returning who had given up their claim to waterfront work, eliminating all hiring at the gate, and requiring all reserve men to be hired through a central dispatching hall. A joint committee thinned the ranks of the some 1,400 men working on the docks, measuring them by American citizenship, marital status, taxpaying history, and physical ability to do the work. Some 750 were selected, and nearly an equal number pooled on a waiting list, the so-called extra board.[15] They chose Frank P. Foisie, Connecticut-born, Harvard graduate, lecturer, and researcher, as industrial relations manager to implement the plan. If anybody came to understand the complexities of job equity on the docks, it was Foisie, but he had great difficulty accepting an independent union as equal partner in the task.

Down the years, the Seattle plan made a serious effort to equalize the distribution of work. It worked most effectively among the steady gangs, less so among the reserve gangs. It vested both the original and final word on hiring in the employer, who could refuse to hire a man without reason. The only appeal from an employer's decision was to the employer himself.

The principal difficulty with the Seattle plan, Boris Stern noted in his survey of longshore conditions, was not "in the scheme per se. It is due primarily to the fact that the plan was promulgated and carried out by the employers against the strong opposition of organized labor. In fact, the scheme may be considered as the result of the protracted fight between the Employers Association of the West Coast and the ILA which culminated in the almost complete elimination of the union from the West Coast."[16] Foisie conceded that it developed out of the 1916 and 1920 strikes but denied it was intended to eliminate the ILA. Had the ILA been more "cooperative," he argued, the relationship might have continued. "We deal around the table by a full valid system of collective bargaining, without a trade union agreement, as such," he claimed. The employers, he said, had dealt without objection with the election of solid slates of ILA men as employee representatives. Nevertheless, Foisie noted that the minutes of the joint committee in 1931 said the employers ten years before had taken the position that "they would not deal with the ILA and their reasons are as real and as vital now as ever." Quigle conceded that finding a job complaint that had been settled satisfactorily to the men was "like looking for a needle in a haystack."[17] E. L. Ridley, onetime employee representative, said Foisie often told men who brought in complaints, "If you don't like it, you can quit." Nor had the employers ever agreed to arbitrate any question. "We managed to settle it without going that far," Ridley said. Another employee representative said they were told they might as well take [a wage cut] because it was going to be choked down their throats anyway. When the employees proposed arbitration, the employers told them there was nothing to arbitrate; the wages came up from San Francisco and they had to take them as they came. Finally, the employers refused to deal with the employee representatives because they had been "instructed as to their actions by the ILA . . . and were not free agents to represent the employees who elected them."[18]

In Portland, too, A. J. Singer, a veteran longshoreman, said he did not know "of a single instance where a complaint by longshoremen has ever been investigated" under the "dummy paper organization" that ran the major hiring hall. "This fact [was] so clearly realized by the workers that long ago they quit attempting to secure redress through this system." Following the 1922 strike, an active blacklist drove many strikers off the front. Only a court action several years later allowed some to return to the docks. But, Singer charged, once the ILA renewed its activity—in 1924 and 1931—the blacklist returned. The Portland employers, too, undertook to equalize earnings but their hall served only longshoremen working aboard ship and slingmen. Dock workers and grain handlers were compelled to seek work—at reduced rates—from dock to dock. And, as in Seattle, a substantial part of the work was distributed outside the employers' "big" hall. Not until 1933 did the Portland employers set up their own employee representation plan. By then, longshoremen increasingly considered the ILA their spokesman, not, as one longshoreman put it, "any gang foreman or anybody the employers picked."[19]

In San Pedro, A. H. Petersen remembered seeing two hundred men "prospecting at one of the Dollar boats, and who have stayed aboard ship and have stayed in the shed and all over there all night long . . . to try to get a job." Perhaps as much as one quarter of the work in the port was distributed outside the employers' Marine Service Bureau. Work out of its hall was supposed to be assigned to registered men who carried the bureau's book, Petersen said, but increasingly it went to unregistered men. Ignoring the employee representatives, employers drew up the working rules; discipline, penalties, enforcement were reserved to the employer.[20]

Eugene Mills, a San Pedro employer, said the employers set up an industrial relations committee on which the various classes of employees—ship, dock, and lumber—were represented. (Petersen said the elections were not generally known; few of the men voted.) In the early years, Mills said, "I will say the boys had a lot of grievances; most of them were petty and easily settled." The committee, though, had not been meeting as often "because the boys have not been doing so much complaining."[21]

Only the Tacoma ILA locals survived the onslaught between 1922 and 1933 in the major Coast ports and that by way of wages imposed by northwest employers; the union did not sign changes in working conditions, nor did employers mention the union. Grievances were handled by a joint committee; the union business agent policed the jobs. ("Jack Bjorklund was a business agent who could put his hand on top of a bar, jump over and knock down four longshoremen," a local history said. He later became secretary of the Pacific Coast District.) The Tacoma locals, too, sometimes with the help of the International union, tried to revive unions in the other northwest ports. Success, says the local history, "was fleeting. . . . The risks were too great. At that time trying to organize a new local led too easily to discrimination in hiring, lost jobs, or blacklisting." As the depression deepened, the Tacoma locals attempted in a variety of ways to equalize work opportunities, both by agreement and unilaterally. But their isolation limited their capacity, if not the will to challenge overwhelming employer rule.[22]

Each port in its own ways during these years had sewn the wind, years of depression fertilized the bitter soil, and the harvest was ripening.

5.

Turnaround

THE ECONOMIC DEPRESSION that swept across the nation in 1929 was "unique," observed historian Irving Bernstein, the only one we call "great."[1] It was unequalled for sheer size—never before had so many been unemployed for so long, never had the nation been so unprepared for economic disaster of such scope and depth. At least 3.25 to 4 million workers were jobless in 1929, according to the government's crude count, which climbed steadily until it passed 15 to 16 million by 1933. National income as well as industrial production dropped by about half. Millions were reduced to poverty and want. A generation (and more) of Americans was deeply scarred by the effects.

"Earnings dropped unavoidably during the depression," Thomas Plant philosophized.[2] The maritime industry added its own peculiar dimension to the impact of depression on longshoremen and seamen. It reduced its workforce, not as in other industries by layoff or discharge, but simply by not hiring. Every man was unemployed at the end of each job; the gap between jobs only grew longer. At the same time, jobless workers from other depression-struck industries crowded into the shape-up. "Where the opportunities open up daily," Frank Foisie observed, "then, obviously, it is happy hunting and open season . . . for men from other industries to come down and cut in."[3] In the decasualized ports, steady gangs shared the scarcity of work. Between 1929 and 1932, average steady gang earnings in Seattle fell 51 percent—from $37.16 to $18.88 a week.[4] In Portland, the decline in earnings was 40 percent.[5] Casual workers, helpless in the face of both the job scarcity and the influx of newcomers, fared worse. Most of the old-timers, the *Waterfront Worker* reported in its first issue, published in December 1932, had been replaced by "sheepherders." The same issue of the *Waterfront Worker* said about 20 percent of the longshoremen in San Pedro were averaging about a day's work a week; the rest about half that time. San Francisco employers had no way of knowing the year-round earnings of even their steady men, but the individual long-shoreman knew.

Earnings already depressed by scarcity of work were further cut by reductions in wage rates: in the winter of 1931–32 from 90¢ an hour to 85¢, a year later to 75¢. "In those days," Roger Lapham remembered, "men were seeking a job for almost anything, and of course we reduced our crew wages when men were willing to go to sea simply to have food and lodging."[6]

Germain Bulcke remembered one ship where a gang was discharging shoes. "Most of the men had a new pair of shoes on when they went off the job," he said. As work slowed down, "it became more prevalent for the longshoremen to help themselves to whatever things they could get at."[7] Men gathered spillage from broken cases and sacks of food. "Of course, sometimes we'd make sure a case or sack broke," he said. Many worked only a few days; many were married and had families "and they found that they needed to do this in order to get by."[8]

"Now comes the question—how do we live?" a longshoreman asked in a letter in the *Waterfront Worker*. "Well, some of us live in the Rich street soup line on skid road. Some of us who are married, work for the Charities and get in return, food that in most cases could not be sold on the public markets, and for this rotten chuck we must work every third week."[9] When Harry Bridges lost his place in a star gang in 1932, he applied for city relief, working for groceries and a few dollars toward gas and light. A construction foreman put him to work as a rigger for a month; at the going rate, he earned three months of food boxes. He added, "I still went down and worked as a longshoreman when I got the chance."[10]

E. F. Ellison, who had formerly worked in the Sailors' Union office, wrote to labor historian Ira B. Cross:

> Our warehouse at 6th and Berry streets has two open sheds with concrete floors. Nightly about twenty men sleep on the concrete. I have asked them why they do not apply to the shelter provided by the Salvation Army, and like organizations, and they tell me that in order to get a "flop" in any of these shelters, it is necessary to spend the entire afternoon "in line" waiting for turn. If a person gets into line after all the beds have been preempted, he is just out of luck, and will have to sleep in the street. Furthermore, if an unemployed comes more than two nights in succession to the same shelter, he is told that he must not wear out his welcome. These men are not hoboes, they are men willing and anxious to work.[11]

The waves of economic depression washed at the footings of the American society, gaining in force and reach each year. The leaders and the traditional wisdom by which the nation had lived were increasingly questioned. Unrest, protest, and demonstrations mounted, anger paralleling growing fear. Reason and good will foundered in a morass of panaceas, overnight cures, and drastic solutions.

Historian Arthur J. Schlesinger, Jr. scanned the national mood. Would there be a revolution?, people asked. The "ordinarily benign" William Green, president of the American Federation of Labor, warned a Senate committee that workers would seize the thirty-hour week by "universal strike" unless Congress enacted it. Edward A. O'Neal, head of the Farm Bureau Federation, declared that, unless something was done immediately for the nation's farmers, "we will have revolution in the countryside within less than twelve months." Schlesinger writes: "In the cities and on the farms, Communist organizers were finding a ready audience and a zealous following." Some Americans became convinced that revolution awaited only the rise of the right leadership. "There'll be a revolution, sure," Schlesinger quoted a Los Angeles banker. "The farmers will rise up. So will labor. The Reds will run the country—or maybe the Fascists. Unless, of course, Roosevelt does something."[12]

Public discussion boiled with formulas for ending and preventing economic depression and "recovering" prosperity. They ranged from crackpot "utopias" to conservative caution, reform to revolution, in every conceivable degree, right and left, of economic and political manipulation. The debate was all too frequently distorted by cries of "red" and "fascist," with little or no intent to distinguish literal political identity or intellectual honesty. It turned raucous, emotional, and irrational, substituting labels for substance, impaling advocates of change before their ideas could be seriously examined.

In November 1932, Franklin Delano Roosevelt overwhelmed the Republican incumbent, Herbert Hoover. Schlesinger capsuled the mood of the country as a new president prepared to take office:

> The fog of despair hung over the land. One out of every four American workers lacked a job. Factories that had once darkened the skies with smoke stood ghostly and silent, like extinct volcanoes. Families slept in tarpaper shacks and tin-lined caves and scavenged for food on the city dump. In October the New York City Health Department had reported that over one-fifth of the pupils in public schools were suffering from malnutrition. Thousands of vagabond children were roaming the land, wild boys of the road. Hunger marchers, pinched and bitter, were parading cold streets in New York and Chicago. On the countryside unrest had already flared into violence. Farmers stopped milk trucks along Iowa roads and poured the milk into the ditch. Mobs halted mortgage sales, ran the men from the banks and insurance companies out of town, intimidated courts and judges, demanded a moratorium on debts.[13]

"Plenty is at our doorstep," the new president said on a cold, overcast inaugural day, "but a generous use of it languishes in the very sight of supply."

The lead story in the first issue of the *Waterfront Worker* in December 1932 was headlined "CHRISTMAS FOR THE SHIPOWNERS." The *Waterfront Worker*, a ragged, bleary mimeographed publication, was "published by a group of longshoremen for longshoremen." Its editors were anonymous, its correspondents shrouded in pen names, for fear of employer retaliation. Mitchell Slobodek, one of its editors, said it sold for a penny on the theory that the price would keep people from throwing it away. In its blunt, inelegant fashion it gave voice to the unending job complaints of the working longshoreman in ways that had been denied him for at least the past fourteen years. "There was an undercurrent of restlessness on the waterfront when we started putting out our paper, but no direction," Slobodek said. "The paper gave one."

"1933 will be the beginning of a new year," the lead article in its first issue said, "and of a new agreement on the 'Frisco' waterfront. It has been decreed that wages will be 75 cents an hour—a 10c wage cut. Coming at the time of the festive season, this wage-cut is a regular Christmas present to the shipowners." The next issue reported that the same wage cut had been imposed in the northwest ports and in San Pedro. "Sheer necessity," Plant said later.[14]

Longshoremen "had to" make their yuletide gift because, the paper said,

> the Blue Book union had betrayed them. But what can be done about it? . . . Some of us have got together, whats to prevent others from doing the same. If you ask this question of your partner the answer will be "Open your mouth and you will get blacklisted." We know this. Its nothing new. Whats to prevent us from organizing small undercover groups of those whom we know on each dock. This is the only way we can lay the basis of a real union and protect ourselves as individuals.[15]

In its February issue the *Waterfront Worker* said it intended to fight: '1. For a deep cut in the new working rules. 2. For more men in a gang. 3. For a real fight against further wage-cuts." And it urged again that longshoremen organize small groups to take the lead in dock action against grievances. Its goals were limited and defensive, only a distant approximation, as it turned out, of workers' expectations, far short of the trade union program it would later support.

The "real union" some of the editors had in mind was not a revival of the "Red Book" union, that is, the ILA, but the Marine Workers Industrial Union (MWIU), a small, active, but ineffective branch of the Red International affiliate, the Trade Union Unity League (TUUL). It pursued the TUUL policy of separate industrial unions, overlapping, duplicating, and competing with the mainstream AFL organizations, in this case calling for one union of longshoremen and seamen—of all marine workers. Later issues of the *Waterfront Worker* acknowledged MWIU help in publishing the paper. For about the first six months the paper touted—sometimes loudly, sometimes subtly—the MWIU as the union for longshoremen, but the longshoremen never responded. Sam Darcy, regional head of the Communist Party, later explained its failures. It had "not a single worker on the docks." As outsiders, the party fell victim to agitation "against our Union and our Party." "Militant phraseology," though mouthed by "reactionaries . . . succeeded in turning the minds of the men."[16]

In midsummer, 1933, the ILA was reborn on the San Francisco waterfront when ILA President Joseph P. Ryan appointed Lee J. Holman organizer. Henry Schmidt recalled, "We sort of streamed into the office and put down the so-called initiation fee, which was fifty cents, got a book, and it was the right time and the right place. It also had something to do with that thing that was called the National Recovery Act, NRA, Section 7a."[17]

Dissent came from surprising directions. Paul Scharrenberg, who had come from the Sailors Union of the Pacific to become secretary-treasurer of the AFL California State Federation of Labor, angrily protested granting a charter to Holman; he insisted it should be offered to the Blue Book union. It will "cause bitter antagonism of the shipowners," Scharrenberg said. Ryan, suggesting Scharrenberg refrain from criticism, telegraphed, "This is the first time I have heard a representative of the Seamen's international union worry about attitude of shipowners."[18] At almost the same moment, the *Waterfront Worker*, supporting the MWIU, reported: "That the stevedores on the San Francisco front have lost faith in the old line craft unions was proven a couple of months ago when an attempt to revive the old Red Book, that is, the ILA, fell through." The scheme of "two old timers" to start up the old union again did not work.[19]

In fact, it did. The *Worker* soon reported 4,000 were signing up in the Red Book union: "In order to break the Blue Book we followed the rest of the stevedores on the Front in signing up for the

ILA."[20] Bulcke remembered: "It went like a snowball and first thing you know ninety-eight percent of all the men working on the waterfront in San Francisco signed up."[21]

Involved in the sharp turnaround in the *Waterfront Worker's* direction was an equally sharp reversal in MWIU—and Communist Party—doctrine. Under pressure from local Communist Party officials, in light of the obvious failure of the MWIU to organize San Francisco longshoremen, and quite possibly in recognition of a fait accompli, party officials waived the policy of organizing their own revolutionary unions and consented to moving party efforts into a regular, old-line local of the International Longshoremen's Association."[22] Members of a rapidly emerging rank-and-file group— Bridges, Schmidt, some Party loyalists, and others—took over the influential little paper, displacing its MWIU emphasis and shifting its editorial support to the now-burgeoning ILA local. Out of this motley group, too, in the months that followed came the leadership and program that set the new course for the longshoremen.

In December 1932, Senator Hugo L. Black of Alabama had introduced a bill embodying the American Federation of Labor's thirty-hour-week formula for halting the depression. It proposed to close foreign and interstate commerce to products from establishments in which any person was allowed to work more than thirty hours a week. On April 5, 1933, with growing public support, the Senate passed the bill, 53 to 30.

But Franklin Delano Roosevelt, a month in office and pushing vigorously for economic recovery legislation, was uncomfortable with the bill. He shared industry's conviction that it was both unconstitutional and unworkable. In its stead, in early May, he sent Congress the National Industrial Recovery bill. It called for the establishment of the National Recovery Administration (NRA) under which business itself, freed from anti-trust restraints, would regulate "unfair competition and disastrous overproduction" through codes of fair competition. At the same time, the codes would shorten the work week and establish minimum wages. To balance the generous grant of economic power to industry, each code would be required to include a guarantee of the right of workers to organize and bargain collectively. When President Roosevelt signed the bill into law on June 16, 1933, Section 7(a) asserted the right of workers to organize and bargain collectively, free of employer restraint or interference. It prohibited any requirement that employees join any company union or refrain from joining a union of their own choosing.

Union fever swept across the land in a contagious epidemic. Organizers from the United Mine Workers strode the rutted roads of the coal camps collecting applications from thousands of miners. In one market after another, the International Ladies' Garment Workers' Union (ILGWU) extended its membership and influence. The Amalgamated Clothing Workers launched a series of strikes and organizing drives that brought in 50,000 new members. Workers in steel, autos, rubber, and radio moved to organize under what the AFL's William Green called labor's "Magna Carta." Union interest emerged in surprising places—among newspaper reporters, movie actors, grocery clerks, and cannery workers. In a major, unprecedented upsurge of unionism, the labor movement in little more than half a year added some 400,000 members. Among those who responded were the longshoremen of the Pacific Coast—San Francisco and Seattle, Portland and San Pedro, and dozens of smaller ports in between—and, in due course, the seamen who sailed the West Coast's merchant fleet.

In the end Section 7(a) proved to be a false dawn. It was often and widely resisted by employers; it failed at moments when it was most urgently needed; it often turned out to be weak and helpless. It was finally knocked down in May, 1935 by the United States Supreme Court. But for the moment, it gave new hope and courage to millions. Its recognition of the right to organize and bargain collectively gave them an effective tool and freed them from apathy, hopelessness, and inaction. It gave rise to a new militance, directed not at revolutionary upheaval but at down-to-earth matters of wages and hours, of status and dignity.

In the face of the ILA's resurgence, the Blue Book retaliated with repeated dues sweeps of the docks, backed by the employers and forcing many to pay up or get out. The longshoremen resisted.

On the Matson dock, called on to show their Blue Books, workers refused and walked off the job. They tore up their books and dumped them on the sidewalk. After a brief conference between Matson and Blue Book officials, the men were asked to return. "Never mind the books," they were told.[23]

At about the same time, the ILA complained to the regional office of the NRA that longshoremen were being denied work because they were not members of the Blue Book union. The Blue Book's preferential hiring clause in its agreement with the Waterfront Employers Union, the ILA charged, was a violation of Section 7(a). (Ironically, the employers later used the same argument to oppose the ILA's demand for union preference and union controlled hiring halls.) George Creel, who had headed the nation's World War I information service and was now the regional NRA director, named a special board to hear the complaint. The board included Rabbi Irving F. Reichert, John A. Pettis, and, notably, the Labor Council's John A. O'Connell. The NRA has no jurisdiction, the board found, since the Waterfront Employers Union was not yet covered either by a presidential or industrial code of fair competition. But in a "purely advisory" ruling, the board held that the Blue Book union was "not a company union and is not under the control or domination of WEU." (O'Connell's participation in the ruling, Eliel later contended, was tantamount to organized labor's stamp of approval on the Blue Book union. O'Connell's response was not unexpected since he had been a prime advocate of the Blue Book's earlier affiliation with the Labor Council.) Its contract, the board concluded, was legal, valid, and enforceable by law. To obtain its benefits, longshoremen must belong to the association. The advisory ruling urged employers, though, to hire members of the Blue Book and ILA without discrimination.[24]

The conflict with the Blue Book union came to a showdown only weeks later also at the Matson dock. Meantime, an internal dispute, rooted in Holman's conservative, slow-moving policies, claimed the attention of the militants. The dispute focused on his efforts to impose a tightly controlled, narrowly restricted constitution on the local. Holman's move was vigorously opposed by the rank-and-file activists now calling themselves the Committee of 500 (its name had no relation to its size). It wanted instead—and in large measure won—more regular union meetings, financial accounting, and a more democratic constitution. It worked to wean the local away from Holman's reliance on the NRA and Section 7(a) to solve the longshoremen's problems. The committee's candidates for the union's top offices were defeated, but it elected two of three business agents and a majority of the executive board, including Bridges and Schmidt.[25]

The Matson dispute sprang from the firing of four longshoremen because, the men claimed, they were members of the ILA. The regional NRA, in the absence of a code, would not intercede. Holman refused help: "We don't want any trouble right now. You fellows had better take whatever action you can as individuals." The local's executive board backed away from Bridges's proposal to strike Matson, but Bridges and his group shaped-up one morning at the Matson dock, buttonholing every man selected for work on the dock, urging him to refuse to go in unless Matson reinstated the four men. "So everybody stayed out," Bridges said. Matson and the Waterfront Employers Union hired men from uptown employment agencies to fill the jobs. Though Holman considered the walkout led by Bridges a "wildcat" strike, he asked Ryan to file a complaint with the NRA's National Labor Board in Washington. Despite the absence of a code, the board reminded Matson that Section 7(a) prohibited discrimination of the kind the men were protesting. Federal Conciliator E. P. Marsh wired Washington: "Resentment at Blue Book organization apparently widespread and union leaders fear men will soon get out of hand." Creel and Marsh feared that "there was a general danger of a tie-up not alone of this entire waterfront but other coast ports." They succeeded in persuading Matson to fire the strikebreakers, reinstate the strikers, and arbitrate the discharge of the four men. In short order, the board ordered Matson to reinstate them. "That reestablished the union on the waterfront. That was the end of the fear and intimidation," Bridges said, looking back. It "demonstrated that you could join the union and wear your button, and if the company tried to fire you we had enough power to tie up the waterfront in order to enforce the demand. From that time on the union was established, it was recognized, it was in business."[26]

The Australian-born Bridges, emerging rapidly as the dominant voice of the group, had come ashore at San Francisco some ten years earlier after years at sea under both the Australian and American flags. On the front, Bridges gained a reputation as both a skilled longshoremen and a persistent (if often frustrated) opponent of the Blue Book union. He was a major figure in the editorial crew that swung the *Waterfront Worker* behind the successful reorganization of the ILA. He was a principal mover in the rank-and-file caucus that pushed an aggressive program. Increasingly his became a major voice in providing leadership and direction of the San Francisco local and, in due course, of the Pacific Coast district, though the strike was well underway before his role was publicly spotlighted. Bridges combined a political radicalism with a hard-nosed, job-oriented trade unionism—an attitude deriving in good part from his earlier trade union experience—as an Australian unionist, with the IWW in a 1921 New Orleans strike, and in his war with the Blue Book. Plant, Lapham, Mayor Angelo Rossi, Joe Ryan, the shipowners, the press, the Chamber of Commerce, and Industrial Association never ceased portraying him as a radical. Bridges did not deny it. But they also often painted him as acting for, if not as an active member of, the Communist Party. This accusation he flatly rejected—a position he successfully sustained later in a long, intensive series of administrative rulings and court decisions. In the battle, he often said, the strikers accepted aid from all sources, including the party, but his attitudes—and the strike conduct—were determined independently and, Bridges sometimes boasted, often well in advance of the party leadership. The key to his leadership rested more in his advocacy of militant tactics and job-oriented goals than in the left wing, political program he espoused, and more in his capacity for acutely reflecting what longshoremen thought and felt than in any dogmatic theoretical formulations.

When the militant's caucus was looking for a meeting place, Henry Schmidt, another of the militants in the longshore leadership, suggested Albion Hall, where he had sung as a member of a left wing German singing society. The caucus's variable membership linked Bridges, Schmidt, Bulcke, other militant rank-and-filers, and a small but indefinite number of Communist Party members (who were longshoremen). The common denominator was resentment of the abuses and inequities that infected their jobs, their exploitation by the Blue Book union, and their interest in a democratic union. Through the caucus, they sought to coordinate their voices on union issues now coming to the fore. It was necessary, Bridges later explained, "to lay down some policy in [the ILA] union to overcome the disruption and wrecking that was going on."[27] The group's existence and membership were kept secret, until some individuals split away and ended its secrecy.

Charges of "radical and communist" domination, a major theme in the employers' propaganda attack, often focused on the Albion Hall group. It was also the setting in part for Sam Darcy's claim that the 1934 longshore and general strikes were "our"—the Communist Party's—strikes, with "Communists and other militant elements" exercising broad, and sometimes decisive, influence.[28] Looking back, Darcy tells of a continuing, informal relationship with Bridges in which they discussed matters of tactics and goals, often reaching "a common view." Bridges would then present their judgement to the union leadership.[29] Bridges recalls working day and night during the period of intensive organizing: "The agenda came out of all of us, with big input from party people such as Darcy."[30] Party members for a time sat in meetings with the rank-and-filers until the caucuses were restricted to working longshoremen. Though outside contacts and discussions continued, Bridges always maintained that the driving force, then and later, was the rank and file.

The revived Red Book union was clearly focused on the job—not revolution. The tactics and strategy of its strike were drawn not from political theory, but from solid trade union precedent and waterfront tradition. They were radical only in their sharp departure from prevailing job practices. Militant, rank-and-file tactics and pragmatic goals, vigorously pressed by the caucus, fueled the longshoremen's drive. They left behind the timid, defensive program initially advocated by the *Waterfront Worker*. They forced the party to change its dual-union policies, abandon the MWIU as the union for longshoremen, and cast its lot with the ILA local. They looked, not merely to resistance, but to aggressive and affirmative steps to correct the evils they had endured. They repeatedly demonstrated, to anyone willing to see, that the cries of Communist domination, so loudly trumpeted by the employers, the press, and government officials, dealt with matters that were no part of the union's job program and aspirations.

Arthur Whitehead had been a longshoreman on the Seattle docks for close to a quarter of a century. In 1931 he, like most of the employee members of the representation plan, belonged to the ILA. When they asked for recognition of the union, however, the employers refused. When employers announced a cut in wages the next year, the employees proposed arbitration. The employers refused. When the employee members asked for a meeting of the employees, Frank Foisie told them he did not think the employees wanted one. The employers suggested Whitehead resign from the employee representation plan. He told them he had been elected by the longshoremen; he would resign when they asked him. In the fall of 1932, a committee from the employers' hall looked up the ILA.[31] "It seems," said Dewey Bennett, who was secretary of the Seattle Longshoremen's Association, "they could not do anything under the present set up and they wanted to know if they could not get the wheels of the ILA working to see if they could not do something for the men."[32]

After the ILA organized in Portland in 1933, the employers countered with an employee representation plan, organized principally through gang bosses and called the Columbia River Longshoremen's Association. In the face of the ILA's repeated requests for recognition, the employers insisted the association was "the only legal union," in the hope that it would meet the requirements of Section 7(a). Longshoremen accused the employers of using labor spies and the blacklist to wean members from the ILA. The employers, ostensibly through the association, revised the port's standard practices. They raised wages and continued to hide behind the representation plan almost to the moment of the strike some weeks later.[33]

The San Pedro local voted in December to take their complaints against the employers' hiring hall, the Marine Service Bureau, to the Los Angeles Regional Labor Board. In January, the board ordered a representation election. Longshoremen registered in the bureau voted 1,262 to 32 for the ILA, but requests for negotiations with the employers went unanswered.[34]

The Tacoma local, lone ILA survivor of the 1920s, had been in recent years the major, sometimes the only, source of organizing efforts on the Pacific Coast. Charters had been issued in Everett and Grays Harbor in 1929, Portland in 1931, Seattle in 1932, and San Francisco in 1933. Incubation periods varied port to port but by the end of 1933, unions of longshoremen from San Diego to Juneau, Alaska, were moving toward joint action under the ILA's Pacific Coast District.[35]

Section 7(a) held out the promise of collective bargaining but, for the longshoremen, the gap between promise and performance was vast. Proposals aimed at gleaning its supposed benefits had been circulated among the Pacific Coast locals, approved at a conference in Portland, and carried to hearings in Washington, D.C. The proposals called for a six-hour day, thirty-hour week, $1 an hour with $1.50 an hour overtime, and preference of employment for ILA members through ILA-operated hiring halls. In a short time, the proposals also became the union's bargaining and strike demands. Shipowners had their own agenda for the shipping industry code but had no intention of discussing it or the union proposals with the union representatives.[36] Unfortunately, some of the longshoremen's own spokesmen did not represent them effectively at the hearings. A. H. Petersen, reflecting the reputed conservatism of his San Pedro constituency, sidetracked the longshoremen's major proposals in favor of a proposal for separate code for the longshore industry. ILA President Ryan, present as an advisor to the NRA, offered his recent settlement with Atlantic Coast shipowners—85¢ an hour and a 44-hour week—as a satisfactory resolution of the labor issues. Characteristically, Ryan missed the point: he ignored the Pacific Coast concern for ILA hiring halls, fair job distribution, and a shorter work week; even his wage proposal fell short.

The longshoremen were also confronted at the hearings with a proposal for hiring halls operated by the government with the help of a joint union-employer board. Its author, Boris Stern, had concluded in a nationwide survey of longshore labor conditions that the methods of hiring longshoremen were "atrocious:" Pacific Coast employer-operated hiring halls had been designed to oust and avoid the ILA as the employees' representative. The ILA on the East Coast accepted the shape-up without quarrel or question. Government operation offered the only answer. From San Francisco, by letter, Jack Bryan, president of the Blue Book union, warned the hearings in Washington that Communists and radicals were intent on breaking up his union, then gaining control of the ILA.[37]

Two weeks later, the Pacific Coast longshoremen met again in Portland. They flatly rejected the Stern proposal. Reports that the employers, too, had rejected it encouraged some to think they might get together. The district officers, with an advisory committee, were instructed to seek coastwide negotiations and, failing that by December 10, to take a strike vote. The vote was never taken; the district secretary said later that Ryan had asked him to postpone it. By that date, however, the Waterfront Employers in San Francisco had "voluntarily" restored the previous year's 10-cents-an-hour wage cut in its agreement with the Blue Book union. San Francisco local called it "a desperate effort to defeat the real wishes of the longshoremen." The increase spread rapidly to the other ports. So, too, did the tactic of avoiding dealing with the ILA. The San Francisco union representatives were told that the employers were "by no means" convinced that the ILA represented a majority of the longshoremen. (Local 38-79 Secretary Ivan Cox wrote to Senator Robert F. Wagner, chairman of the NRA National Labor Board, that the Blue Book was made up of 40 percent of the gang foremen, 2 percent of the longshoremen, in all, about 10 percent of the total.) Portland employers had their newly formed association to deal with. In San Pedro the employers ignored the overwhelming vote for the ILA; the local NRA labor board was helpless to do anything about it. Seattle employers dealt, too, with their own employee representatives.[38]

Bridges and his allies swung the San Francisco local behind Bridges's proposal for an early, rank-and-file convention of the Pacific Coast District, to meet in San Francisco February 25, 1934. Bridges and Eugene Dietrich were dispatched to the northwest (on a per diem of $6.80 a day—a longshoreman's base pay—for train fare and hotel rooms) to urge the proposal and to encourage election of rank and file delegates.

6.

THE BIG GUNS

SAN FRANCISCO BAY, historian Lucille Eaves noted, lies where "the mountains crowd close to the oceanside and where but few indentations permit a safe entrance for commerce."[1] Millions of dollars of gold from the Sierra foothills funneled through that "safe entrance" to the outside world; food, supplies, and mining machinery made the return trip. Commerce with the goldfields broadened rapidly to include the burgeoning produce and expanding needs of the great inland valleys—wheat, a swelling flood of farm products, and a growing trade, foreign and domestic, in industrial raw materials and consumer goods. Lumber from the coastal forests flowed through the numerous ports of the northwest. A steadily increasing stream of oil and citrus helped San Pedro, the coast's second busiest port, to challenge San Francisco's dominance. The new canal across Panama speeded the growing traffic between the Atlantic and Gulf coasts and the Pacific. Through the Pacific ports an expanding trade reached out to the Far East and the Pacific rim.

By the spring of 1934, twenty ports served 1,366 miles of Pacific coastline. More than 6,500 vessels and 159 steamship lines were doing business out of these ports; 12,000 longshoremen handled the cargoes, and thousands of seamen, licensed and unlicensed, sailed the ships. The industry's influence spread out from the docks, to shipbuilding, ship repair, and ship supply; uptown to drays of every kind, trains and trucks, warehouses and processing plants, suppliers and users. In turn, the distribution network spread goods and work and profits far inland. A large percentage—at times a majority—of the area's income and jobs was related to the movement of cargoes across the docks. The shipping industry was, in short, a rich and muscular economic force, strategically placed. Its influence reached far beyond the docks to widespread industry, agriculture, and finance, and to government at every level.[2]

It was also a predatory industry. Down the generations, it captured a net of government protection, later reinforced by outright government subsidy, that effectively safeguarded its profits and made multimillionaires of its owners. Coastwise trade—coastal and intercoastal—was reserved by law to American vessels flying the American flag with American crews. Behind the protective barrier, operators could afford to incur higher costs than foreign operators for their ships and their labor (though restrained later by the competition of trucks and railroads). American shipowners in foreign trade had no such monopoly; they faced extensive low-cost, low-wage competition of foreign-flag operators. To meet it, though they made up only about one fifth of the nation's merchant marine, they were lavished with ships, construction and operating subsidies as if the nation's existence depended on it—which was the impression the industry labored tirelessly to maintain.

Under the pressures generated in World War I, between 1918 and 1922, the United States government built 7.250 million tons of steel shipping and nearly a million tons of wood and concrete. Lines established and operated by the U.S. Shipping Board were turned over to the shipowners to operate until they were ready to buy them. When that time came, the ships were sold at bargain-basement prices, on the most favorable terms, for a small fraction—as low as a dime on the dollar—of their cost. Beginning in 1928, under the Jones-White Act, foreign trade operators were paid rich operating subsidies in the form of payments for carrying the U.S. mail.

Shipowners claimed the subsidies were intended to maintain American standards of wages and living conditions aboard American ships against foreign competition. In reality, despite the subsidy, the operators continually pushed seamen's wages toward foreign-flag levels. One analysis showed that subsidized operators paid an average monthly wage, for example, of $34 for an ordinary seamen, $55 for an oiler. Wages on the same vessels when they were operated by the United States Shipping Board had been $47.50 for the ordinary seamen, $72.50 for the oiler. Shipowners collected, one report said, "a subsidy two or three times greater than the total annual wages, from the masters down, of their entire fleet."

Pacific Coast shipowners shared in the government bonanza. Dollar Lines—originally the bailiwick of the belligerent Captain Dollar—organized the Admiral Oriental Line with a $500 cash investment, operated an Orient service with government-owned ships, and paid off the remaining $499,500 of capital stock with its profits. It was paid $19.1 million in mail subsidies. It bought ships that cost $32.5 million for $5.6 million. Four officials of the Dollar company—R. Stanley Dollar, J. Harold Dollar, Herbert Fleishacker, and H. M. Lorber—shared salaries, bonuses, and profits totaling $14.7 million. R. Stanley Dollar was paid $698,750 in commissions and expenses (including, a union report noted, $210 for railway passage that had been provided free). Four San Francisco-based companies collected construction and reconstruction subsidies totaling $112.5 million and mail contracts worth $76.1 million.

Foreign trade shipowners were by no means alone. Companies that were protected by the exclusion of foreign-flag shipping from coastwise trade did well. Matson Navigation Company between 1920 and 1935 earned $29 million in profits, paid $16 million in cash dividends, and $27 million in stock dividends, paid off its funded debt, and increased its net worth from $10 million to $29 million. (Between 1920 and 1932 the monthly wage of a second assistant engineer for Matson dropped from $200 to $140.) American-Hawaiian Steamship Company, though it had its ups and downs, still paid $6.5 million in dividends between the depression years 1930 and 1936.

In March 1934, with events moving toward a showdown, the shipowners were well entrenched and fortified in depth. For some fourteen years, the employers had exercised virtually unchallenged sway over a disorganized, captive work force. Subsidies and protection fed their coffers. They had, no doubt, been buffeted by the

depression, but their defensive measures gave them measurable relief. They cut wages on the ships and on the docks. Lack of employment for the men who handled their cargoes and sailed their ships
imposed no burden; workers were unemployed from the moment
the job or trip ended. If ships did not sail, seamen ashore cost the
companies nothing. Longshoremen simply shaped-up again for increasingly scarce work. But now, plainly, shipowners felt threatened
by the upsurge of the workers' concerted action. The industry's
fundamental assumptions were being challenged vigorously and in
unaccustomed ways. Shipowners prepared to deal with the challenge: to defeat it totally, if they could; to evade it, wherever possible; to shape it to their own ends as circumstances permitted.

In the 1916 longshoremen's strike, and again in 1919, San Francisco's waterfront employers had been vigorously reinforced by the
Law and Order Committee, later the Industrial Relations Committee, of the Chamber of Commerce. Through these committees, in
keeping with the nineteenth century San Francisco tradition, the
most powerful elements of the business and financial community
joined forces to support embattled employers and to defeat the
workers' unions.

They rallied in 1921 when building trades workers angrily protested a 7.5 percent pay cut. The employers retaliated with a general lockout. When the Building Trades Council offered a month
later to accept the cuts, the builders announced the workers could
return only under an open shop. To enforce the open shop and to
complete the decimation of the building crafts' unions, the leaders
of the city's construction, manufacturing, retailing, railroad, bank-
ing, and insurance industries banded together in 1921 in the Industrial Association of San Francisco. By rigid controls on credit and
materials, the association imposed the open shop—embellished as
the American Plan—on the construction industry, contractors as
well as workers. For the next dozen years, the association maintained its rule on the city's building industry and extended it where
it could to other industries. Wages and conditions were set by "impartial" wage boards. The association claimed that it would "consider" problems affecting the building trades or other unions but it

would sign no agreements and insisted that the unions' "unrestricted and arbitrary power" must be curtailed. The association recruited workers, trained apprentices, operating a hiring hall, and broke strikes. It claimed that it hired union men on equal terms with nonunion workers, though as individuals and not through union halls. Union men, on the other hand, were forced to give up or conceal their union cards to obtain work.

Managing Director Albert E. Boynton, a former state senator, held "almost the complete rein of authority" in the association. William G. Storie, a onetime staff member, remembered him as dynamic, meticulous, and energetic. He "would even go through the offices to see whether No. 2 or No. 3 pencils were used and search the waste paper baskets to observe whether the carbon paper had been used sufficient prior to being discarded."[3] But to Henry Melnikow, Boynton "was a bit stuffy. . . . He felt he had the right principles and the right thoughts and that everybody ought to recognize it and bow before it."[4] Boynton was surrounded by men who had played key roles in earlier episodes of anti-unionism: Atholl McBean; Frederick J. Koster, the barrel magnate who had headed the Law and Order Committee; Paul Shoup of Southern Pacific; Wallace M. Alexander of the shipping firm of Alexander and Baldwin; and Colbert Coldwell, representing real estate interests. Others would move into active leadership but the association provided continuity for the city's powerful anti-union tradition. In a carefully staged public transaction, it was assigned the role of premier strikebreaker in the summer of 1934, but its part in the planning and preparation for the strikes, if not secret, went largely unreported.

The National Recovery Administration and Section 7(a), the association contended, had changed little. Labor's claim of new rights was "without foundation in law or fact." The American Plan "open shop" and "properly conducted" company unions were legal, now as in the past. The association reiterated the rule laid down by General Hugh S. Johnson, the NRA administrator, that employees cannot be required to belong to a particular union. Nor could individual employees be barred from bargaining as individuals. "Senator Boynton," said Storie, "figured [Section 7(a)] was a passing development and not to be taken too seriously." The association's

stand was consistent with widespread opposition to the national recovery program and Section 7(a) among business—and Republican—interests. The association also was not greatly impressed by
the feeling of some important businessmen that FDR and the NRA
were useful.[5]

Opposition to the Roosevelt administration made close allies of
major elements of the press. William Randolph Hearst, the powerful publisher who had vigorously supported Roosevelt's election—
once John Nance Garner of Texas had been added to the
ticket—was suffering from disillusion. He was not so much worried
by the administration's "lunatic fringe" as "incensed against them."
"I feel sure," he wrote to John Francis Neylan, a onetime Hearst
publisher, now his legal counsel, and soon to be an important player
in the summer's strikes, "revolution against the revolutionists is
gaining strength every day."[6] Hearst's five newspapers were flanked
on the coast by such ardent Republican, anti-FDR, usually anti-
union voices as the *San Francisco Chronicle*, Joseph Knowland's *Oakland Tribune*, and, probably the nation's foremost advocate of the
anti-union open shop, Harry Chandler's *Los Angeles Times*. Lorena
Hickok, an observer reporting to Roosevelt aide and advisor Harry
Hopkins, was informed "newspaper publishers have been getting
together in more or less secret sessions and laying plans publicly to
rid [California] of Communists, but privately to fight Roosevelt."[7]
Waterfront employers shared the anti-FDR outlook. Roosevelt and
his Secretary of Labor Frances Perkins were intent on unionizing
"all industry," the shipowners' lawyer, Herman Phleger, contended; "to accomplish this they used their governmental power to
favor the unions in every labor controversy."[8] Roger Lapham was
convinced the Roosevelt administration was committed to the
workers and unions. "Labor was given all the breaks," he later told
an interviewer, "and to my way of thinking [the federal govern-
ment] didn't hesitate to use any methods to build up organized
labor." But to Lapham the longshoremen's leadership "went beyond the aims of the usual accepted labor leadership. It was to get
power. To get control."[9]

Such was the climate in the early spring of 1934 as the waterfront employers sat down to plan their resistance to the chal-

lenge—or threat—posed by the longshoremen. They were prepared, they made clear, to live with the International Longshoremen's Association (ILA) but only under carefully tailored conditions that would insure weak unions, no unions, or, perhaps, survival of their current employee-representation plans. These conditions called for the reduction of unity to port-by-port levels, evasion or denial of exclusive representation, and retention of the employers' unilateral control over vital job decisions.

To insure these—and no worse—results, employers were prepared to go to some length, as George Creel, the World War I propagandist who served as NRA regional director, wrote to the National Labor Board in Washington: "They gave me to understand confidentially that even if they lost two or three million, it would be worth that to destroy the union." "We planned well in advance," Thomas G. Plant told an interviewer. Plant had been elected president of the Waterfront Employers Union of San Francisco in 1933, soon after reorganization of the ILA got underway. He brought an extensive background in shipping to the job; he had worked as clerk, roustabout, super-cargo, and port agent. He had operated shipping for the United States Shipping Board and ran a postwar fleet of ships (the results had been "disastrous," he said). Through much of his twenty-eight-year career he had been employee and associate of Roger Lapham in the American-Hawaiian Steamship Co. Plant retained a sentimental affection for the days of sail and the shipmasters who sailed the ships. His work on the docks had been arduous, the hours long with no overtime pay, but he had loved the job.[10] Melnikow, a frequent opponent, described him as "rigid and fairly inflexible but as honest as could be. . . . If he made a promise he kept it. But it was impossible to make a promise [in negotiations with the ILA] that was acceptable."[11]

In a memo to WEU members, Plant outlined the steps in the employers' plan: the WEU would establish a recruiting hall for strikebreakers and establish and maintain housing and feeding facilities aboard properly equipped ships. Employers were asked to survey their organizations for permanent employees who could be used to teach unskilled men. Labor, he thought, "apparently is available to any degree or extent it may be desired. It should not be necessary to hire any professional strikebreakers." He cited the vast numbers of unemployed and college students. He anticipated few defections among seagoing crews.

The employers "would not hire one armed guard," Plant said. "We were going to depend on the city to provide all the protection necessary." Mayor Angelo Rossi had no doubts, either, he said. "He called the police chief and as a matter of fact they wanted us to proceed just that way because they didn't want us to have armed guards. It was fully shown that the job was theirs of providing [the strikebreaking operations] with the necessary protection."[12] The police department told shipowner and Industrial Association representatives that it would assign an adequate force to "take care of the entire situation without any additional expense to the Waterfront Employers' Union." These would include mounted police on the Embarcadero, a sufficient number of radio cars, and the police boat. The police asked the WEU to keep them informed on ship movements and indicated their willingness to patrol piers where loading was going on and escort men being transported along the waterfront. The WEU would be responsible for policing the housing ships but, otherwise, the shipowners would place the entire situation in the hands of the police.[13] (In mid-June, Plant sharply reprimanded Eugene Mills of the Marine Service Bureau in San Pedro after the WEU membership "expressed themselves very forcibly on the subject of expense at San Pedro. . . . The item of guards, cost and boarding, amounting to about $100,000 is one we think should be borne by the city. Here, the police in ample numbers are supplied without cost."[14]

In addition, before, during and after the strike, the Industrial Association maintained undercover surveillance in unions it suspected of communist leadership. Paul Eliel told the LaFollette Committee in 1940 that surveillance had originated in the association's efforts to maintain the open shop in the building trades. It flared up, William Storie said, during the waterfront strike. (Association representatives admitted to the committee that reports and correspondence relating to a wide range of its activities, including its labor spying and strikebreaking, had been destroyed.)[15]

7.

DEADLINES

ALMOST THE FIRST decision of the twenty-seventh sometime-"annual" convention of the Pacific Coast District International Longshoremen's Association, when it opened in San Francisco February 25, 1934, was to telegraph ILA President Joseph Ryan: "You are urgently requested to attend this convention . . . It is imperative you attend. Situation is critical." Ryan replied that he had more critical business in Washington, opposing the longshore provisions of the proposed shipping industry code. The situation, Ryan advised, "gives your district opportunity to go limit in your demands stop . . . take whatever action you see fit to force employers to accept same stop you will have full backing of International." Be militant but conservative, he added. As the ten-day convention developed, Ryan beat a confused retreat from militancy, advising "no drastic action" until the code was signed—on March 22, he expected.[1]

But the delegates, largely rank and file led by the San Francisco contingent, moved to bring the employers to the bargaining table, by strike if not by negotiation. They expected nothing from the proposed code; instead, they restated their rejected code proposals as negotiating demands: a six-hour day and thirty-hour week; $1 an hour straight time, $1.50 an hour overtime; and ILA-operated hiring halls and preference of employment. They set a March 7 deadline for negotiations with the shipowners. Ryan promised "all possible pressure" on the Pacific Coast shipowners' eastern representatives. The delegates asked the National Recovery Administration's George Creel to arrange a meeting with the employers. Without a code, Creel replied, no action was possible but one was expected soon. The delegates, not satisfied to wait, asked the shipowners through the Waterfront Employers Union of San Francisco to sit down with their committee. The WEU agreed to meet only on behalf of the San Francisco employers, but it offered to ask employers in other ports to join them.

On March 5, the day of the meeting, Ryan wired the convention that he was having difficulty arranging a meeting with the shipowners. With radical leaders in control of the international on the Pacific Coast, expressing their dissatisfaction with the conservative leadership, Ryan reported, the employers are taking the position that they "may as well meet the situation now no matter what the cost." If that is the case, Ryan suggested the "loyal" ports negotiate "conservative" agreements, leaving the "radical ports to take whatever course they see fit." The delegates voted unanimously to inform Ryan that "each and every and all locals on the Pacific Coast are loyal."

That morning, too, Bridges proposed a set of instructions to the committee that would meet the San Francisco employers within a few hours. The committee should insist: "1) That they can deal only as a district. 2) Recognition embodying our original demands. 3) That we will not arbitrate these demands on the grounds we have nothing to arbitrate. 4) That in the event that these things do not receive favorable consideration by the employers by March 7th we shall take strike measures to gain them, with a time limit of 10 days. 5) That no separate port agreements be signed." Paddy Morris of Tacoma, acting as convention chair, read the fourth item as a call for a strike no later than March 17 if the employers failed to meet their demands. After considerable debate the delegates amended it to call for a strike vote—not a strike—by March 17.

The committee reported the next morning that the employers were willing to recognize the ILA as the representative of a majority of the longshoremen, but only for the port of San Francisco. "We realized," the committee reported, "that the employers were organized up and down the Pacific Coast and we had similarly taken a leaf out of their book and organized likewise." The union committee told Plant how, in the northwest, when any advance in wages or hours or working conditions was proposed, workers were told it was entirely a matter for San Francisco to decide. The committee suggested the San Francisco employers invite the others to "sit down here and talk things over."

Plant, speaking for the WEU, told the ILA committee the union proposal that the employers hire only members of the ILA was unacceptable. It would constitute a closed union shop in violation of Section 7(a), as construed by General Johnson, the NRA administrator, and it would unlawfully discriminate against nonmembers of the ILA and coerce them in their choice of bargaining representative. The shipowners, of course, had not allowed Johnson's ruling to interfere with their closed-shop arrangements with the Blue Book union or with the employee associations in Portland and San Pedro. Organized labor in general had heatedly opposed the general's interpretation, contending that minority recognition undercut the majority union and handed employers a ready means of using one group of workers against another. President Roosevelt, with the final word, had been quoted on both sides of the issue but finally had allowed Johnson's interpretation to stand.

The employers also raised the issue of "radicalism" in the ILA. They charged that sixteen of the fifty-five delegates to the convention were Communists. "They want to know," the committee reported, "if we represent the rank and file or somebody else is representing the rank and file." Bridges replied from the convention floor: "We all are radicals." The delegates had voted down the "conservative" policy that would have required them to wait for a shipping industry code. "We shouldn't take any notice of what the shipowners think or say about us. They would shoot us if they had the chance or could get away with it without being discovered. We are putting them on the block and we should keep them there." Bridges was convinced the union would have to force the employers to deal with the union as a district. It must pursue a course, Bridges declared, "to get what we should have and not what they want to give us. If they won't consent, we must force it."

The convention's final action ordered a strike vote unless the employers complied with the union demands by March 7—the next day. If the union demands were not met by March 22nd, a strike would be called in all Pacific Coast ports at 8:00 A.M., March 23. In its final hours, too, the convention instructed the newly elected executive board to have all Pacific Coast locals convene port-by-port conferences of all marine unions and marine workers, organized and unorganized, to organize united support behind the union's demands.

Longshoremen voted in mid-March to strike, 6,616 to 699. The ballot put the question ambiguously: "Members in favor of calling a strike for recognition of the International Longshoremen's Association, effective 8 A.M. March 23, will vote yes. Members against a strike at that time will vote no. If the employers have agreed to collective bargaining before March 23rd, this ballot is void." Frequently in the weeks ahead the employers argued that the ballot sought only recognition, made no mention of wages or hours, that the walkout was being continued for purposes that went beyond "recognition" and was, therefore, unauthorized.

Advertisements in the daily newspapers on March 19 and 21 and a lengthy statement by Plant on March 20 launched the employers' propaganda offensive. Somewhat tentatively, the WEU restated its willingness to negotiate for the port of San Francisco, as it had voluntarily in the March 5 meeting despite the absence of a code; its qualified "recognition" of the ILA; its inability to negotiate for the employers in other Pacific Coast ports; and its conviction that the union demand for a "closed shop" would be "clearly unlawful." Most of all, the WEU contended, the men do not "clearly" understand—and it questioned whether they had been told—these "facts." It would be "regrettable," one ad wound up, if a strike should result where the employers are unable to concede the union demands. "Remember [the ad said] that if you strike, it is your own job and your own livelihood that you give up. The ships will be kept working."[2]

Local 38-79, too, prepared for battle. Bridges proposed the creation of a strike committee, made up of delegates from steady gangs on each dock, as well as from the casual gangs and casuals. The committee's some fifty members made Bridges its chairman. Henry F. Grady, a University of California professor serving as chairman of the NRA regional labor board in San Francisco, called on the committee to delay its strike. Henry Schmidt remembered him painting "a grim picture," warning, " 'There's liable to be violence. . . . Some of you are liable to be killed.' "[3]

Delay was also being urged from other directions. On March 22, William Lewis wired Ryan: "The sentiment of the men is so strong that a strike cannot be averted unless the President intervenes." The National Labor Board confidentially wired the San Francisco regional office that President Ryan was seeking conferences with Pacific Coast steamship interests to work out an agreement: "Pending developments believe strike will not be called stop." Creel urgently and confidentially asked President Roosevelt to intervene: "I have assurances from International Longshoremens strike committee that they will agree to your request stop Means ruin to Pacific Coast stop Employers confident of victory and actually eager for conflict feeling loss of millions amply compensated by destruction of union stop Longshoremen equally confident and neither side considering public interest."[4] President Roosevelt responded immediately. He urged Lewis as president of the Pacific Coast District to suspend the strike. He promised an impartial investigation by a board empowered to conduct hearings and make recommendations for peaceful settlement by direct negotiations. Lewis agreed at once. The strike vote, he told the president, "represents the deepest conviction of 12,000 workers that justice could not be had except by showing our economic strength." But the strike was being postponed in view of the President's pledge of an impartial commission and the belief that "the evidence of the justice of our cause is bound to change present unbearable conditions. . . . With every assurance of loyalty and esteem."[5]

Some longshoremen doubted that District President Lewis had authority to postpone the March 23 walkout, but they nevertheless continued working. George Creel at the NRA summarized up the situation: Both sides, he said, had wanted a strike—the employers were willing to risk millions to destroy the union; the radical leaders were committed to the strike by "their own reckless utterances on the floor of the convention." President Ryan was incapable of holding back the West Coast radicals. If the National Labor Board were to be effective, Creel wrote, it must overcome the Johnson interpretation of Section 7(a). Coast employers are using it to destroy unions—"this is not an interpretation, but a nullification. As long as it is permitted to stand, collective bargaining will only be a sorry joke."[6]

8.

THE APRIL 3 DISAGREEMENT

ON APRIL 3 at the National Recovery Administration's regional labor board in San Francisco, officials of the International Longshoreman's Association and the Waterfront Employers' Union shook hands on a written but unsigned agreement. "Let's be friends," said Judge Charles A. Reynolds, one of the mediators. "Let's make it a gentlemen's agreement, and we will not sign it." "To show good faith and good feeling," Thomas Plant later added.[1] It came after four days of hearings conducted by the mediation board named by President Roosevelt within hours after District President William Lewis called off the March 23 strike. In addition to Judge Reynolds, who was the regional labor board chairman in Seattle, the board was made up of the regional labor board chairmen in San Francisco, Dean Henry F. Grady, and in Los Angeles, J. L. Leonard.

Rather than tackle the substantive issues themselves, the mediation board had sought instead to establish a procedure for resolving them. It had proposed port-by-port elections to determine if the ILA represented the longshoremen. Employee and employer representatives, under an impartial chairman, would undertake to settle local disputes and grievances. A coastwide board, with employer and union representatives from each of the three Pacific Coast states, would be responsible for coastwide conditions—such wages, hours, and working conditions "as may be common to all ports."

The WEU continued the evasive tactics that had frustrated earlier talks. It offered to recognize the ILA as the "majority" union, but it would also recognize "the known spokesmen" of any other "bona fide" groups of longshoremen. It promised it would not offer any minority group more favorable conditions than those accepted by the ILA. It recognized that a "dispatching hall" must be established to obtain a more equitable distribution of work, but it could be neither employer- nor union-controlled. It offered to accept provisions of the still-unsigned shipping code calling, in case of deadlock, for a locally appointed mediation board, followed, if necessary, by national mediation, appointed in Washington. Finally, WEU insisted, "because of local differences each port's problems must be handled separately."

The mediators recommended acceptance. Lewis, along with other district officials, thought the proposal useful. Bridges led the dissent, not least to employer plans to deal with a minority union—a blatant open shop. Nevertheless, negotiations under the agreement started the next day, April 4.[2]

At the moment when a strike had seemed unavoidable, an unhappy John O'Connell of the Labor Council had sought the intervention of ILA President Joseph Ryan. The council had learned of the proposed strike only the night before it was to take place. O'Connell doubted that Local 38-79 could afford a strike involving several thousand men; it would as a result seriously involve the labor movement. In any case, O'Connell wrote, Lee Holman believed the local union officials "are communistically inclined and the decent element in the organization are not in favor of their methods." Holman said it was a mistake for San Francisco to negotiate for the entire coast; each port should deal for itself. O'Connell strongly urged Ryan to "come here and take hold of the situation."[3]

Local 38-79 itself dealt with Holman. The local's executive board accused him of "insubordination and malfessance [sic]," sending telegrams without the sanction of either the Pacific Coast District or the local union. "He did not carry out the mandate of the convention of the Pacific Coast District and has been constantly violating the confidence invested in him," the executive board charged. Holman, "ill from overwork," appealed to Ryan. The action was a reprisal for his stand against the strike, he claimed. Convervatives did not favor the strike, nor did important labor leaders or public opinion. He strongly urged Ryan to "take the bull by the horns" and deal "with this mob of radicals." Conservatives did not attend meetings, he said; they were too tired from working. Radicals directed the union's affairs through "secret" meetings. His solution, he told Ryan: no meetings except on rare occasions, mail reports on financial affairs, and secret ballots on vital questions. He asked Ryan to restore his pay; "otherwise cannot hold the fort for the ILA very long. I shall be compelled to do next best thing in order family not starve."[4] On April 19, it was announced that Holman had been suspended permanently and barred from holding office for one year.

Lewis brought the first direct information on the April 3 agreement to Local 38-79's April 9 meeting. Waving a paper at the members, Lewis reached feebly for a light note, "Well, here's the damned thing I sold you out for." A longshoreman asked, "Is the 'damned thing' even in writing?" "No," Lewis replied, "it's a gentleman's agreement." The longshoremen hooted.[5] From Portland, a telegram to Bridges expressed Local 38-78's dissatisfaction with "Frisco settlement" and expressed its willingness to strike for complete recognition. Two days later, Lewis put his optimism into a letter to Pacific Coast District locals: "I [confidently] expect that all questions will be finally settled in 10 days. . . . we have accomplished the main desires of our membership. We have gained full and complete recognition of the ILA on the Pacific Coast. Also, under the arrangements with the San Francisco employers, which will apply to all other ports, we have secured a closed shop, if the membership lives up to its responsibility."[6] But ten days later, negotiations were close to deadlock. San Francisco had obtained a closed shop and recognition was complete only if employer recognition of minority groups, such as the Blue Book, was ignored. The settlement's adoption in the other ports was, at best, uncertain.

Renewed negotiations with district officials quickly ran aground. The union insisted that any agreement on wages must bind all Pacific Coast ports. The WEU flatly refused. After two days of wrangling, Dean Grady advised the ILA that the demand violated the April 3 agreement. He suggested confining its attention to the San Francisco situation or sending in a new committee for that purpose. After about a week, a new committee signed in. "We spent, I guess, the better part of each and every day except Sundays in negotiations," Plant recalled. The new committee quickly agreed on a temporary forty-eight hour ceiling on work in any one week, a maximum of fifteen hours on any one shift, and at least eight hours rest between shifts. With ILA consent, the rules were made immediately effective.

Discussion turned to limiting the work force. The employers wanted to close the waterfront as of June 30, 1933, to bar the men who had flooded the waterfront in the latter half of the year, but no agreement was reached. A hiring hall was discussed; the employers brought in Frank Foisie to share the Seattle experience. Work on revising working conditions and port practices went ahead. Wages proved a barrier. The union advanced its $1-an-hour proposal; the employers contended the increase of 10¢ an hour in December, 1933 was as far as they could, or should, go. They referred the wage question to "local mediation"—two representatives of each side, labeled the committee of two-and-two.

At the Local 38-79 meeting on April 29, district officials undertook to explain the difficulties being encountered in the negotiations. Bridges objected that the employers were losing the men's demands in a maze of negotiations, that months of talk had no other purpose than stalling for time to weaken the men's stand. Indeed, the union's original demands—$1 an hour, union hiring hall and union preference, the six-hour day and the thirty-hour week in a coastwide agreement—were nowhere to be seen.

The employers were told the next day that "unless something definite shall have been arrived at by the joint committee of five-and-five [the main committee] and the committee of two-and-two, by Monday Evening Eight P.M., May 7th, 1934; negotiations shall be discontinued."[7]

Restlessness on the waterfront grew during the April negotiations. Eliel later charged it was largely because the men were, at best, only sketchily informed about the situation. He added, "radical agitation on the waterfront began to assume alarming proportions." The flood of leaflets, broadsides, mimeographed circulars, and other materials, he said, was rising.[8] The president's mediation board returned to the negotiations, meeting in two sessions daily. Efforts to move the dispute to national mediation were rejected. The employers asked the ILA to join them in a joint statement to the men of the results of negotiations thus far. The proposal was delivered by hand to Lewis, but the bearer was told there would be no reply. A WEU advertisement complained that the agreement for a peaceful settlement had been "abandoned." Means for a peaceful settlement were still available; failure to use them was a violation of the April 3 agreement.[9]

Wires from Ryan's New York office urged other locals to ignore the San Francisco local. U.S. Senator Robert F. Wagner, chairman of the National Labor Board, urged further delay to allow the mediation board an opportunity to reconsider the matter. Dean Grady, flying back from Washington, wired for a delay. Afternoon newspapers on May 8 reported the strike would begin the next day—and recalled the "violence and bloodshed" that had characterized the 1919 strike. The WEU phoned union officers for confirmation. Chief of Police William J. Quinn organized a special force to augment the harbor police and issued orders "to bear down hard on any threats of disorder." The ILA strike committee adopted a motion to reinstate the committee in the "present emergency." Harry Bridges was unopposed for chairman.

"What else we could have done to avert the strike, I do not know, except outright capitulation to union demands," Plant said later. Lewis told the *San Francisco News*, "No one, not even President Roosevelt, can stop this strike now except an agreement on the part of our employers to conform to our demands."[10]

9.

STRIKE

"THE MEN DID not turn to on May 9th."[1]
So Thomas G. Plant described the start of the strike of some 12,000 longshoremen at ports from San Diego to the Canadian border. The coast "is 100% out," ILA Pacific District President William Lewis told the San Francisco strike committee. The strike, a union statement said, is intended "to get all the things that the government, itself, has advocated and after every means available under the NRA for an amicable settlement have been exhausted."[2] The shipowners counterattacked. They slammed tight the heavy steel gates on the docks and reinforced them with barbed wire. Police took up stations along the piers; the few radio cars reinforced mounted and motorcycle policemen patrolling the front. Newspaper ads called for strikebreakers.

In Portland, two crews of gang bosses stood by for emergencies. Otherwise, longshoremen—estimated at from 1,100 to 1,500—stayed off the docks. A newspaper told the men that, unless they reported for work by 8:00 A.M. the following morning, they would be fired. The employers counted heavily on unemployed workers to move the port's cargo. Teamsters were refusing to cross the longshoremen's picket lines; sailors, bargemen refused to work cargo and members of the United Licensed Officers balked at furnishing steam, tending hatches for strikebreakers, or assisting in moving scabs. By the end of the first day, thirty-one ships were tied up at

Portland docks. The Portland City Council wired President Roosevelt, asking him to intervene personally in the dispute which, it said, would affect all classes of the population unless settled immediately.

On the first day of the strike, when Tacoma employers called for the National Guard, the Central Labor Council—ILA District Secretary Paddy Morris was its president—warned Washington Governor Clarence Martin "to keep his hands off or there would be a general strike from Bellingham to Portland."[3] In Seattle and Oakland, as in Portland, teamsters were refusing to haul cargo handled by strikebreakers. In San Francisco ILA President Lewis, after meeting with Teamsters Local 85 president Michael Casey, was confident the truck drivers would support the strike.

A majority of longshoremen joined the strike in San Pedro, though members of the newly formed Longshoremen's Mutual Protective Association of Los Angeles and San Pedro continued to work. The militantly open shop Merchants' and Manufacturers' Association opened recruiting stations for strikebreakers in Vernon, Wilmington, and in the Rosslyn Hotel in downtown Los Angeles. Strikebreakers were housed on moored ships or behind stockades. Police forces in harbor communities—as in other ports up and down the coast—went on strike duty; leaves, holidays, and vacations were canceled. Within days three hundred policemen were patrolling the San Pedro strike area, along with an equal number of private guards and deputies. The police force eventually reached a strength of some seven hundred, many of whom received additional pay from the waterfront employers.

"We planned [to open the docks and employ strikebreakers] well in advance," Plant said. "In fact, much before the strike we had two ships"—the *Diana Dollar* and Matson's *Wilhelmina*—"outfitted so that we could house and take care of strikebreakers."[4] On the first day of the strike, the employers opened a recruiting office at 23 Main Street. The police had promised protection for the new hires, a WEU statement said, as well as for regular longshoremen who reported for work. They would be lodged on the docks where they worked so there would be "no need to cross picket lines."[5]

LONGSHOREMEN WANTED
EXPERIENCE DESIRABLE BUT NOT NECESSARY

an ad in the next day's papers said. The number of recruits mounted rapidly and "without difficulty," though, Plant added, they sometimes had trouble reaching the recruiting place. Within days, the employers claimed hundreds of strikebreakers were at work; by the end of the month Plant said 970 men were living on housing vessels.

The strikebreakers, Plant said after the strike, "were nearly all Americans, nearly all citizens of San Francisco, nearly all family men, and in the large majority of cases men who had been on relief, willing to work and satisfied with the conditions under which they were employed."[6] On the other hand, Theodore Durein recorded his experiences as a strikebreaker—most of the time as a pot-washer in a housing ship's bakery—in *Reader's Digest.* He described strikebreakers as "mostly pasty-faced clerks, house-to-house salesmen, college students and a motley array of unemployed who had never shouldered anything heavier than a BVD strap before in their lives."[7] Among them were platoons of husky football players from the University of California, recruited by their coach, William "Navy Bill" Ingram. One of them, though, was rescued from scabbing by his irate father who managed to get aboard the housing ship. The son apologized when he reappeared in his father's tow: "I didn't know I was doing anything wrong. The coach said that working on the dock was a good opportunity to keep in shape for football." His father contributed $100 to the strike fund before he left.[8] Durein said some of the "hard nut" strikebreakers imported from San Pedro had been guaranteed their return fare. He also met an analytical chemist, a bacteriologist, two members of the California bar, and five school teachers. "They were the softies," he added. Said one premedical student: "I'd rather have salt on my torn body, but God, I have to be a doctor." His earnings of $150 paid for his return to college.[9]

F. J. McGowen, general manager of the Outer Harbor Dock and Wharf Company at San Pedro, recalled that some of the men housed in a company camp "had not eaten for weeks; some of them had not worked for months and years. When they first came to us they were in pretty bad shape. After we got a couple of weeks' food into them and a place for them to sleep, they began to improve. . . . After sixty days . . . the men we took in and trained were better than the longshoremen are today."[10] Durein claimed that, as strikebreakers hardened, they, too, achieved the competence of the old hands—except in stowing cargo which, he concluded, called for years of experience and "a sixth sense."

"We lived in luxury," Durein wrote. Comfortable quarters, daily changes of linen, fresh towels; generous meals—steak, strawberries, and ice cream; two nightly movies, newsreels and cartoons; and weekly boxing bouts. Banks established weekly office hours to receive the better than $90 a week the men were earning. They could buy beer by the case, tobacco, clothes, shoes, etc., at the ship's store. Gambling flourished every night. "All this was free . . . Our enormous pay checks were clear profit."[11] A student committee appointed by the president of the University of Washington reported that employers were offering students board and room and wages higher than those paid longshoremen. Said the committee: "Excellent food, brand-new sheets and blankets and first-class Negro valet service convinced many [once aboard a housing vessel] that the life of the longshoreman was not as bad as they believed."[12] Durein would not guess "what it cost the shipowners to keeps us in the style to which we were utterly unaccustomed." He was sure, though, that the shipowners had "decided to work their ships at any cost save that of giving in to the strikers."[13]

Some twenty-five strikebreakers on the McCormick docks in San Francisco, according to the local ILA's second strike bulletin, decided to quit their jobs. If they came off, could they have protection? They asked the ILA's speedboat crew by semaphore.[14] In addition to the speedboat pickets, the strikers patrolled the waterfront by automobile. The auto patrols carried a full load of pickets—the so-called "sanitary" or "clean-up" squads armed with baseball bats and rocks. "Many are the cases of strikebreakers who were beaten by striking pickets," said Herbert Resner in a Work Projects Administration-supported study of law enforcement in the strike. "A police report of July 20, ten days before the strike ended, listed 195 strikebreakers and 'innocent bystanders' injured from the time the strike was called."[15] Durein said he was reminded daily that "several thousand half-starved stevedores patrolled like vultures across the Embarcadero. Their favorite trick, when they captured a strikebreaker, was to put his leg across the curb and jump on it. Or kick his teeth out." (In one such case, though, the strike committee was sufficiently angered with the beating of a strikebreaker that Bridges with one of the pickets boarded the ship where the man was working to apologize and offer to pay his dental bills.)

To onetime Harvard President Charles William Eliot, the strikebreaker had been "a pretty good sort of hero."[16] Strikers saw him differently. Durein reflected the employers' view when he wrote, "We were moving cargo, and moving it fast. We were making it possible for the employers to hold out and finally break the backbone of the strike." During the strike, Thomas Plant said, strikebreakers performed longshore service "to a very high degree of excellence." To the striker, though, strikebreakers were traitors to their own kind, collectively and individually—the enemy, without principle or decency. They were the assault troops in the employers' war to disarm the strikers in their fight for a decent living.

Strike violence is almost invariably the product of a clash between two, sharply conflicting, powerfully asserted rights. The employer claims a right—ordained from on high, at least since the start of the Industrial Revolution, sanctioned by the ruling wisdom and later by law—to unfettered use of his property; open access to labor, transport, and commodity markets, and to conduct his business without (or with as little as possible) interference. To defend that inalienable right, the employer feels he has a prior and unlimited claim on the authority of the city, state, and nation. Pacific Coast shipowners invoked that right in justifying their employment of strikebreakers and in planning and carrying out the forcible openings of the strike-locked ports under the armed protection of the police in the face of certain resistance, violence, and bloodshed. Employers were accorded generous support by government at many levels in that purpose. Restrained only by the feeble strictures of Section 7(a), they brought every weapon to bear, confident that their hostility was proper, lawful, and just.

The strikers assert a conflicting right. They withhold their labor because they are dissatisfied with the terms—wages, hours, recognition, status—under which it was being bought. By doing so, they do not quit their jobs; instead, they assert a proprietary interest in them. By doing so, they seek to concentrate attention on their grievances and to negotiate some amelioration. Their labor is the workers' basic source of economic influence with the employers, their ultimate source of equality at the bargaining table. The use of strikebreakers is a declaration of war, not only against the strikers' demands; it hits with unmitigated economic—and as it turns out, political—force at their right to withhold their labor until better terms can be negotiated.

When the WEU opened its strikebreaker recruiting office, Henry Schmidt remembered, "Our guys organized a parade. . . . The dope was, 'Don't do anything, just march by there.' . . . After we peacefully marched past this place and turned the corner to the left and were marching back towards the waterfront, the police attacked us."[17] The *San Francisco Examiner* had a different view: five hundred men broke through police lines at the WEU headquarters on Mission Street, threw rocks and swung clubs until police disbanded them. At the request of the police, the WEU moved its recruiting operations nearer the waterfront because of the difficulties in protecting the recruits. In the first days of the strike, police had broken up a crowd of strikers, reported to be "menacing" two hundred strikebreakers being trucked to the Embarcadero to board the *Diana Dollar*. (The other housing ship, the *Wilhelmina*, was stuck on a sandbar while being towed from Antioch.) Police dispersed a crowd of strikers, too, at Pier 35 where strikebreakers were loading a Grace ship. After the confrontation at the WEU recruiting office, Chief of Police William J. Quinn declared, "From now on, strikers will be shown no quarter."[18] Quinn's declaration was a perhaps unwitting admission of what quickly became the fact: the police even more than the strikebreakers became the strikers' chief antagonist. The role of the strikebreaker was soon stabilized and contained, while police came to serve, day by day, as the employers' virtual private assault force. When the clashes came, as they did, the police—not the strikebreakers—were pitted against the strikers.

Schmidt described the pattern: "Somebody came up with the idea of parading up and down the waterfront, taking a soap box along and when we got to the end of the line get up on there and make a speech." Led by a striker carrying an American flag, bearing placards denouncing scabs and calling for "full recognition," the marchers paraded from the Ferry Building to Fishermen's Wharf or south to the Dollar docks at Pier 48. To avoid automobile traffic, they moved on to the sidewalk. "Then police got orders to chase us off the sidewalk. . . . They were looking for an opportunity to break up these marches. Every once in a while we would go over on the sidewalk and they would raise hell. There would be some horse cops around and they would ride into us and scatter us all over the place. Then they would arrest some people."[19]

The ILA's defense committee, headed by Eugene "Dutch" Dietrich, spent much of its time at the Hall of Justice, bailing out strikers. The committee was helped by Elaine Black and attorney George Andersen, representing the International Labor Defense, a Communist party agency, as well as its own attorney. Dietrich told Resner that bail was set rather high in the early days of the strike but somewhat lower as it went on. Still, bail was set at $2,000 on charges of riot, $5,000 on charges of kidnaping a strikebreaker, and $10,000 on assaults to commit murder. Later many of the radicals swept up by police were held as "$1,000 vags"—a device of doubtful legality for holding as "vagabonds" on $1,000 bail persons for whom no other charges were at hand. Strikebreakers were held on relatively low bail—$20 to $100, the latter in cases of assault with deadly weapons. Arrests of strikers were numerous, but charges were often dismissed. Two men were sentenced to ten days in jail for violating the anti-picketing ordinance; eighteen were dismissed. Of thirty-two men charged with violating the city's anti-handbill ordinance, eleven were dismissed. The police proved unusually sensitive to a handbill showing the two men killed in the July 5 battle, along with a photo of police firing teargas. Nine strikers were promptly arrested. Dietrich said ILA attorneys quickly moved for jury trials to allow a cooling off period. The record of the police and the police courts in relation to arrests of strikers and in the vigilante raids during the general strike, however, was sharply different.

In cases involving both the strikers and the radicals,[20] a representative of the Industrial Association usually sat at the elbow of the deputy district attorney responsible for the prosecution. The association claimed, the Resner report said, its attorney was present to remind judges that the businessmen of San Francisco were watching their activities and expected them to "enforce the law" (much as Captain Dollar said he had intimidated a judge in an earlier strike). In appealing to employers for information concerning assaults and threats, the association said "Attorney Charles Brennan is vigilant but cannot prosecute cases he does not hear about." Brennan, referred to, at least by the *Oakland Tribune*, as "special prosecutor," both defended strikebreakers and helped to prosecute strikers.

> Resner's report concluded: The law was a major force in the campaign to break the strike . . . . The conclusion seems inescapable that the charge made by the workers during the strike was true; the law was used as a strikebreaking agency. . . . unlawful arrests, unlawful searches and seizures, setting of bail in unreasonable sums, unfair trials, convictions without proper or sufficient evidence and in some cases without even a day in court, denial of counsel, deportation of workers, interference with picketing and distribution of strike bulletins, and other devices just as effective in breaking strikes. . . . in their official capacities, many [police, district attorneys, judges and others] are subject to censor. They forgot that they represented the workers as well as the employers.[21]

In the aftermath of the 1901 teamsters' and waterfront strike, Teamsters, Local 85, had been nailed down by a contract clause that read: "The Brotherhood of Teamsters and Auto Truckmen are not in favor of sympathy strikes and will do everything they can to avoid them." That clause was much in the minds of the leaders of the Industrial Association, the longshoremen, and Mike Casey, longtime president of Local 85 and a veteran of the 1901 strike, as teamsters prepared to take action on the 1934 strike. The question was set for a special meeting Sunday, May 13.

The longshoremen's strike committee sent its own representatives to make sure that the teamsters knew of its willingness to negotiate wages and hours, as well as its insistence on the closed shop. Casey and his associates asked the teamsters for a declaration that they would haul cargo to and from the pierheads, but would not enter the docks. The members rejected their proposal; instead, they shouted approval of a resolution "not to transport merchandise to or from the docks." It was not, Casey emphasized to the *Chronicle* afterward, a "sympathetic strike," but "a definite boycott of the waterfront." He explained, "our action was taken for protection of the men. If we continued to haul cargoes to the pierheads, our men might become involved in fights and injuries might result."[22] After the meeting, a number of union drivers joined the longshoremen in a picket parade along the Embarcadero. Eliel called it "a definite vote of sympathy in support of the strikers" by a "substantial number" of teamsters. Oakland teamsters took similar action the next day, and the Seattle teamsters on May 15. When Los Angeles teamsters voted to refuse to haul cargoes to and from the harbor areas, vehicles were put under police protection. An ILA statement exulted: "With the Teamsters behind us we've got them licked. We are sitting on top of the world. There are 2500 freight cars sidetracked between San Francisco and San Jose and they can't move until we give in." Southern Pacific reported the 388 cars held up were more than twice normal.[23]

Police broke up a gathering of pickets—some estimates said five hundred—at the Luckenbach docks where black longshoremen were working. For the moment it spotlighted a potentially heated issue. In the past, black workers had been widely used as strikebreakers, only to be fired once the strike ended. In the 1919 longshoremen's strike, black strikebreakers had been imported from and returned to New Orleans. At least two racially segregated gangs of black men worked during the Blue Book years. Early in the strike, an ILA strike bulletin warned that the shipowners were "circulating rumors that the ILA will not accept Negroes. . . . This is a deliberate and vicious lie." It would accept any worker who had worked in the area for at least one year. It pointed to a Negro delegate to the coastwide convention, five black members of the strike committee, and black members who "speak at all strike meeting[s]." Before the strike ended, the black gangs joined the walkout.[24]

The state of California owned and operated the Belt Line, the short-haul railroad that linked the Embarcadero docks with the main line. The men who worked the line, though union members, held civil service status; strike action would cost them their pensions (a relatively rare benefit in 1934) and seniority. The strikers parked their cars across the tracks and sat down on the rails in front of approaching locomotives to halt the movement of freight cars. With the teamsters' boycott of the waterfront, freight cars became an even more important link in the port's crippled operations. The crews, one observer said, welcomed the delays and interruptions; "they went through the motions of work with no enthusiasm and considerable discontent." P. W. Meherin, president of the Board of Harbor Commissioners, the state's operating agency, warned that, unless the interference was halted, he would ask the governor to put militia on the waterfront to insure free movement.[25]

Meantime, aid for the strikers continued to mount. Boilermakers and machinists voted sympathetic strikes against ships worked by nonunion labor, ashore or aboard. Pacific Steamship Company was first among a number of lines to cancel calls at ports in the northwest until the strike was settled or adequate protection was provided for employees on the vessels. Matson transferred its San Francisco calls to Los Angeles where it claimed operations were "almost normal" by the month's end. In San Francisco, fifty coastwise and forty-four offshore vessels were tied up; thirty had arrived since the strike began. One line reported it had 10,000 tons of cargo immobilized on the dock, with perishables intended for transshipment spoiling. The teamster boycott blocked delivery of substantial quantities of cargo addressed to uptown and out-of-town "marks." While the employers claimed an ample supply of men working the ships, the strikebreakers worked best at unloading, not loading. Cargo continued to pile up and congest the terminals; in the weeks ahead, that roadblock would become the shipowners' overriding concern. On May 15, for the first time in San Francisco's history, no freighter sailed from the port.

10.

The Strike Spreads

In the early days of the Gold Rush, one ship's master in San Francisco Bay found that sailors were asking $300 a month to take his ship to sea, with "ham, eggs, butter, soft tack and canned meats and all the liberty we want in port." The captain sold his ship and headed for the goldfields. Shipowners in the years that followed, however, used other, harsher methods of dealing with their crews:

> The sailor had been abused on shore and exploited at sea. He had been robbed blind by crimps, sold aboard ship for "blood money," kicked and beaten and driven, as Richard Henry Dana put it, "at the will of the master or the whim of a mate." If he refused to work, it was mutiny. If he quit his job, it was desertion. He had no private life ashore—the boarding house masters and their runners saw to that. His life at sea was made up of dingy, airless, cramped forecastles, bad food—prison food was better, one sailor swore—and hard work. He worked twelve or fourteen hours a day in fair weather, around the clock in foul. He had no assurance his ship would stay afloat; inspection for seaworthiness was unknown, safety at sea ignored.[1]

The seaman's relations with his employer were casual and constantly changing. He was paid off at the end of a voyage, usually without assurance he would make the next trip. Organization was especially difficult since a large and varying proportion of the prospective members was always at sea. In 1885, with a shoreside committee to look after their affairs, seamen put together the Coast

Seamen's Union, later the Sailors' Union of the Pacific (SUP). Almost from the day of its inception, the union fought a long series of violent battles with the shipowners, with control of the hiring hall always a major, if not the leading, issue.

Early in that long line of battles Andrew Furuseth joined the union. Furuseth had been a clerk in an Oslo grocery store before shipping out at the age of nineteen. He landed in San Francisco in 1880, sailed on lumber schooners, and worked as a fisherman. In 1886 he became secretary of the union and, with only two short breaks, served until his death in 1938. Under Furuseth the SUP established its place in West Coast shipping. Notably, too, under Furuseth seamen won a large measure of liberation in the LaFollette Seamen's Act of 1915. It ended many of the seamen's peculiar legal liabilities and introduced minimum food and living allowances and manning and safety standards.[2] "Ascetic, aloof, and at times melancholic," Selig Perlman and Philip Taft described him.[3] Thomas Plant remembered Furuseth as "a wonderful person. . . . He was tough, but he was a gentleman. He lived completely alone in a tiny room on the Embarcadero, scrupulously neat and clean, never profane, and honest, but hard."[4]

In 1921, a combination of the shipowners and the United States Shipping Board wiped out the unions on the ships. Faced with a demand for sharp reductions in pay and a 50 percent increase in hours of work, six unions of officers and unlicensed seamen left their ships on strike. Though the board made tentative gestures toward a settlement, the private operators declared an open shop. Once again, men were shipped through the employer-operated Employment Service Bureau. Originally instituted to provide strikebreakers during the 1919 longshoremen's strike, now it turned exclusively to shipping seamen, once again using the so-called continuous employment and discharge book, the hated "grade" books. The "grades" were tabulated and circulated through similar offices in other coast ports.

"There seems to be no question," Paul Eliel cautiously noted some years later, "that in some instances, the service bureau and the discharge book were abused and both favoritism and blacklisting were not unknown."[5] Unionism among the seamen survived mainly under an agreement with the Shipowners' Association of the Pacific Coast, principally operators of coastal lumber schooners. Plant recalled how Furuseth frequently visited his office, asking "if we wouldn't recognize him" or take some of the men, "but we never saw our way clear. . . . Furuseth was in no position to exact [what he wanted] and we didn't want to be bound by any contracts or obligations. Our own consciences were clear; we were paying the highest wages in the industry. And continued to do so during the Depression. Why saddle yourself with an obligation if you don't have to have it?"[6] "The highest wages" continued to sink from 1921 to 1934. Plant's company, American-Hawaiian, led the industry in a series of wage cuts in 1931. Overall, by 1933, wages had fallen, by generally accepted estimates, about 50 percent. Reduced wages were accompanied by a general deterioration of working conditions. Like the longshoremen, through the open-shop years, the unlicensed seamen had accumulated their own bill of grievances extending over the full range of job conditions.

Licensed officers, too, saw their pay and conditions deteriorate. In the 1921 strike the shipowners had gutted the Marine Engineers' Beneficial Association (MEBA), which had existed continuously in San Francisco since 1882. Sam Kagel, a young economist (later a lawyer and a well-known arbitrator) associated with Henry P. Melnikow in the Pacific Coast Labor Bureau, told the National Longshoremen's Board that, after the 1921 strike, engineers had been required to maintain membership in the American Society of Marine Engineers—$10 initiation fee, $1 a month dues—to obtain a job; even with it, if he belonged to MEBA his job was in jeopardy. As far as the engineers knew, Kagel said, the society made no attempt to improve wages, hours of work, or job conditions. On the contrary, hours were stretched out—engineers worked anywhere from eight to sixteen hours a day, and were often called out after their regular shifts for "field days," repairing or overhauling equipment that ordinarily would have been worked on by another engineer. The pay of a first assistant engineer, for one, fell from $222.50 a month in 1919 to $167 in 1933.[7]

Licensed deck officers, too, were compelled to join a "company" organization during the open shop years—according to E. B.

O'Grady, representing the National Organization of Masters, Mates and Pilots (MM&P), Local 90—and swear they had no connection with an American Federation of Labor union. Deck officers were concerned by the deterioration of legal safeguards and standards that had once prevailed on the ships. And now, O'Grady said, they "embraced an opportunity to seek improvement."[8]

After the longshoremen had rejected efforts of the Marine Workers' Industrial Union San Francisco to organize the docks, the MWIU turned its attention to the seamen. On the heels of the longshoremen's May 9 strike, the MWIU began clamoring for seamen to join the fight. A leaflet signed by the "United Front Seamen's Strike Committee and Marine Workers Industrial Union" urged seamen to strike "in support of the longshoremen and for your own demands." The MWIU has declared its own strike, it said; the International Seamen's Union (ISU, embracing the Sailors' Union, Marine Firemen, Oilers, Watertenders and Wipers Association, and the Marine Cooks and Stewards) had done nothing. An ILA strike bulletin reported that MWIU had called for a strike May 12 on all ships in the harbor, the call issuing from a conference claiming to represent some three hundred employed and eight hundred unemployed seamen. The ISU told the *Chronicle* that it had taken no action on supporting the longshoremen, though the ILA had discouraged the MWIU's ambitions to organize the seamen as it had already stifled MWIU's efforts to organize the longshoremen. "Once the seafaring men came off their ships they went back into their old unions," Henry Schmidt said.[9] From the first day, as ships came into port, seamen began to walk off in rapidly mounting numbers, officers as well as unlicensed men. Newspapers reported four thousand sailors and firemen joining the strike. Next day, they added seven hundred cooks and stewards to their count. On May 16, the three ISU unions, in Paul Scharrenberg's words, "having lost all hope in federal mediation, promises made under the NRA, etc., joined with the longshoremen to obtain results by the only method still available for obtaining results."[10]

Though they had gained little attention, the seamen's unions earlier had pressed their claims to consideration. On August 31,

1933, the ISU had demanded "redress" from the shipowners. The shipowners did not reply. On November 10, the same demands were presented to the hearing on the shipping code in Washington. The code was "still unfinished business." On January 11, 1934, the ISU asked for a hearing before the National Labor Board but, without a code, the NLB disclaimed jurisdiction.

Three days after its strike action, the ISU asked the Pacific Coast District of the ILA to agree that neither of them would return to work until the demands of both have been met. Within days, the Masters, Mates and Pilots and the Marine Engineers Beneficial Association announced their numbers were joining the strike. Shipowners belittled the impact of the strike call on the ranks of their licensed employees. Herman Phleger, the shipowners' attorney, doubted the seamen's economic power. "The sailors unions were totally unorganized, but when they saw that the longshore workers were making progress, the leaders of the sailors union, desiring to obtain the same results that the longshore workers might, participated in the strike."[11]

Before two weeks had passed, the count of strikers neared 22,000: 12,000 longshoremen; 5,000 from the Sailors Union; 2,100 from the Marine Firemen; 1,500 from the Marine Cooks and Stewards; 900 from MEBA; and 200 from MM&P.

In the fall of 1933, B. H. Barker, vice president of Federal Laboratories, Inc., had enthused to his field representatives across the country over the opportunities that lay ahead of them: "Prison outbreaks, labor strikes, bank robberies and disturbances of all kinds are of such frequency that the field for our activities is almost unlimited." Federal's activities consisted of supplying tear gas, riot guns and projectiles, and a wide assortment of arms to police departments and, as it turned out, to the nation's major industrial employers for use against picket lines, mass demonstrations, and assorted mobs, as well as escaped convicts and bank robbers. Their effort, Barker told his salesmen, had produced "unlimited quantities of tear gas business." Now, "the present-day trend of criminal activity" offered those in "disturbed areas the chance of a life time."

After all: "Strikes cannot be broken with one or two grenades or a .38 shell. It is essential that this idea be put across."[12]

Joseph M. Roush, Federal's San Francisco representative, and Ignatius H. McCarty, salesman for Federal's rival, Lake Erie Chemical Co., had been working diligently to cultivate the goodwill—and business—of the San Francisco Police Department. Roush had for months past been servicing, without charge, the department's arsenal. McCarty, on the other hand, was aware that Chief of Police Quinn held an order from "public-spirited citizens" directing him, McCarty, to deliver up to $50,000 worth of gas on the chief's order without expense to the taxpayers. On May 13, Quinn gave McCarty an initial order for $5,500 worth of gas. It was delivered the next day. McCarty told his boss that the "public-spirited citizens" in this instance was the Waterfront Employers' Union but warned him that advertising the information would violate the confidentiality which was a condition of sale.

Roush, though disappointed, was not idle. In early July, Federal delivered some $18,000 of gas equipment to the police department. Adjusted for returns, the bill finally totaled $13,809.11, mainly for more than 1,000 long-range gas projectiles and several hundred grenades. When McCarty learned that the city was being asked to pay Federal's bill, he protested; it had been ordered without competitive bids or formal authorization. Unless the Federal order was revoked, McCarty threatened to make public his own dealings with the WEU. McCarty wrote his company's head office that he had been approached, at the mayor's suggestion, by a representative of "the people who had purchased the gas." He explained "that if the unions or other people found out that they donated this equipment it would raise hell." McCarty's protest produced a method of payment that drew again on "public-spirited citizens." As a result of discussions between Barker, Federal's vice president, and Ashfield Stow, assistant to Thomas G. Plant, Barker would put an invoice in escrow with the Bank of America at Montgomery and Market streets; Stow said he hoped someone would go in and pay it. Within two days, an unidentified person paid the full amount in cash and carried away the invoice.

Spasms of violence erupted. In San Pedro, picket lines scattered across the considerable distances within the port grew, by one estimate, from 300 to 1,800. On May 15 pickets surrounded—some reports said "stormed," one said "demonstrated"—a stockade housing some 400 strikebreakers. Private guards fired on the pickets. Twenty-year-old Dick Parker, who had joined the union only the day before, was shot through the chest and killed. "Dickie was a good boy," his mother said, "he gave me the last money he earned." Thousands of strikers and supporters joined in funeral services and a parade. A second striker, John Knudsen, died from a bullet wound received in the same conflict.

Strikers in Portland rallied outside the employers' hiring hall where they were hiring strikebreakers. Pickets halted and threatened to overturn buses brought in to haul strikebreakers to the docks. Strikers blocked gang bosses, bus drivers, and guards from escaping from the hall for several hours until police escorted them through the pickets. The employers' plans to house strikebreakers on the steamer *Admiral Evans* were disrupted when pickets forced twenty-four private guards off the ship—one was thrown overboard and five were badly beaten. Efforts to work cargo were frustrated by the refusal of firemen to supply steam. The small force of strikebreakers quit work by the third morning. Employers announced their intention to open the port on May 14. Police were put on full emergency status. Employers demanded National Guard, as well as police, protection. The Portland Central Labor Council countered with a declaration that it would advocate a general strike if the Guard were called out to police the waterfront. Efforts to work ships in Portland (and Seattle) were abandoned.

In Oakland, strikers boarded the steamship *Oregon Maru*, injuring six strikebreakers, one "seriously." One worker was thrown into the bay, followed by a shower of scrap iron. Drivers of privately owned ambulances, saying they had been threatened with death if they responded, refused for some hours to carry away the injured men. The *San Francisco News* quoted the ILA as blaming the Communists for the threats. Strikers, too, had pursued two busloads of strikebreakers headed for the Alameda waterfront.

"One day we started out to march south from the Ferry Building," Henry Schmidt remembered. "I was marching with Johnny Olsen with about fourteen or fifteen marchers ahead of us. And then there was the flag, and the guys up front swung onto the sidewalk." Newspapers reported a ship working at Pier 18 was the strikers' goal; the *Diana Dollar* housing strikebreakers also was tied up at nearby Pier 22. Bridges remembered that he and a handful in the middle of the long line had planned to charge into Pier 38 and "scramble all over the dock." Instead, a force of policemen, mounted and on foot, met the picket parade, perhaps a thousand strong—a "mob," the *New York Times* called it—at Pier 18. John Shoemaker, a big, blond, muscular longshoreman leading the parade, sent a runner back for instructions. Told to keep moving, Shoemaker took the initial brunt of the police charge. He managed to pull two policemen from their horses before going down under their clubs. "Shoemaker got beat up," Schmidt said, "and Willie Christensen got beat up—he was too heavy to get out of the way, anyway." The bare-fist battle was broken up by a barrage of tear gas and gun shot and, Schmidt said, "we were scattered in all directions." The *San Francisco Examiner* described the scene: "Gas bombs exploded; a sawed-off shotgun roared; clubs smashed against heads, and cobblestones flew along San Francisco's waterfront yesterday as police and strikers clashed in the fiercest battle yet produced by the coast-wide maritime strike." Police fired shotguns directly into the crowd, discharged their revolvers in the air, and, for the first time, used the recently acquired tear gas to disperse the pickets.[13]

Captain Arthur DeGuirre, commanding the Harbor District, said the parade had started out "about as usual," but when it was opposite Pier 18, "the strikers became a howling mob. They began to surround the police cars and tried to drag the inspectors out. From then on it was a case for everybody for himself."[14] Chief Quinn told the *Chronicle* that, henceforth, the pickets must remain on the "town" side of the Embarcadero, an extra-wide street's width from the piers. Lieutenant Joseph Mignola, who ordered police to fire their weapons, told reporters, "If the strikers come back for more, you'll find some of them in the morgue next time."

The ILA angrily protested to the San Francisco Board of Super-

visors: "For no reason whatsoever the mounted police this afternoon rode into the parade and attempted to disperse it. The attack
was carried out by the police with tear gas, drawn guns and revolvers. Several men were shot, and many clubbed and beaten to the
ground, and even after they were lying unconscious on the sidewalks, were kicked and beaten by the police." Supervisor Andrew
Gallagher (a union official in private life) questioned whether the
police chief had the right to restrict the pickets to one side of the
Embarcadero, whether the police department was being used, and
whether there was too much unnecessary brutality. The board authorized Mayor Angelo J. Rossi to appoint a committee of five to
investigate and report the "truth" to the public. The mayor made
no appointments; the protest was never investigated.[15]

On May 17, Edward Francis McGrady flew into town. He was
assistant for labor to General Hugh Johnson, administrator of the
NRA; assistant secretary of labor and principal troubleshooter for
Secretary of Labor Frances Perkins; and a labor lobbyist who held
the respect of the labor movement's main line leadership. McGrady
had earned his labor spurs as a high official of the pressmen's union,
his political credentials as a member of the Boston Common Council and the Massachusetts House of Representatives, and as a legislative representative for fourteen years of the American Federation
of Labor under Sam Gompers and William Green. He had been
mentioned frequently as Roosevelt's choice—they were old
friends—for secretary of labor, but the post went instead to Perkins.
Johnson admired the way McGrady had helped to nurse the National Industrial Recovery Act through Congress and took him into
the NRA as his assistant. Perkins later brought him into the labor
department. McGrady's labor philosophy, developed in the shadow
of the cautious Gompers and the slow-moving Green, shared little
common ground with the left wing or militants. Though his labor
connections and government credentials were impressive, local
longshore leaders only reluctantly put up with his intervention.

McGrady promptly went into a series of closed-door talks—
with the president's mediation board, a committee of businessmen.
The next day, he asked the waterfront employers and strikers to
give their committees full power to act—that is, authority to sign

an agreement without ratification by their respective members. The employers hedged their consent with renewed insistence on open shop, employer-controlled hiring halls, and elections in each port to choose the longshoremen's bargaining representatives. The longshoremen, for their part, reiterated that any agreement must be approved by the rank and file, and that the shipowners must meet the demands of the other striking maritime unions. A resolution by Local 38-79, Bridges the major protagonist, nailed it down—an action, Eliel noted, that brought Bridges his first public notice. McGrady responded with an angry outburst:

> A strong radical element within the ranks of the longshoremen seems to want no settlement of this strike. I have observed that the Communists, through direct action and by pleas in the widely circulated Communist newspaper here, are trying to induce the strikers to remain out despite our efforts to arbitrate. We are very far from a settlement. On Friday we believed the executive committee of the ILA had power to act for the strikers along the entire coast. But that same night the rank and file of the strikers stripped them of that authority. The executive committee appears to me to be helpless to do anything with the men they represent or to combat the radical element in the longshoremen's union.[16]

Repercussions were widespread and immediate. Secretary Perkins, unpersuaded by the red scare approach, apparently let McGrady know her doubts. Whether as a result of her phone call or because he changed his mind, in his nightly phone call to the National Labor Board, McGrady reported "three hundred communists among the men—not much violence but much talk." Some employers, he said, "seized on this for a red scare" and were talking of forming a Vigilance Committee. McGrady's attitude now was more in keeping with the view developing in Washington that the "red scare" was less significant than employer (and sometimes union) intransigence. Marvin McIntyre, FDR's secretary, alerted by McGrady's charges, asked the Labor Department for information on reds on the waterfront. The department responded that it had investigated two cases in connection with the strike. One, Frank Cameron, had entered unlawfully in 1923, had served in the army, and had remained in the United States since. The only "communis-tic" connection in the second—Harry Bridges—was that two wit-nesses in his incomplete naturalization proceedings were reported to have been political candidates of the "communistic party." Its only direct report, the reply added, "is quote he is captain and chief agitator in longshoremen strike unquote." The report reinforced the skepticism of Perkins and the White House about "communist" control of the strike.[17]

J. W. Mailliard, Jr., president of the Chamber of Commerce, quickly renewed the attack. The strike was no longer a conflict be-tween employer and employee but a rapidly spreading conflict be-tween "American principles and un-American radicalism." Its leaders do not desire a settlement. They "are responsible," he went on, "for the violence and bloodshed which is typical of their tribe." There is no hope for peace "until Communistic agitators are re-moved as the official spokesmen of labor and American leaders are chosen to settle their differences along American lines."[18] The In-dustrial Association joined the chamber in a substantially identical telegram to President Roosevelt. In Los Angeles, Roger Lapham told the Ad Club that the strike leaders were "communists out and out . . . They want to break down the walls of government."

McGrady's eruption undercut what little confidence the strike leaders had in him. His outburst coupled with Mailliard's attack drew heated replies. The ILA publicity committee insisted the men were striking only for what the NRA offered. A small number of men "are interested in Communism, that is their privilege. Never-theless . . . a great majority of the striking longshoremen are adher-ents of conservative political parties." A member of the district executive committee replied: "Any strike in history is a conflict be-tween the pocketbook and the capitalist and the stomach of the employee." The April 3 agreement had been "openly flaunted" or "nullified" by employers and their agents, not the union. "The ex-ecutive board of the ILA and the members of the ILA," A. H. Pet-ersen, the board member said, "are a true cross-section of Americanism."[19]

Nudged by Secretary Perkins, McGrady brought the parties to-gether on May 19 for the first time since the strike began. (The

Industrial Association was represented on the employers' side of the table. Bridges, chair tilted back against the wall, was a "mute observer.") The mediators proposed tripartite control of the hiring hall, with the U. S. Employment Service as a third and controlling party. Neither side welcomed the suggestion. The union feared shipowner domination; the employers considered it an indirect closed shop.

On May 24, preceded by a widely known and unsavory reputation, Joseph P. Ryan, president of the International Longshoremen's Association, arrived in San Francisco. In a confusing statement, he declared the most important issue in dispute was the recognition in collective bargaining of the ILA. The WEU was puzzled; it had already recognized and was now willing to bargain with the ILA, it said, but if Ryan meant a closed shop, there was little hope for a settlement. The WEU charged Ryan's lapse to "a woeful failure" of the Pacific Coast unions to keep the head of the union informed.

Ryan had gone to work in New York as a longshoreman in 1912. He worked his way up in the union movement to become ILA president, then president of the Central Labor Council of New York City. When he landed in San Francisco in 1934, he stepped into a waterfront world almost totally unlike the one from which he hailed. Accustomed to "painted neckties, pinstriped and elegantly tailored double-breasted suits, flashy diamond rings," as historian Irving Bernstein pictured him, Ryan ran the New York waterfront at a "rather spectacular level of corruption." Annual dinners or campaigns against Communists on the waterfront provided funds for his plushy style. On the docks, he fully accepted the shape-up, reportedly cutting in local union officials on the job rackets and kickbacks and cooperating with gangsters moving in to control waterfront jobs. When a civic committee concluded that the waterfront provided a lucrative field for racketeers and that the shape-up was responsible for evil waterfront conditions, one voice—Ryan's—objected that it was unfair to the waterfront employers. Strikes in the east, shipowner lawyer Phleger commented, "were usually settled between Joe Ryan and the representatives of the steamship companies and . . . rumor was that Ryan was susceptible to being influenced by payments to him." It did not help matters that the Pacific Coast District, by an agreement of twenty-five years' standing, had virtually complete autonomy over its own affairs. Neither the international union nor Ryan had had any substantial part, let alone control, in the district's long and turbulent history. Nor, in the light of his commitment to the pierhead shape-up, did Ryan understand the West Coast concern with their own hiring halls. His foot-in-the-mouth declaration on his arrival was not the first, nor the worst, in a continuing series of misadventures.[20]

McGrady quickly started talks that afternoon. There, the employers met—for the first time, they claimed—a demand that the strikes of the maritime unions must be settled before the longshoremen would return to work. Two days were taken up, Plant explained, with the employers reiterating "their utter inability to do anything about it." The proposal was withdrawn after the president's mediation board assured the maritime unions that it would use its prestige and influence to insure "proper attention" for their demands. Ryan explained: "We are not going to leave any men in the lurch if they struck in sympathy with us. But if they struck because of grievances of their own it is up to their locals and internationals to settle them." He warned the employers that, if they continued their present course, they would be faced at once with the grievances of every trade welded together in a transportation organization. Ryan added: "We don't give a hoot for the closed shop. All we are interested in is recognition and preference" of employment. It worked on the East Coast, Ryan argued, why not here? By way of answer, the San Francisco local that day reaffirmed its demands for the union hiring hall, the closed shop, and its solidarity with the striking maritime unions. "The workers are going to hold out for nothing less than a closed shop," Bridges said. McGrady commented: "As long as both the strikers and shipping men are willing to sit down around a table and talk things over, it is far from hopeless. I'm here to bring peace, if possible—and I'm convinced it it possible."[21]

Now, Ryan and Plant, as a committee of two, put together a proposal covering the four major ports. Next morning, even as strikers and police battled at Pier 18, long distance calls secured the participation of operators at other ports. Ryan was pleased: "This gives us exactly what the longshoremen have fought for and is all we want." As Bill Lewis later remembered it, "it was a glorified company union proposal."[22] Again, the employers had done little more than refine their persistent refusal to accord the longshoremen equal status at the bargaining table.

The proposed agreement would recognize the ILA, port by port, as the collective bargaining representative of the longshoremen, but with an escape hatch for nonunion workers. Rules governing registration and hiring would be determined jointly, but hiring halls would be maintained by the employers who would pay all expenses and be responsible for registration and dispatching records. The ILA would be allowed representatives in each hall to see that there was no discrimination in registration or hiring against any member of the ILA. Disputes on hours and wages would be submitted to arbitration. Perhaps most of all, it dealt, not with the Pacific Coast District, but with Ryan who had neither standing nor authority as its representative.

The end of the strike, if not here, was near, newspaper headlines proclaimed. The San Francisco strike committee disagreed. It argued that the members would not welcome the hiring hall, since it remained under the employers' "absolute control." It gives the employer the right to hire whomever he pleases—"militant leaders of this strike would never be hired on the San Francisco waterfront again." It does not grant recognition to the ILA as "sole representative of the men." Strikebreakers would be retained or, at best, would be discharged one day, rehired the next. It warned that the unions outside the maritime industry would "probably be involved." "The possibility of a general strike along the Pacific Coast is a certainty." In any case, even if it were acceptable, the longshoremen could not return to work until the striking maritime unions obtained satisfactory settlements.[23]

San Francisco Local 38-79 in a special meeting emphatically rejected the agreement. Henry Schmidt remembered a longshoreman known as "Pirate" Larsen—he wore an eyepatch—standing alongside Ryan at the podium. A member of the Albion Hall caucus, an ally of the Bridges-led militants, Larsen summed it up: "You know, fellows, this guy is nothing but a fink and he's trying to fink all of us." Schmidt added: "That finished Joe Ryan." When the chairman called for the "ayes" in support of the proposal, the minutes noted that "not one single sound was heard." To the call for "no," the minutes said, "the twenty-five hundred members present with one voice shouted 'no.' " Even so, the local scheduled a secret ballot vote.

Ryan headed for the northwest to try to rescue the proposed pact. He called it "a long step"—not all that had been asked but with concessions "which we wanted badly." It was necessary, he added, to bring in Los Angeles, where the employers were "not so enthusiastic about it." An ILA man in the hiring halls, he thought, would create "what amounts to the closed shop."

Going into a meeting with the northwest strike committee, Ryan said it was up to the northwest locals to "save [the San Francisco] local from itself." The strike committee listened patiently to Ryan's defense, asked some questions, then flatly turned it down. Some locals shouted down the proposal; in others, the executive boards refused to submit it. In San Pedro, the local union turned it down, too. So did Joseph Banning, a local shipowner who insisted that Los Angeles employers would negotiate only with San Pedro longshoremen, excluding the strikers. In Seattle, Dave Beck, the teamster chief, recommended the Seattle strikers make their own settlement. Anti-union merchants and shippers in Los Angeles, he said, would never stand for union labor. Ryan now withdrew his support, endorsed the demand for a closed shop. "I have a different slant on it," he said. By May 31, the proposal clearly had been overwhelmingly rejected. The San Francisco vote, 2,401 to 78—the only formal vote—was the final touch.[24]

11.

THE THIRD DISAGREEMENT

ON A CORNER near the Embarcadero, not far from Local 38-79's headquarters on Steuart Street, on the morning of May 30, a crowd of some 250 young people stood "irresolute and confused." Along the nearby waterfront and streets hundreds of policemen waited—on foot, horse, and motorcycle, in squad cars. Young William "Billy" Newman clambered up on Jack Allen's shoulders to explain why, this year, there would be no meeting as there had been in previous years. "Comrades and fellow workers," he said, "This meeting is called for the purpose of . . ." At that moment, Newman said, three mounted policemen and "a good number" of uniformed and plainclothes police charged. Watching from a window in the ILA hall, longshoremen Henry Schrimpf said, "I have never seen anything like that attack upon these kids. . . . It was nothing but murder. . . . These cops just slugged and beat everybody they could reach."

The young people had come together in what had been intended as an observance of National Youth Day, sponsored primarily by the Young Communist League (YCL). After a meeting at 765 Howard Street, said twenty-one-year-old Jean Rand, a YCL member, the crowd had wandered down toward the Embarcadero. They had no police permit for a march, but had walked toward the Embarcadero, "just to hold a peaceful meeting," she said.

Police clubs and clouds of tear gas scattered the crowd in every

113

direction. Newman remembered police beating him on the arms and shoulders before arresting him. Louis Goldblatt, later secretary-treasurer of the International Longshoremen's and Warehousemen's Union, who had come up from Los Angeles with a number of young radicals to join the observance, took refuge in a doorway. Rand was badly gassed. Fifteen-year-old Leonard Pressel, no job, no money, "on the bum," bumped into a carload of police, was club-whipped until he passed out, then taken to jail. He had, he said, no knowledge of the meeting or its purpose.[1]

In the confusion of the attack, the police charge swept over and injured many bystanders. The newspapers were equally random in their reports. The *News* called it a demonstration of "striking longshoremen;" it was not, as the *New York Times* reported. The *News* counted one unidentified sixteen-year-old girl and twenty-four men hospitalized with head injuries. The *Chronicle* said nineteen persons had been treated; two youths "were reported to have been shot and subsequently spirited away." Harry Bridges testified later that a number of the young people, frightened, uncertain—"I would say, young boys and girls about sixteen or seventeen"—had been hidden from the police in the ILA hall.[2] Henry Schmidt also witnessed the attack from a window in the ILA hall. "Isn't that a helluva way to treat those kids," he commented to a longshoreman alongside him. "Ah, hell," the guy said, "They're just a bunch of Commies." Some time later, Schmidt again was watching police chase "several hundred guys" with tear gas and shotguns, among them the man who had watched the police attack the "Commies." Schmidt watched him run into a second bunch of cops and start to jump the fence. At that moment a cop fired—"That guy's ass was riddled with buckshot." Schmidt said he never got around to asking the guy how he felt about the police after that.[3]

Paul Eliel later echoed the Chamber of Commerce belief that the demonstration was "engineered by Communists and Communist sympathizers." It was, of course, sponsored by the Young Communist League. The chamber said it was intended to provoke a police attack; Eliel argued it was designed to influence San Francisco longshoremen to vote the next day against the May 28 proposal, though the results of that vote were virtually foreordained.

(Hindsight suggests the police attack itself may have been intended to influence the longshoremen's vote—but for the proposal, not against it.) It might have had an "adverse effect" on longshoremen's reactions in other ports but, Eliel conceded, the final result would not have changed.[4]

The police attack on the youth demonstration opened a new, increasingly tense stage in the conflict. As the strike tightened its grip on the ports—and economies—of the northwest, shipowners and city officials responded with growing force. Shippping was completely tied up. Early efforts to operate with strikebreakers had been frustrated—both by the absence of police protection and by the strikers' vigorous picketing. Sawmills, logging camps, industrial plants, and pulp and paper mills shut down. Grain shipments from Spokane were halted. One report said lumber mills in Longview had laid off three thousand workers because they were unable to ship or receive lumber. Ship operators were canceling calls to northwest ports because authorities failed "to provide adequate protection."

Mayor John F. Dore of Seattle urgently asked Secretary of the Interior Harold Ickes for federal troops, not alone to free thirty-seven ships tied up in Elliott Bay but especially to feed and supply Alaska (then a territory of the United States). The start of the fishing and canning season was near. Alaska, isolated and dependent, would quickly need supplies. A temporary agreement allowed one vessel to depart for Alaska. Soon after, the ILA reached an agreement with the Alaska operators to resume operations. It was no precedent for the rest of the coast; the employers belittled it as no more than a temporary truce. Nevertheless the Alaska operators did agree to hire only members of the ILA through the union's hall. Ship's crews would also be hired through their respective unions. Men working the Alaska service would not be required to handle cargo trans-shipped from any unfair dock or vessel.

Mayor Dore followed his appeal to Ickes with an announcement that he was preparing to "open the port." That meant, everyone understood, police protection for strikebreaking operations. (Frank Foisie reassured Thomas Plant in San Francisco that Seattle shipowners had no intention of "substituting their own police for public police protection.") From San Francisco, Edward McGrady asked Dore to hold off as long as the parties were "seated around the table attempting to reach an amicable agreement." Dore angrily replied: "Who is this man McGrady that should be trying to run our business for us? We are not going to paralyze our business and industry to make things easier for him." Ryan advised the Secretary of Labor that barricades had been erected on the Seattle waterfront and four hundred special police had been sworn in. The *Seattle Times* underscored the mayor's anger. A front page editorial warned labor that its "attempt to make Seattle a closed port, with business dominated by labor—without regard to the welfare of the city as a whole—will meet" the same "inglorious end" that befell the Seattle general strike in 1919. If armed guards were used to protect strikebreakers "and some of our men get shot down and clubbed," Ryan bluffed, he would order a sympathetic strike on the eastern seaboard.

McGrady returned to Washington soon after the longshoremen emphatically rejected the May 28 proposal. He planned to present the entire situation to President Roosevelt and secure "his interest and intervention. . . . I intend to propose to the Administration that the Employment Service take over the operation." Presumably he referred to an earlier scheme for government operation of the Longshore living halls. The Waterfront Employers' Union wired McGrady June 5 that, unless men went back to work promptly, "it will be necessary that steps be taken to move cargo by other means and this may well precipitate extension of difficulty violence and perhaps bloodshed to the public detriment." Government supervision, it went on, "may be the solution." A headline in the *Chronicle* bloomed: "Peace Looms;" the proposal for government control of hiring halls is "gaining momentum." McGrady called Ryan for the union's reply. "We have no objection," Ryan said, provided all other groups in the industry are subjected to similar regulation. Supervise dispatching of ships, as well as of men, and distribution of cargoes—"give the employers as much supervision as the longshoremen are to receive."[5]

Ryan's erratic course left confusion in its wake. On June 1, he proposed that the District executive board sign agreements with any employer who agrees to recognize the union and hire from its halls. Next day, the *Examiner* reported that Ryan was talking with shipowners in an effort to convince them to extend to the West Coast the union preference granted on the East Coast, though the WEU made clear that it considered preferential employment no different than the closed shop. San Francisco Local 38-79 answered Ryan by reaffirming its "determination to accept no agreement which did not involve the entire Pacific Coast." Ryan's speech to the local was cut short by "a chorus of boos and catcalls" and he left almost at once for Seattle to take part in the Alaska negotiations. When ILA officials in Seattle were reported willing to consider a government-supervised hiring hall, Ryan said the ILA would not consider "piecemeal settlement." Confusion was further confounded when Lee J. Holman, the deposed president of Local 38-79, announced that McGrady's plan for government supervision would be satisfactory to his group of several hundred "conservative" longshoremen. Ryan protested any dealings between the WEU and Holman's group; the WEU said no talks had been held, and none would be held as long as negotiations continued with the ILA. (Holman had been arrested the night before for carrying a gun without a permit and discharging a firearm within the city limits. He explained that the car in which he was riding had been attacked by a gang of men; he had fired through the rear of the car in an attempt to frighten the gang away. The charges were not pressed.)

"Old Mike Casey," recalled Henry Schmidt, "was entitled to be famous. [He was] the type of [man] who had relations at City Hall." Schmidt had been chosen to carry a proposal (inspired by Bridges) to the Teamsters' executive board aimed at tightening Teamsters' support for the strike. To Schmidt's suggestion that the teamsters elect a rank-and-file strike committee, Casey blandly replied, "We're mindful of the suggestion that the brother from the longshoremen made, but we are accustomed to making our own arrangements."[6] Casey was a big man, white-haired, pink-jowled, wearing a heavy mustache. At the time, he had some thirty-four years in the union movement behind him. He was highly regarded in his own union, in the labor movement generally, and by a wide cross-section of business and civic leaders. He had helped to organize Local 85 in 1900, led its bloody fight for survival in 1901, and brought it through the trials of the American Plan and open shop 1920s. Mike, said a prominent San Francisco businessman, "was the product of evolution. He was radical when young and conservative . . . as he aged and achieved his objectives."[7] Teamster employers, Henry Melnikow said, "did not want the Industrial Association to break down the Teamsters' union. They felt they were getting along all right and attempts to break that down might do more harm than good." That feeling, perhaps, was an important reason why Casey had established a respectful, trusting relationship with Senator Albert Boynton and Paul Eliel of the Industrial Association. "I think they were able to call upon the Industrial Association for information," Melnikow said, "and . . . kept in touch with them."[8] (When Eliel published his book on the 1934 strikes, Bill Storie, a ranking staff member of the association, said Casey was angered by the inclusion of some conversations which, he felt, had been off the record. Casey swore he would never enter the association's offices again, and, Storie said, "he never did."[9]) Melnikow added: Casey "had a sense of how far leadership should go and that on basic things they should keep their ears to the ground."[10]

Now, Casey's leadership skills were being strenuously tested as Local 85 met for a fresh look at the strike situation. Since May 13, teamsters had refused to haul any cargo on to—or from—the docks. They left it in the street; officials and strikebreakers worked it the rest of the way. The longshoremen, though, quickly realized that, with the help of the Belt Line Railroad and extra freight cars, freight was leaking from the tied-up docks. It was hauled off to industrial sidings; from there teamsters handled it without regard to source. But longshore pickets tracked the cars and confronted the teamsters with the violations, in effect, of their waterfront boycott. While longshoremen, as well as some teamsters, sought to outlaw all hot cargo, wherever they found it, Casey and his associate, John P. McLaughlin, fought to prevent any deeper involvement in the strike.

The June 7 meeting, however voted to clamp down: it resolved to put a stop to handling any freight handled by strikebreakers. The action, Eliel said, "changed the whole course of the strike and led directly to the general strike." Eliel claimed "that even in the more conservative unions the traditional 'boring-from-within' tactics of the Communists had been successful in creating sentiment in favor of the longshoremen."[11] But Eliel's single-dimension observation ignored the emerging class ties that linked teamsters and longshoremen: on-the-job camaraderie, family, school, neighborhood as well as economic concerns. In a letter to the secretary of the National Labor Board in Washington, Eliel, strongly denying that he is anything of a "Red-baiter," said Casey "has absolutely lost control of the Teamsters' Union and he is unable to lead it any more. He used to be able to drive it."[12] Casey never gave up control, Sam Kagel said. Now deeply involved in the strike leadership, Casey retreated from his personal inclinations to limit the teamsters' involvement but when you see "an avalanche coming," Casey told Kagel, "you get out of its way."[13]

The Industrial Association had been involved in the shipowners' preparations for the March 23 strike deadline. In mid-May its representatives turned up alongside the waterfront employers in the mediation sessions. The association initiated a series of meetings with businessmen on strike developments. It attempted, and failed, to influence the teamsters' policy toward the strike. Its steps restated its established role in mobilizing the business community against the threat, real and imagined, of union organization. It had been for close to thirteen years the prime keeper and practitioner of the city's American Plan, open-shop policies. Now these steps were leading the way to the full exercise of the association's specialized strikebreaking skills.

The association plainly held the confidence of the business community. Its some eight hundred members included Bank of America, Anglo-California, Wells Fargo—every major bank; six major insurance companies, nine public utilities including Pacific Telephone and Pacific Gas & Electric; the Hearst newspapers, radio stations, railroads, including Southern Pacific. Its permit system enabled it, through the open-shop years, to dominate the city's construction industry, reducing the once-powerful building trades unions to impotence and controlling the builders' labor policies as well. It successfully frustrated the bitter efforts of carpenters and plumbers to reestablish their unions. The association extended its open shop policies to other San Francisco businesses. Though it refused to deal in any way with unions, as such, it managed to impose an accommodation on much of the remaining, viable union movement. Now it proposed to put the force of the city's business community behind the shipowners to crush the strike.

Its early role in the waterfront strike was given little prominence. A meeting with businessmen on May 13 started word filtering through the business community. A second meeting, assembled by the association and the Chamber of Commerce, called for a committee of seven "to act on behalf of the business community as an agency for the purpose of determining strike policies." The committee met representatives of the shipowners, Dean Henry Grady, and Assistant Secretary of Labor McGrady. A meeting on June 5, with about a hundred businessmen present, decided, Eliel reported, "to place the full responsibility of the waterfront strike in the hands of the Industrial Association in cooperation with the shipowners"[14]—the association's apparent goal all along. The decision freed WEU to focus on bargaining, and the Industrial Association, with wide backing in the business community, to carry out its plans to end the strike by other means.

On June 12, J. W. Mailliard, president of the San Francisco Chamber of Commerce, formally asked the Industrial Association immediately to determine "a method of ending this intolerable condition." In a carefully stage-managed exchange of letters, Mailliard recited the employers' grievances, noting that some $40 million worth of merchandise lay on the docks, in the warehouses, and in the holds of ninety-six ships stalled in the bay by the strike. Freight entering the port had dropped another $40 million worth in the month following the strike. San Francisco's shipping was being diverted to Los Angeles. Teamsters and warehousemen had been intimidated by threats of violence by the strikers and many have been thrown out of work.

The ILA angrily denied his charge that control of the union had been taken over by radicals. A secret ballot vote, by a huge margin, had rejected the May 28 agreement and endorsed unity with the seamen. Mailliard's earlier and similar charges had been repudiated by Assistant Secretary of Labor McGrady and the WEU's President Plant who had found the ILA's district executive committee to be "true" AFL representatives. The union has "given in to the shipowners on every single point excepting the question of hiring halls and recognition of our union."

John F. Forbes, president of the Industrial Association, next day delivered the preordained response: the association accepts "the responsibility for determining a method of ending the intolerable conditions." The association still hopes for an amicable settlement, he declared, but it "intends to take whatever lawful steps are necessary to protect the economic interests of this community and to restore to the people of San Francisco that security to which they are entitled."[15]

Tensions built and events quickened in the early weeks of June, moving inexorably toward shattering, for better or worse, the unstable deadlock that gripped the situation.

Seattle Mayor Charles Smith proposed to San Francisco Mayor Angelo Rossi that the mayors of Pacific Coast cities develop a plan for common action. Mayor Rossi held him off, doubting that it would be productive. Days later, Mayor Smith announced that he would assume command of the city's police department and promised police protection for anyone loading or discharging cargo. He was joined by the newly formed Tacoma Citizens Emergency Committee and the mayors of several smaller ports. In Portland, the union and employers were working on a local settlement.

Early in June, too, Acting California Governor Frank Merriam paid a visit to San Francisco. Shipowner Roger Lapham welcomed Merriam to his office. "We told him . . . what we thought were the conditions, and he was simpatico," Lapham recalled.[16] Merriam was markedly different from the man he succeeded, Governor James Rolph, who had become ill. As former mayor of San Francisco and a onetime member of the Shipowners' Association, Rolph had often stood with the unions—and vigorously—against the Chamber of Commerce, its Law and Order Committee, and other anti-union employers. Merriam had succeeded the ailing Rolph in an acting capacity; upon Rolph's death in June, Merriam became governor. Soon after the visit to Lapham's office, Merriam denounced the "Communist agitators" and "fomentors of industrial hatred" who were responsible for the unrest in San Francisco and for agricultural strikes in several parts of the state.

Now, San Francisco Mayor Rossi took a hand in the situation. He was untested in the field of labor relations. He had not hesitated, at the outset, to assure the waterfront employers of the cooperation and protection of the police department. Beyond that, his attitude was unclear. Angelo Rossi was the son of a grocer, born in the foothills of the Sierra. From a start as a street corner flower peddler in San Francisco he developed one of the city's leading floral businesses. He entered City Hall by the way of the Downtown Association, a political alliance of small, independent businessmen. Now, he called in the waterfront employers, the ILA, and prominent leaders in the city's unions. The newspapers reported that "nothing of importance was accomplished," but the meeting brought Joe Ryan back to San Francisco.

From Portland, based on a proposed settlement developed by the Portland employers and the local ILA, predictions had come of an early settlement—"perhaps by nightfall." Ryan was dubious: "We'll be lucky if we reach a settlement by nightfall of New Year's. . . . We almost had a settlement in Seattle, but the employers were stubborn. And the entire coast ILA membership is united in insisting that the strike not be settled on a separate basis." But he also said that he agreed with Mailliard that radicals controlled the local strike situation: "They say that Communists are leading this strike. That is true. That's because [the employers] won't meet the terms of persons like myself and William Lewis. . . . But they have nothing at all to do with the settlement of it."[17] So saying, Ryan presented Rossi his latest peace offer. Its principal feature was a preferential union shop, based on nineteen years of East Coast experience, Ryan pointed out. Plant dismissed it as nothing new—

"We do not feel calling the closed union shop by a different name will contribute to the settlement of this controversy." But Plant also noted that Ryan had approved a settlement proposal in Portland, as well as a similar proposal in Seattle, providing for no discrimination between union and nonunion men. Yet, he refused to offer similar terms to the San Francisco employers.[18]

That same morning the Industrial Association convened an unusual meeting in its offices, in pursuit of the advice of its recently hired public relations counsel, McCann-Erickson, Inc. The association, the agency recommended, should establish its own identity, not representing one side or the other, but concerned with the welfare of the community. It urged meeting with both parties to establish that policy. A McCann official expressed surprise "to find great reluctance . . . to meet or confer directly with the strikers."[19] Senator Boynton explained that the shipowners might be unwilling to have the association meet the strikers—"it was their fight and they should not be interfered with." At the same time, the association telegraphed urgent appeals to President Roosevelt asking for his personal intervention, to Secretary of Labor Perkins and Assistant Secretary McGrady, and to members of Congress asking their intervention with the President, all seeking somehow to compel acceptance of the May 28 agreement. Through a committee of publishers, the day's newspapers blossomed with look-alike editorials also stressing acceptance of the agreement.

Gathered with Industrial Association officers and staff were Ryan; Michael Casey, president of the San Francisco Teamsters' Union, and John P. McLaughlin, its secretary; and Dave Beck, president of the Seattle Teamsters' Union. Representatives of the strikers were notably absent. After discussing the strike situation, Ryan was asked whether any agreement that was satisfactory to him and to the representatives of the teamsters would be accepted by the rank and file of the longshoremen. Ryan, according to the files of the association, "made a most emphatic statement in the affirmative." Casey and McLaughlin also gave assurances that, if an agreement satisfactory to Ryan was reached, the teamsters would immediately begin to haul all freight from the waterfront.[20]

The meeting reconvened later that afternoon in Mayor Rossi's office. The group now also included Bill Lewis, J. E. Finnegan, and A. H. Petersen, the latter two members of the ILA district executive board; the WEU's Thomas Plant and Herman Phleger; and Judge Charles Reynolds and J. L. Leonard of the president's mediation board.

Any terms of settlement requiring ratification by the Coast membership of the ILA was "an evident impossibility," said Plant, asking, "what's the point of negotiating an agreement, only to have it rejected as soon as it is announced?" Ryan replied, "I give you my unqualified assurance that I can make an agreement on behalf of my membership that will be effective." He could "exercise the necessary authority;" if he did not have it, he would assume it. Plant had (or could get) similar authority to negotiate an agreement that would bind his principals. Ryan was backed by assurances from the teamster officials that, if an agreement satisfactory to Ryan were reached, trucking operations would be resumed. With those assurances, Plant and Ryan went into executive session.[21]

They moved their private talks to Plant's home. Before evening they had reached a tentative agreement. A few remaining questions were deferred until final adjustments could be made and final consents obtained. Next morning, June 16, after some minor changes, Plant and Ryan signed the document. Mayor Rossi hastily summoned the group that had met in his office the previous day for the formal signing. T. G. Plant signed for the employer associations of the four major ports. Joseph Ryan signed for the ILA; J. J. Finnegan for the Pacific Coast District. The guarantee of observance was signed by Michael Casey, president, and John P. McLaughlin, secretary, of the San Francisco Teamsters' Union, and Dave Beck, president of the Seattle Teamsters' Union. Observance by the Waterfront Employers' Union was guaranteed by John Forbes for the Industrial Association of San Francisco. Both Lewis, the ILA district president, and Petersen, a member of the district executive board, refused until the agreement had been ratified by the longshoremen. Under the ILA constitution, their signatures could—Ryan's could not—bind the Pacific Coast District.

Once again, the agreement offered the ILA open shop recognition. It called for "joint and equal" control of employment policies and management of hiring and dispatching halls. Local wages, hours, and working rules, would be established by a joint labor relations committee. Deadlocks would be broken by arbitration. Registration of new men would be cut off as of December 31, 1933; no additional men would be hired without approval by the joint committee. Expenses of the hall and its staff would be shared; nonmembers would be required to pay a pro rata share of the expenses. Sympathetic strikes of any kind were prohibited.

The newspapers proclaimed the end of the strike—except the *News.* It said the agreement turned on a vote by the ILA locals and its acceptance would be "difficult." But Mayor Rossi congratulated the participants. Finnegan commented the agreement marked the first major union entry into Los Angeles harbor. Beck said the strike was over; he was flying back to Seattle. Ryan described it as "the best agreement for settlement of this coastwise strike that could be reached."

Their conclusions stood, at best, on a shaky foundation. Plant and Ryan and the City Hall group had acted on the belief that the agreement was binding, despite repeated assertions that Ryan had no authority to sign on behalf of the district and that the strike would not end without the members' ratification. Casey said the teamsters would return to work Monday, no matter what the longshoremen did. But it quickly became apparent that longshore leaders, local and coastwise, recognized no peace. Ryan told Plant the next day that Bridges had been waiting for him when he returned to his hotel. You may have thought you executed an agreement, Bridges told him, but Ryan would find out that he had no control over the situation and the thing would not stick. Ryan told Plant he had never been talked to in his life the way Bridges talked to him at that time.[22] To reporters, Bridges said the men would return to work if the agreement was approved by a two-thirds vote of the entire Pacific Coast membership. And, as expected, the seamen's unions vowed their strikes would continue.

A tumultuous meeting of the San Francisco longshoremen the next afternoon in Eagles' Hall emphatically rejected the agreement. Men packed the hall early; latecomers waited in the street. Anti-agreement sentiments were loudly voiced, backed, some said, by threats of violence. Ryan, a half hour late, was greeted by a storm of boos and catcalls. His efforts to swing the meeting toward acceptance were received with unrestrained dissatisfaction. Judge Reynolds, who attended the meeting, said Ryan, "faced not only with apparent open opposition of the majority of those present but also by the possibility of physical violence being done to him . . . veered away and practically surrendered to the will of the more radical longshoremen in control of the meeting." In an "extremely stormy meeting, through jeers and boos," the minutes noted, "President Ryan unflinchingly finished his discussion." Bridges challenged Ryan's secretive conduct of negotiations and his failure to consult the strikers. The men shouted down a proposal for a secret ballot, then unanimously rejected the agreement. It was rejected the same day, too, by the locals in Portland, San Diego, and Tacoma. In San Pedro the vote was 638 for acceptance, 584 for rejection.

An ILA statement said the membership "refuses to return to work until satisfactory settlement is made with the other maritime unions out on strike." No agreement was broken because no agreement existed, said Ralph Mallen, the local's publicity chairman. "International President Ryan had no power to sign any agreement, but merely assumed that power." Mike Casey said, "We will make no move until the situation clarifies. . . . But sending teamsters to the waterfront today would only result in confusion and possibly worse. After today it might be another story."[23]

12.

R ᴇᴀᴅʏ ! A ɪᴍ !

"Tʜᴇ ꜱᴛʀɪᴋᴇ ꜱᴇᴛᴛʟᴇᴍᴇɴᴛ blew up yesterday with a loud bang when the longshoremen unanimously refused to accept the agreement made for them by the International President, Mr. Ryan. They now stipulate they will not settle anything unless all the other marine unions now on strike are included and taken care of." The Industrial Association's publicity agent, author of this memo to the New York office of McCann-Erickson, sensed in the purported settlement a purpose beyond ending the strike. The many guarantors who promised the shipowners and longshoremen would perform seemed "ridiculous," the memo said, "but seems now to serve the purpose." This report from the LaFollette Committee was one of a long series of "violations of the rights of free speech and assembly and undue interference with the right of labor to organize and bargain collectively." United States Senator Robert M. LaFollette of Wisconsin headed the subcommittee which, historian Irving Bernstein noted, exposed "with sensational impact, the grim underside of corporate labor relations policies."[1] When it published the McCann-Erickson correspondence, the committee suggested that the dealings with Ryan were utilized mainly for their value in justifying the association's ongoing preparations "for a violent struggle."[2] The employers may have been prepared to live with the June 16 agreement, but its emphatic rejection by the strikers, as they saw it, gave a kind of absolution for their plans to open the port, however drastic the consequences.

On the day that had been scheduled for the return to work, the signers of the June 16 document gathered again in the mayor's office. "Mr. Casey stated that he was helpless," Thomas Plant remembered, "his men had been threatened and intimidated, and that he could not get them to go back again. Ryan told us . . . the situation was hopelessly out of hand, that the Coast locals, particularly the San Francisco coast local, was completely in the hands of Communists and radicals, and that he was helpless in the situation.[3]

Nevertheless, the Waterfront Employers Union (WEU) called on the Industrial Association to demand the "guarantors make good on their guaranty." The agreement, the WEU insisted, was "in no way contingent upon ratification by the union membership." Nor was it contingent on settlement of the strike demands of the seamen. It was negotiated only on the basis of assurance of Joe Ryan and the teamster leaders that they could make an effective agreement. Now, the WEU said, it is plain the ILA plans to continue its strike until the demands of the other unions have been satisfied. The WEU has no authority to negotiate the demands of the sailors and other marine workers; Ryan had known that as far back as May 27. Repudiation of the agreement was "convincing evidence" that the radicals and Communists who dominate the ILA are not interested in industrial peace; "rather their avowed purpose is to provoke class hatred and bloodshed and to undermine the government." To reinforce its efforts to obtain compliance with the June 16 agreement, the WEU halted cargo movements with strikebreakers for nearly two days until, Paul Eliel said, it was "futile to wait for further consideration."[4]

In Portland, Mayor Joseph Carson said he was "damned tired" of being patient; it was "no longer a virtue." He promised the city government would use "every force at hand to resume business." The police chief asked for nine hundred extra officers; the employers announced they would open two hiring halls. The Citizens Emergency Committee in Tacoma advised "5,000 workers" thrown out of work by the strike that it was prepared to open the port. In Seattle, Mayor Charles Smith put a police guard on a pier where longshoremen were loading an Alaska-bound vessel. Charging Smith with bad faith, the strikers closed down the Alaska operation. At the Milwaukee dock the next morning, truckloads of strikebreakers were met by the longshoremen's "flying squad," backed by some four hundred Tacoma strikers. A conference among the longshoremen, the scabs, and local police relieved the scabs of their pistols, blackjacks, tear gas canisters, and baseball bats. Then they climbed aboard the trucks and returned to Seattle. In Tacoma, the citizens' committee won an agreement from the City Council setting aside a pier for scab ships. But the decision was reversed and, in the same mysterious way, pickets disappeared from the Port of Tacoma piers. From Los Angeles, and employer spokesman said, "Since the union has repudiated its leaders up and down the coast the employers feel justified in carrying this fight to a finish and have called off all negotiations."[5]

In San Francisco, Ryan advised the longshoremen at their Sunday afternoon meeting—after they had rejected the June 16 agreement—to "get your proposals together and present your demands jointly in a body. I was not aware the strike was so widespread or I would not have agreed to the peace plan which I must say wasn't bad." It was not a fight of the maritime unions, the *Chronicle* quoted him, but an open fight between organized labor and the open shop. He had thought it was "purely a longshoremen's proposition. . . . Now I find out no matter what I might have got, even the original demands, they could not accept it because they had promised the other maritime unions to remain out until the demands of all were met." A joint committee is the answer.[6]

Two days later, a letter to the WEU, over the signatures of H. Bridges, chairman, and Harry M. Espy, secretary, announced the formation of the Joint Marine Strike Committee. Its purpose, the letter said, "is to carry on all future negotiations for a settlement of the strike."

The striking unions had been in almost constant touch with each other from the start, meeting daily in informal sessions. Now, Sam Kagel remembered, at the suggestion of Harry Bridges (or perhaps of Randolph Meriwether of the Marine Engineers) the joint committee formally brought them together in a united front.

It was made up of five delegates from each of the striking unions: the ILA; the three unions of unlicensed seamen: the Sailors (SUP), Marine Firemen (MFOWW), and Marine Cooks (MCS); two unions of licensed officers: the Masters, Mates and Pilots (MM&P) and the Marine Engineers (MEBA); and the Machinists, Boilermakers, and Ship Clerks. The Marine Workers Industrial Union (MWIU) asked to join but, after a vigorous debate, was rejected. A delegation headed by Bridges asked the teamsters to send delegates to the committee but the invitation was refused. Casey reportedly told Bridges: "Our refusal to handle goods in the waterfront is sufficient assurance that we support you."[7] As Plant remembered it, "word came that a total of ten unions which were on strike in San Francisco had consolidated and had appointed, or the people themselves had appointed themselves, to serve on what was known as a joint marine strike committee.[8]

The committee moved quickly, in its words, to "provide means by which the employees can return to work." To that end, it would exert every "honorable effort" to meet the employer groups in the marine industry that have refused to meet with the authorized representatives of these unions. It wired San Francisco Mayor Angelo Rossi that it was empowered to negotiate a satisfactory settlement and would "be pleased to accept your gracious cooperation" in that effort. And it set a rally for the Civic Auditorium which, though it was not billed as such, conceivably could serve as a trial balloon, if not a launching pad, for a general strike.

Plant promptly told the joint committee that the WEU "cannot possibly have any authority or jurisdiction" to deal with matters affecting machinists or caulkers, or the management of all vessels flying the American flag. They were, he emphasized, only a small group of vessel operators and agents, foreign and domestic, whose vessels trade in San Francisco, and of contracting stevedores. The mediators had assured them the seamen's demands would be handled through the regular channels of the federal government. Those means are still available, Plant said, and no other means exist.[9]

Mayor Rossi attempted to get talks restarted, but Plant had a prior word. "I advised you over the telephone," he told the mayor, "that it was utterly beyond my power or that of the WEU to discuss the demands of the joint committee." With that, he withdrew. Bridges commented, "It's up to the employers. We found a way to get together and agree on what we wanted. There is no reason why all the employers can't do the same thing." Paul Scharrenberg, speaking for the three unlicensed seamen's unions, noted that since August 1933 the seamen have been rebuffed. "Will Mr. Plant please advise us where this machinery can be found to furnish redress for the seamen's well-founded grievances?"[10]

San Francisco's Civic Auditorium was packed the night of June 19—ten thousand in its seats and more in every foot of standing room. (No vessel had sailed through the Golden Gate that day for the first time in forty-five years.) One estimate guessed strikers made up 40 percent of the audience, families, friends, and the general public the balance. A noisy mix of boos and cheers greeted the appearance of Mayor Rossi, escorted by Police Captain W. T. Healy, and interrupting Bridges's review of the strike. Captain E. B. O'Grady, of the Masters and Mates, banged his gavel hard, asking "a respectful hearing and a courteous welcome." He was only partially successful. The mayor was frequently, and similarly, interrupted as he declared he would work for peace without bloodshed and violence. His promise to help the American Federation of Labor (AFL) brought renewed jeers. His advice was "keep cool. Win without violence." His departure won another round of cheers and jeers. Following the mayor, a series of speakers—including Harry Jackson of the Marine Workers Industrial Union—rehearsed their unions' grievances and their strike goals. Several urged a general strike as the only action that could win the strikers' demands.

Almost as if in answer, front pages of the city's newspapers on June 21 again in editorial unison demanded implementation of the June 16 settlement. Their first venture in wolf pack journalism the preceding Saturday had urged acceptance of the May 28 agreement, though, at that moment, Plant, Ryan et al. had been moving toward still another agreement. Now, they embroidered the theme of accepting the new agreement with appeals to return to work; failure to do so would lead to "bitter and disastrous warfare." The common front had been organized by John Francis Neylan, a prominent and influential lawyer, one-time publisher, and confidante to publisher William Randolph Hearst. The early efforts of Neylan's committee may have been somewhat out of joint, but they loudly reiterated the employers' contention that the union's intransigence was proof enough of the "radical and Communist" leadership's evil intent.

The speeches at the Civic Auditorium rally echoed a few evenings later in the weekly session of the San Francisco Labor Council. Conservative delegates took special umbrage at the presence at the rally of Harry Jackson of the MWIU; it created a wrong impression that the strikers had made common cause with the communists, they argued. They objected, too, to the left wing proclivity to label Ryan, Casey, and their associates as "fakers" and "sellout artists" and to extend the derogatory labels to those, like Edward Vandeleur, the council's president, and John O'Connell, its secretary, who frowned at the rising talk of a general strike. Objections were raised, too, to the reception of Mayor Rossi who was voluntarily attempting to find a way to peace. A resolution repudiating "all communist organizations" and denouncing their attempts to exploit the strike for making converts to communism provoked a long and angry debate. Supporters of the resolution were playing into the hands of the Industrial Association and the shipowners; opponents were supporting communism, if not communists. The final vote— 129 to 22 for the resolution—"strongly" advised the longshoremen to cut all ties with the communist element on the waterfront. A week later, ILA Local 38–79 replied that it had endorsed the council's resolution; a member "who refuses to abide by this advice shall be held to trial on charges of insubordination and, if found guilty, will be liable to expulsion."[11]

Unions locked in bitter dispute—battles for their lives, it often seems—never cease to search for allies. They call initially on those whose support has strategic value—the longshoremen's apppeal to the teamsters or their backing for the seamen, for example, or their forlorn hope that the East Coast longshoremen might somehow be brought into the fray. Beyond that, unions look to others whose support means more in terms of financial aid, public relations, and morale-building, and less in direct economic pressure on the antagonistic employer. As the scope of the alliance broadens, as the unions and workers beyond both the immediate and related industries are brought into disputes, as strike support becomes increasingly general, its impact on the immediate economic issues is inevitably diffused; its indirect moral, persuasive influence heightened. A general strike in these terms is an ultimate expression of support, a demonstration of common class concerns. The general strike as a political weapon, as an instrument of revolution, however, would be of a different order; its genesis, reach, and goals are of other kinds; it is a class concern of an almost totally different orientation. It would seek to control instruments of government, the media, and the economy itself. When the San Francisco general strike did come, it was clearly a statement of support of the first kind, despite the inordinate efforts of the employers, the Industrial Association, and the newspapers to define it as the second.

The longshoremen's strike was barely three weeks old when Ralph Mallen, the ILA publicity chairman, touched on the possibility of a general strike. Some local unions invoked the possibility in letters to the city's unions—some, Sam Darcy said, at the instigation of the Communist Party.[12] The ILA strike committee had proposed a twenty-four-hour work stoppage. On June 11, the ILA asked unions throughout the area to consider a sympathetic strike in support of its strike. The June 19 mass meeting was, Sam Kagel has suggested, a testing ground for the idea.[13] A leaflet circulated in advance of the meeting urged "a solid front of all workers" as the necessary response to the Chamber of Commerce-Industrial Association plans to use force to break the strike. More than one of the speakers called for a general strike. Machinists, Lodge 68, informed the San Francisco Labor Council that on June 20 its membership had voted to participate in a general strike if the unions affiliated with the Council deemed it necessary "to aid the striking unions on the waterfront."[14] Still, when an ILA delegate, Charles (Curley) Cutright, raised the question in the June 29 Labor Council meeting, it was met with applause that Eliel called "only scattered" and the ILA Strike Bulletin "a wave." The butchers' representative declared that if the employers attempted to open the port, union workers in the city's meat jobbing houses would be called out. The teamsters' joint executive board told the council that it had taken a stand against a general strike and had asked its affiliates to take similar action. Other unions would also look at the possibility in the days immediately ahead, but it was at the moment little more than a distant rumbling.

The city's employers were by no means of one mind about how to break the deadlock. "There were a number of people, particularly Thomas Plant and some of his associates, who felt that this particular situation should be met head on," Bill Storie, at the time a staff member of the Industrial Association, later an employer representative, recalled. "There were a number of other individuals, I think some of them in the department store group and city officials, who thought that the matter should be temporized with and not brought to a head. This occasioned many meetings . . . violent disagreements and, on occasion, people walked out of the meetings. It was finally decided, however, the issue must be met squarely."[15] "There is nothing left we can do," Plant said. "There is nothing we intend to do. We have conceded everything we can possibly concede." The Industrial Association was working "assiduously," Eliel said, on plans to move waterfront freight but "had nothing to discuss at the time."[16]

To handle the freight operation, the Industrial Association set up the Atlas Trucking Company. In its name, Storie found a warehouse on King Street that would be used to hold freight moved from the docks. The company bought trucks and other equipment. A meeting on June 18 of some 150 representatives of business and industry provided customers for the cargo-moving service. "Plans to break the strike and open the port by force," the *Examiner* reported June 24, "were laid at a two-and-a-half hour conference . . . by representatives of the police, the State Harbor Commission, the Industrial Association and the Chamber of Commerce." Chief Quinn said the police would "do everything possible to handle the situation." While policemen would not ride trucks, every available officer would be detailed to "give necessary protection."[17]

Flanking support was provided by Acting Governor Merriam who suggested to the Board of Harbor Commissioners that it could remove cargo from the docks at the consignees' expense and make the docks available "for the service of the public." Later, he suggested that, to protect state property, the commissioners could hire temporary wharfingers, toll collectors, and special policemen if conditions made them necessary. Board President P. W. Meherin commented that no state property had been damaged and there was no occasion for guards.

As its plans took shape, the Industrial Association kept closely in touch with the teamster leadership. Initially it had warned that if the teamsters' boycott of the waterfront continued, the association would find other means of moving the freight. It added assurances that the union's longstanding place in the city's industry would be respected, that the Atlas operations would continue only as long as the emergency required, and would be disbanded the moment normal operations resumed.

Meantime, continuing efforts to find a way, if not to a settlement as such, at least to a method of working out a settlement, were momentarily derailed when Secretary of Labor Perkins telegraphically asked Plant if employers would submit "the one point still in dispute"—control of the hiring hall—to federal arbitration. Plant hastily and at some length explained that there was more to it than that. The demand for the settlement of the seamen's disputes and the rejection of the June 16 agreement were also involved. Her help in persuading the men to return to work and implement the agreement would be welcome, said Plant. Mike Casey got on the phone from the Industrial Association's office (with Paul Eliel listening) to AFL President William Green, asking him to explain to Secretary Perkins that the stumbling block was the demand for parallel settlement of all strikes. The next day, Casey left a long message for the secretary, saying that the major issues were "recognition" and suggesting a preferential shop as on the East Coast; no discrimination against strikers and the discharge of all strikebreakers; and settlement of the claims of the other marine organizations.[18]

Now the Industrial Association announced that trucking operations would begin "probably within a week"—possibly June 25, at the latest June 28. The ILA denounced the association's "plans of violence." It asked Mayor Rossi to act "to avoid a situation where a small group of shipowners can defy all law and order and utilize the police force of San Francisco to carry out their selfish aims." Albert Boynton, association managing director, replied that, for forty-seven days, the strikers had been responsible for every act of violence; the association's efforts to end the strike peacefully had exhausted "every avenue of appeal and conciliation." The association, he said, would do "whatever is necessary" to restore the use of the port of San Francisco "to the people," relying on the constitutional protection guaranteed for "the lawful conduct of lawful business."[19]

Mayor Rossi had phoned Secretary Perkins June 22 to advise her that "the authorities" intended to open the port on June 25, "even though that involved the possibility, which he recognized, of bloodshed." Rossi told Charles E. Wyzanski, Jr., solicitor for the Labor Department, that he thought the issues covered in the June 16 agreement "and any other issues" could be arbitrated; the employers would "stand" on that basis and "reasonable" labor leaders would agree, though he doubted the radical element—Communists and "an alien leader whose name he didn't give me"—of the longshoremen would accept it. Wyzanski asked if a presidential board could handle the situation. Rossi said he thought it could and added that he would urge postponement of any attempt to open the port until President Roosevelt returned to Washington on June 26.[20] To the press, Mayor Rossi said he had been in touch with Washington and that he expected "advice" not later than June 25.

Next day, a committee of businessmen, headed by Leland W. Cutler, former president of the Chamber of Commerce, told the mayor that the patience and temper of the city's businessmen were near the breaking point. "If conferences are unproductive," Cutler said, "we will have to have our cargoes moved. If this is necessary we want your fullest cooperation. This is not an ultimatum, but a report of the temper of thousands of citizens who feel . . . steps should be taken, under proper protection, to open the port."

Opening the port is no simple matter, Rossi told the committee; the real battle was against communists, not the labor unions. "There have been those right here in my office who do not want to settle the strike," Rossi said. Although he held the key to the situation—any movement of freight required the help of the police—he asked a delay: "I beg of you, gentlemen, not to do it." He pleaded for "another 24 hours" to allow Edward McGrady, who had just returned, an opportunity to ask the men to go back to work "while the President appoints a Board to give them a square deal." Rossi improved: "Let us avoid bloodshed—the entire coast is watching San Francisco."

The Industrial Association grudgingly yielded. It regrets, President John Forbes said, "the seemingly interminable delays caused by repeated and futile negotiations. . . . the time for such delays is past." The port should be opened; negotiations can go on thereafter. Mayor Rossi, Forbes said, must feel that his appeal for a delay rests on grounds "superior" to the rights of citizens "to go about their regular business."[21] That night, the president acted.

Efforts of workers to claim the union rights promised by Section 7(a) ran aground on the twin rocks of the employers' stubborn resistance and the absence of effective enforcement powers. By the end of 1933, Senator Robert Wagner of the National Labor Board as well as the AFL were convinced that the intent and purpose of Section 7(a) needed to be restated. Efforts to move such a bill into law quickly became entangled in an intricate legislative snarl. In the spring of 1934, President Roosevelt cut across the tangle by signing Public Resolution No. 44, a temporary measure intended to effectuate Section 7(a) by providing a ready tool for mediating the industrial conflict rising across the nation. Within the week, it was invoked to create the National Longshoremen's Board. The resolution empowered the board to investigate the dispute; to subpoena, with the backing of the circuit courts, documents and witnesses; and to conduct elections of collective bargaining representatives.

The clamor for presidential action in the Pacific Coast waterfront strikes was loud and insistent. On June 21, the San Francisco Labor Council called on the president to "act quickly"—the employers' efforts to move freight under police or military convoy would lead to a general strike. Wire services reported that the president had been inundated by appeals from San Francisco and other ports for his intervention. His office advised Governor Merriam that all appeals were being put before Secretary Perkins. On the evening of June 26 the President named the new National Longshoremen's Board.

Archbishop Edward J. Hanna, its seventy-three-year-old chairman, was a familiar figure in San Francisco. Born and educated in America, he studied also at the Vatican and Cambridge. He came to the city in 1912, served as auxiliary archbishop, then archbishop. Active in civil affairs and in the liberal National Catholic Welfare Conference, he was frequently involved in the city's labor relations. He had been a member of a hundred-man "advisory committee" to the Chamber of Commerce's Law and Order Committee. He chaired the 1921 arbitration board whose controversial wage cut provoked a building trades strike that became the pretext for inaugurating the open shop in the city's construction industry and for organizing the Industrial Association. He served the association, too, as chairman of several subsequent so-called impartial wage boards that fixed wages under the open shop; eventually he withdrew, perhaps because of union criticism. The archbishop "was a man of great mental powers," Henry Melnikow said, "and also curiosity." (He quizzed both Melnikow and Harry Bridges on the origin of the word "fink" that was so widely used during the strike. Bridges dismissed it as a "colloquial expression"—waterfront workers know its meaning, he said. Melnikow's further research, spurred by the archbishop's question, suggested it may have derived from a man who shanghaied sailors in New York or a person of loose moral character associated with a house of ill fame.)[22] Roger Lapham thought the archbishop "a very fine man" and "generally for the underdog." He felt, though, that "he'd aged a bit . . . he wasn't as fully alive to the situation as he would have been some years before."[23]

Oscar K. Cushing was a prominent San Franciscan, scion of a forty-niner family and a practicing lawyer since 1894. He had been president of the Legal Aid Society and served on a state commission to study unemployment and on the State Emergency Relief Committee, which administered a $20 million unemployment relief bond issue. (Archbishop Hanna had also been a member.) Cushing served as the National Longshoremen's Board's legal officer and often presided over its public sessions. He proved, Melnikow said after the lengthy post-strike arbitration, to be a devotee of the single tax with "an instinctive sense of the equity of distribution of production." Looking back, Roger Lapham thought "toward the end . . . [Cushing] was somewhat biased." Edward McGrady, the third member, Lapham believed, was merely carrying out the orders of Secretary Perkins.[24]

Cushing was seen as a more than usual liberal representative of the business community. The presence of Archbishop Hanna (who could hardly be accused of sympathy for communists) was intended, said one commentator, to divert the employers' focus from the "red" issue to a fair settlement. In the main, the board was well received. Joe Ryan said, "If they can't settle the strike nobody can." Mayor Rossi felt, "Anyone who objects to this set-up doesn't want peace." Confronted by McGrady, the strike committee had some reservations. Its chairman, Harry Bridges, was suspicious of the sponsors of the board members. McGrady replied, somewhat evasively, the president had been in touch with the situation and knew whom he wanted to appoint. When McGrady asked whether the maritime unions would return to work and leave their disputes in the hands of the board if the longshoremen's strike were settled, the strike committee sat silent. And when he asked if they trusted him, he was told emphatically, the *Examiner* reported, "No, we don't trust anybody."

McGrady got the board off to a fumbling start on its overloaded agenda by reopening the question of who represents the longshoremen. The employers claim, he said, the waterfronts are "stacked" with latecomers who are not really longshoremen, who had never worked at the craft. The board's first job is to find out who the real longshoremen are and whom they want to represent them. "If McGrady had carefully studied what would antagonize the men most," observed historian Mike Quin, "he couldn't have done any better."[25]

In an atmosphere tense with renewed threats of a forcible opening of the port, the board dug in. It met with the strike committee, shipowners, and the Industrial Association. It won a delay in the scheduled port opening to June 29, and subsequently another, no less grudging postponement to Monday, July 2. Out of its discussions, it became clearer, McGrady said, that the major stumbling block was the parallel settlement of the maritime union strikes. The

WEU maintained to the board the "practical impossibility" of such settlements, supported by a letter from foreign trade operators contending that the seamen's dispute did not concern them and affirming their willingness to work under the June 16 agreement.

Joe Ryan introduced a new, but then ineffective, note, by proposing jointly managed hiring halls with ILA dispatchers, the latter bound to dispatch nonunion, as well as union, men. Initially billed as a proposal from a strike committee of 100, it turned out to be a proposal from the executive board and strongly opposed by "left-wing members of the union." Ryan's proposal came on the heels of a fresh blast against Bridges. "It looks like Bridges doesn't want the strike settled. My firm belief is that he is acting for the Communists." The employers reportedly asked with whom they should deal—Bridges or Ryan? Ryan responded, "If I ever designate Bridges to speak for the longshoremen, I'll let you know." With that, he left town. "I've done all I can—I'm going home," said Ryan.[26] The joint strike committee, by way of reply, voted confidence in Bridges's leadership. It set a meeting on June 30 and appointed a committee "to contract all unions in the city and discuss the question of a general strike."

And now, Andy Furuseth of the International Seamen's Union, this "gaunt, lean man, lion-hearted and kindly, with a mane of white hair, and eyes burning sincerity," as the *Call-Bulletin* described him, came to San Francisco. For years he had been the seamen's legislative representative in Washington D.C., responsible for legislation that freed seamen from the harsh nineteenth century laws of the sea. He sat in with the joint strike committee, telling it "confidence and justice" could settle the strike within twenty-four hours "without bloodshed." The International Seamen's Union, he told the board, would accept joint hiring halls, but "absolutely opposed" employer operation. The men would return to work pending arbitration but only after the seamen had chosen bargaining representatives in an election. On June 29 he led a walkout of the marine unions from a session with the board. "The owners won't meet with us and nothing can be done until they do," he said.[27]

13.

B LOODY T HURSDAY

THROUGH THE MORNING of Monday, July 2, thousands of longshoremen, seamen, teamsters—strikers, sympathizers, the merely
curious—clustered on the Embarcadero.[1] By early afternoon, a
dense crowd (the *Chronicle* said 1,500; the ILA strike bulletin,
20,000) expectantly faced the docks around Pier 38. "Huddled four
deep, approximately 4,000 strikers along the waterfront eyed the
Matson and other docks, waiting for the port to open," the *News*
reported. A few clutched clubs or stones. The outnumbered police
"grinned at the strikers." Mounted police stirred restlessly as their
horses fidgeted. From Rincon Hill above the Embarcadero a gallery
of hundreds looked down on the tense scene. Doors of the dock
were partly open, motorcycle cops waiting on each side. Overhead
two planes circled. One bore the letters S.F.P.D., the police department's one-plane air patrol. (It had only a one-way radio; it could
receive orders, hear alarms, but its only communication with the
ground was by a handwritten note, weighted with a rock and
dropped as near as possible to the closest policeman.) The other
belonged to Universal News Service. On the ground, news photographers and newsreel cameramen cruised slowly by. From his seat
on the crowded top of a freight car, one striker wondered, "Will
they try to move the trucks?" and realized that the same question
was on everybody's mind. What do we do? he asked an older man,

a squad captain. "Use your own judgment," the man replied, "but I reckon we'll try to storm those trucks."

Word of the Industrial Association's intention to open the port that afternoon was spread wide. The newspapers, radio stations, and word of mouth had alerted the entire city. At 3:00 P.M., they announced, a parade of trucks, under heavy police protection, would enter Pier 38, load, then deliver the merchandise to the Atlas warehouse on King Street.

At 10:00 A.M., while the Industrial Association's crew prepared for the afternoon's work, John F. Forbes, the president, and Albert Boynton, the managing director, personally announced the association's plans to Archbishop Edward Hanna. They expressed "entire sympathy" with the National Longshoremen's Board's efforts to find a "peaceful solution" of the labor difficulties. But, for fifty-five days, at a cost of approximately $1 million a day, the right of "the people of San Francisco" "to the free use of the public streets and wharves in the normal transaction of lawful business" has been denied. That was a matter, in the association's logic, separate from the longshoremen's strike. It would therefore resume operations on the waterfront that afternoon. Chief William Quinn had been so advised by special messenger. Now Forbes and Boynton headed for the City Hall to deliver personally a similar announcement to Mayor Angelo Rossi.

At the City Hall, still hoping the violent clash could be avoided, the mayor brought together top city officials and heads of the Chamber of Commerce with the two messengers from the Industrial Association. The mayor asked for more time. The Industrial Association's spokesmen reiterated its brief for opening the port. They added that the drivers operating the trucks would not be armed; they had no intention of provoking violence. The association was confident of the protection the police would provide. Any efforts to interfere with the movement of freight, it concluded, would make it "obvious to all" that the longshoremen "are being made the tools of agitators and Communists, who have gained control of the union and are using it and its members to obtain their revolutionary end." Nothing was to be gained by further delay. Its plans had been laid; it had conceded four previous postponements; now it was "impossible" again to defer.[2]

The mayor argued that a postponement would open the way to a new possibility of settlement. The board had been in touch with Labor Secretary Frances Perkins and was awaiting instructions; it had asked no action be taken for another day. The mayor could not see that either the merchants or the city would suffer by acquiescing in that request. Finally, the hands on the clock moving inexorably toward 3:00 P.M., the Industrial Association officers agreed to delay the port opening until noon the next day if the mayor would put his request in writing. At 2:42 P.M., the mayor's office announced that the operation had been postponed.

Word of the postponement seeped through the waiting crowd on the Embarcadero and slowly it began to disperse. In the late afternoon, when the crowd had almost totally dissipated, a string of trucks, with motorcycle police escort, suddenly appeared on the Embarcadero. The initial surge of the remaining pickets was blocked by mounted police. The doors opened, then quickly clanged shut behind the trucks. Fearing an effort by the pickets to rush the dock, a police captain told pickets the drivers had left the dock by launch, the trucks were not being loaded. He took a committee of pickets inside to verify his statement.

Meantime, the board had appealed to all parties to submit all issues in dispute to arbitration. The grievances and demands of the maritime unions would be taken up as quickly as the longshoremen's case was completed. The board would conduct elections to determine the workers' bargaining representatives and use its "good offices" to make it unnecessary for seamen to apply for work through the employer-operated Marine Service Bureau. If the parties responded by midnight, July 5, arbitration of the longshoremen's dispute could begin the next morning. Twice, the board had asked the longshoremen to take a new vote on the June 16 agreement; twice they had refused. Now he hoped the board would receive favorable replies to its appeal for arbitration by Thursday night, three days off.

The crowd began to gather early on Tuesday, July 3, despite Chief Quinn's warning to bystanders to stay away from the waterfront. The strike committee had sent out a call to all unions for reinforcement, and thousands of union members were responding. Rincon Hill again was black with pickets and spectators. Mid-morning, the police began to clear the growing crowd from the area surrounding Pier 38—the McCormick dock—and the route to the King Street warehouse. A string of empty freight cars cut off approach from the south; a line of police cars—"bristling with revolvers, riot guns, and clubs," one observer noted—blocked the north flank. As the deadline approached, police lines cleared uncounted thousands from the Embarcadero between the barriers and either side of King Street. At noon, motorcycle police kicked up their bike stands and waited, one leg over their bikes. The crowd waited as moments ticked by.

At 1:27 P.M., the steel doors of Pier 38 rolled up. A string of police cars led the way for five old trucks, two men on each truck. "They look scared," said one reporter. A thunderous shout greeted the clumsy, little parade as still more police—on horses and motorcycles and in cars—joined the escort. The crowd surged forward. Barrages of tear gas opened the way for the trucks. The police moved on the crowd, nightsticks flailing. Slowly, the crowd fell back, breaking up into smaller, rock-throwing clusters, fleeing in retreat. Sounds of revolvers and riot guns echoed over the clash. Pickets fell back to 2nd and Brannan streets, some to Townsend. Bricks and stray bullets crashed windows; one stray bullet penetrated a window of the American Trust Co. at 3rd and Townsend streets, wounding a teller.

Henry Schmidt took a stand near a pile of bricks close to Pier 38 where the street bends toward Townsend, one of "a substantial number of men." Police started chasing them from the brick pile; "that's when they got the bricks." Germain Bulcke was with a group retreating from the "real bullets and buckshot" fired by the police. Running up Rincon Hill Bulcke was hit by an unexploded tear gas shell. He picked up the shell and threw it back into the police where it exploded. Bulcke and a small group of pickets stopped a flatbed truck loaded with rice coming down towards 3rd Street. He and his partner jumped on the back end and started dumping 150-pound bags of rice on the street. When a little coupe

Early in the strike, longshoremen pickets parade along San Francisco's Embarcadero. Strike leader Harry Bridges is in a cap to left and rear of "We want full recognition" sign. ILA Pacific Coast District President William "Burglar Bill" Lewis is in front row, second from left. (Photo courtesy of San Francisco Public Library.)

Police herd longshore pickets in clouds of tear gas on the waterfront. (Photo courtesy of San Francisco Public Library.)

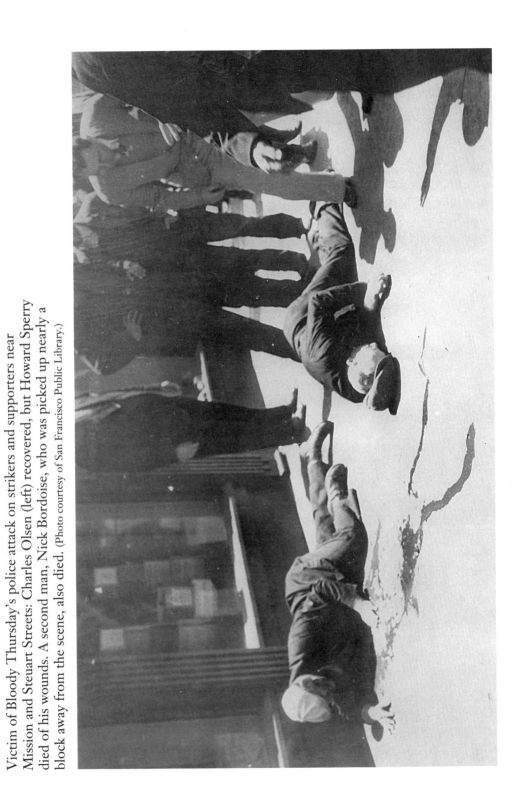

Victim of Bloody Thursday's police attack on strikers and supporters near Mission and Steuart Streets: Charles Olsen (left) recovered, but Howard Sperry died of his wounds. A second man, Nick Bordoise, who was picked up nearly a block away from the scene, also died. (Photo courtesy of San Francisco Public Library.)

Longshoremen fashioned a crude memorial to the victims, labeling it a "police murder." (Photo courtesy of San Francisco Public Library.)

The funeral cortege, the hushed, dramatic escort of the bodies of the Bloody Thursday victims, makes its way west up Market Street. (Photo courtesy of San Francisco Public Library.)

The National Longshoremen's Board had been named to mediate the waterfront strike by President Roosevelt only days before Bloody Thursday: (from left) Assistant Secretary of Labor Edward F. McGrady, Archbishop Edward J. Hanna, and Oscar K. Cushing. (Photo courtesy of San Francisco Public Library.)

Police at the Communist Party headquarters, 121 Haight Street, after it had been hit in the daylong red raids, on the second day of the general strike. (Photo courtesy of San Francisco Public Library.)

Striking seamen toss their fink books on a bonfire to put a finishing touch on their strike. Seamen's leader Andy Furuseth is at right, cigar in hand. (Photo courtesy of San Francisco Public Library.)

Strike leader Harry Bridges talking to reporters during strike.
(Photo courtesy of San Francisco Public Library.)

pulled up alongside the truck, Bulcke carefully laid a bag on its top. "I guess they had a pleasant surprise when they got home—150 pounds of rice," he said. The truck was one of several trucks waylaid by pickets that had no connection with port-opening operation. One explanation said the drivers wore no teamster buttons.

Near 3rd and Townsend, police kept a quiet, sullen crowd at bay, watching the trucks drive into the King Street warehouse. Suddenly, the crowd launched a barrage of bricks and began moving on the warehouse. "Chief Quinn's car sped up, rocks pelting it, one narrowly missing the chief," the *News* said. Gold braid glistened in the sun as blue uniforms rushed in to reinforce hard-pressed police lines. Rocks gashed faces, bricks ripped uniforms, but the police piled in, clubs swinging. The pickets melted away. "No jeers or oaths were hurled at police by the strikers. The burly, lithe seamen and stevedores were strangely quiet as they battled the police."

Observing tear gas lingering in the air around the railroad station at 3rd and Townsend streets, the *Chronicle*'s Neil Hitt found it amusing: "What must be the impression of people arriving in San Francisco for the first time?" Pat Frayne, usually a sportswriter for the *Call-Bulletin*, compared his seat on Rincon Hill to the press box in Berkeley's Memorial Stadium. ILA and ISU union buttons became "college colors"; exchanges of smoke and tear gas bombs between strikers and police were "forward and lateral passes." "It's a dangerous game," Frayne wound up.

The five trucks made eighteen round trips that afternoon, then, punctually at 5:00 P.M., knocked off. They had been manned, the shipowners' attorney, Herman Phleger, recalled, by a group of young business executives. The first trucks were driven by Reed Funsten, president of a large wholesale dry good company; James Folger, president of the Folger Coffee Co.; and Ward Mailliard, scion of a prominent business family. Their first cargoes included packaged birdseed, coffee, and automobile tires. The hired strikebreakers were paid $20 a day, plus meals and quarters. (Pay for teamsters was $5 to $7.50 a day.)

The count of the injured clearly was incomplete. The *News* counted nine injured policemen, two men shot, and eleven others given hospital treatment. Unknown numbers of the injured were moved to ILA headquarters or given other private treatment rather than expose them to possible arrest. One man, described variously as a strikebreaker or a former sailor and found some distance from the scene of the clash, died. Among the injured, the *News* reported, was Ignatius McCarty, Lake Erie's man in San Francisco. The tear gas salesman, "employed by the police department," was slightly gassed when a picket threw an unexploded tear gas bomb into a radio patrol car where he was sitting.

An ILA statement issued at the end of the day read:

> The Industrial Association has accomplished what they set out to do. They have incited a riot and guerrilla warfare that has spread over the entire industrial section of the city. They have put on a demonstration that will get them no place. . . . They still haven't opened up the port. . . . Striking pickets were clubbed down and rode over by the police who a short time ago were supposed to be the friends of these same workers. This strike cannot and will not be settled by force.

The operation, Bill Storie commented later, "was purely a strategic move." It was significant, he thought, as a show of strength in the face of the longshoremen's picket lines. "From there on, there were no definite plans made (and after all, I did have charge of that warehouse) to make any shipments out of it." It was intended "to bring the whole matter to a head. Which it sure as heck did."[3]

Governor Frank Merriam told Mayor Rossi he was prepared to call out the National Guard at the mayor's request. The mayor replied, "if the time comes when [Chief Quinn] cannot handle the situation, I will take up the matter with him."

"THE PORT IS OPEN," the Industrial Association proclaimed in ads in the Fourth of July newspapers. Goods are moving and will continue to move until "citizens are at full liberty to move their own goods without interference," with credit to the "full protection of the authorities." Fifty-six days of strike, "accompanied by rioting, assaults, arson and violence," can no longer be tolerated. The waterfront is public property and all citizens are entitled to use it lawfully without interference, "whether or not a strike is in progress."

While the Industrial Association shut down its operations for the holiday, Matson Navigation Co. was readying a freighter for a 4:00 P.M. departure. Part of its intended cargo was fourteen cars of perishable commodities and a shipment of infantile paralysis serum. When the Belt Line attempted to spot the cars on the Matson dock, pickets swarmed over the train and forced it to halt. The train crew quit, the *Chronicle* reported, saying their lives would be jeopardized if they continued to try to move the train. Governor Merriam ordered Arthur Pidgeon, the Belt Line superintendent, to ask the ILA to permit the train to continue. Twice, Pidgeon put the governor's request to Bridges, who referred the question to the Joint Marine Strike Committee. Both times, the committee refused. Governor Merriam told the strikers every effort would be made to operate the Belt Line; unless they modified their stand, he would call out the National Guard. The Guard, he said, is ready. "Strikers, having refused to arbitrate, must take the consequences."

Pidgeon then attempted to borrow crews from the city's other railroads; they refused, citing their contracts with the railroad brotherhoods. By midnight he managed to obtain a nonunion crew for one train and it succeeded in hauling the cars into the dock. As the train left, however, a switch was thrown that derailed several of the cars.

"This latest move of the Shipowners, San Francisco Industrial Association and the police has been definitely taken to break the strike through intimidation and terror," the Joint Marine Strike Committee declared. It called on all AFL local unions to send delegates to a conference in Eagles Hall on Saturday, July 7, "to discuss and prepare for a general strike of the workers in the Bay Region."

"We certainly fooled the strikers," the *News* quoted the Industrial Association's managing director, Alfred Boynton. "We got five more trucks into the pier before 6 a.m. Only a few pickets around . . . not enough to do any damage." At 8:19 Thursday morning, the first of the association's enlarged fleet of trucks rolled out of Pier 38 with strike-locked cargo for the warehouse on King Street. Lines of police—"mounties, motorcycle, and just plain flatfoots' with extra long nightsticks dangling from their belts," one eyewitness said—held the swelling crowd, tense and silent, to the far side of the Embarcadero. A police patrol car came screaming down the Embarcadero, the witness said. A police captain jumped out, ordered, "OK, boys, let 'em have it." Tear gas bombs were fired directly into the crowd; mounties charged. An elderly man went down, blood streaming from his head. The crowd retreated up Rincon Hill, police following.

Donald Mackenzie Brown, described in *Scribner's Magazine* as "a small investor," drove up Harrison Street that morning to the top of Rincon Hill. An object "whined ominously" over the heads of the motley crowd of "hangers-on, the sympathizers, and curious," he said. The sound of gunfire could be heard over the crest of the hill. Below, about fifty police officers at the base of the hill faced a charging crowd of "several hundred strikers, men and boys, some in old coats, some in shirtsleeves.... They hurled rocks. They picked up the tear-gas bombs and threw them back at the police. But the bombs came thicker and the shots faster. Four strikers fell in agony, Brown said. Then the ranks broke and the men streamed up the hill with police in pursuit on foot and horse."[4] Watching the bloody battle from a window in the American-Hawaiian Steamship Co. office in the nearby Matson building were Roger Lapham, president of the American-Hawaiian; Frazer Bailey, who headed Matson Navigation Co.; Tom Plant, president of the Waterfront Employers Union; and shipowners' attorney Herman Phleger.

Henry Schmidt left ILA headquarters on Steuart Street that morning, walked around the corner to the Embarcadero. "I saw small trucks and I saw tripods and cameras mounted on the truck beds and newspaper people all around. There were police and they were there with their shooting apparatus. I'm pretty sure I saw one of those tear gas salesman who was all equipped with a face mask ... it was obvious that there was going to be some shooting." Word got around the action would be on Rincon Hill. There, Schmidt rounded up a group of men and put them to work building a barricade. "I thought, well, when there's a revolt like this you get on the barricades." They used "a lot of stuff in a lot where construction was going on—I would call it now an imitation barricade." Bridges later added that the barrier and bricks had turned away two charges, on horse and on foot, by the police. But when mounted policemen charged up the hill, Schmidt recalled, "we gave up this job. . . . We removed ourselves by running as fast as we could."[5]

Throughout the morning and into the afternoon, police and strikers and sympathizers battled. "The furies of street warfare raged for hour piled on hour," the *Chronicle*'s Pulitzer prize-winning reporter, Royce Brier, wrote. "Don't think of this as a riot. It was a hundred riots, big and little, first here, now there. Don't think of it as one battle, but as a dozen battles." But battles or riots, they were lopsided contests. Against the tear gas grenades, riot guns, and revolvers of the police, the pickets were virtually weaponless, grabbing at bricks or stones, pieces of lumber or construction scraps. Against the police mounted on horses and motorcyles, and in squad cars, the pickets could only run, in panic and terror, from their constantly reinforced and heavily armed attackers. "Noon came," Brier reported. "Napoleon said an army travels on its belly. So do strikers and police, and even newspaper men."

By early afternoon, several thousand—the police report said six thousand—strikers had gathered in Steuart Street, between Market Street and Howard, near the ILA hall. Police pushed on the massed pickets from either side, tear gun squads, rifle and shotgun men, and mounties, compressing the crowd toward the intersection of Steuart and Mission. Two inspectors, the police report said, responded to a call for all radio patrol cars to report to the area. They found themselves surrounded with threatening strikers, showered by bricks and rocks. They fired two shots from a shotgun, the report goes on, and several shots from their revolvers at men attempting to overturn their car.

Germain Bulcke was in a service station across the street. He saw a car in the middle of the intersection, saw two policemen jump out, fire into the crowd, and leave as suddenly. Bill Caves, a sailor, and E. Wheeler, a longshoreman, said they saw a car in the middle of the intersection, surrounded by strikers and onlookers. A man carrying a riot gun stepped out of the car, looked around, then fired—first at the southwest corner, then at both corners to the north, then to the southeast. His first shot drew a shower of rocks; both men were sure no rock was thrown until after the shot had been fired. On the second shot, Howard Sperry and Charles Olsen dropped. A third, Nick Bordoise, was also shot; he was picked up nearly a block away. "He must have dragged himself there from the scene of the shooting," said Chief of Inspectors Charles Dullea. Sperry and Bordoise died; Olsen recovered. Police disclaimed any knowledge of who fired the fatal shots. Four captains, a lieutenant, seven officers, three inspectors declared "they [did] not know who fired the shots, if any were fired." Coroner T. B. Leland concluded the deaths were the result of "justifiable homicide by an unknown officer in lawful performance of his duty in suppressing a riot."[6]

Soon after, Wheeler saw men emerge from the ILA hall to carry three wounded back to the hall where a doctor could provide first aid. Police objected, insisting—at gun point—the men had to be taken to an emergency hospital. The men were carried out again. When a fourth injured man was carried in, a plainclothesman fired directly into the stairway. Police threw tear gas. When men started to run out they were ordered back in. A witness added: "At the height of the attack, the headquarters telephone rang. 'Are you willing to arbitrate now?' said the voice on the wire." In the confusion, a man rattled the door, yelling to let him in. Schmidt heard somebody say, "Don't let him in; we don't know who it is." Then the individual at the door turned sideways. "Everybody said simultaneously," Schmidt remembered, "let him in. It's the 'Limey.' And here was Harry [Bridges], crying like a kid—tear gas."

Panic gripped the east end of Market Street that afternoon, too, threatening to engulf commuters heading for the ferries. Three men—Joseph Roush, salesman for Federal Laboratories, and two uniformed policemen—started lobbing long-range gas shells across Market Street into the Seaboard Hotel, near the waterfront. (Roush's competition, Ignatius McCarty, had advised his home office that the police were concerned by a giant slingshot, put together by the longshoremen from inner tubes and 2-foot by 3-inch poles, throwing a 1- to 3-pound cobblestone 300 to 400 feet—it made short-range projectiles dangerous to use.) One long-range projectile struck James Engle, a 26-year-old longshoreman, as he emerged from the hotel. An eyewitness said Engle half rose to his feet, felt the side of his head with hand, looked at the blood, and collapsed. "His arms and legs flapped like a chicken whose head has been cut off." Roush reported his marksmanship to his superior: "During one of the riots, I shot a long-range projectile into a group, a shell hitting one man and causing a fracture of the skull, from which he has since died. As he was a Communist, I have had no feeling in the matter and I am sorry that I did not get more." The vice president replied: "The report is splendid and we think enough of it to excerpt a large portion of it to send out to the men."[7] In fact, Engle did not die. Tracked down by the LaFollette Committee, he said he had stopped to talk to a friend, had noticed but paid no heed to the group of men across the street. There was no disorder or rioting. "Next thing I remember is that I was lying in the gutter." Engle added that he was a member of the ILA but not then or ever associated with any communist or radical organization.[8]

No one was exempt who came within range of the battle. Joe Rosenthal, a newspaper photographer who later won worldwide fame for his World War II photo of the flag raising at Iwo Jima, was beaten on the Embarcadero. He told Bridges biographer Charles P. Larrowe he had been "stoned by strikers, tear gassed by police, and beaten so badly that he was hospitalized for a week." Two passengers on a Market Street streetcar were wounded by stray bullets. Many injured were treated at ILA headquarters (where a doctor was on duty) but, when it came under police attack, were removed to a number of places, including headquarters of the Communist Party on Haight Street. George Hedley, an official of the Pacific School of Religion, had spent some ten days at this point on the waterfront talking with union officers, strikers, passersby. He insisted that the police were invariably the aggressors; he never saw a weapon in the hands of a striker. "Such rioting as occurred," he argued, "was the direct product of their own aggression." Chief Quinn said later that "at times it looked quite bad . . . we were faced by from five to seven thousand infuriated men bent on" wreaking havoc with the nonunion men, then the steamship companies' property; "after that, only the imagination can determine what they would have done in the way of sacking San Francisco."[9]

That afternoon, Bridges headed a delegation from the striking unions protesting to Mayor Rossi that the police were being used to drive the men back to work by force and to crush organized labor. The mayor said the men could return to work tomorrow if they accepted the National Longshoremen's Board proposal to arbitrate. The strikers refused bluntly to discuss the board's proposals. The talk turned to violence against strikebreakers. Aren't they entitled to protection? One striker replied, "If you were walking through a park and saw a snake, you'd kill it. Any man who destroys the social conditions built up by organized labor is in that class." The mayor questioned the double standard. Looking at Bridges, he said "There may be men in this room who are not even citizens. Yet these men are entitled to protection, too, and will get it." The police, he insisted, would continue "to protect life and property without discrimination."[10]

At the end of the day, the *News* counted two men killed by bullets, another by injuries, thirty-one others shot, and untold numbers clubbed, gassed, beaten, and stoned.

Governor Merriam had ordered mobilization of the National Guard at midday. "Forbearance with the longshoremen in San Francisco," he said, "has passed the point of common sense and good citizenship." Fifteen hundred troops were ordered to duty; the governor promised five thousand more if they were needed. If they were not enough, he would enroll willing citizens to meet any emergency.[11] In overall command was Major General David Prescott Barrows, onetime United States Army officer and veteran of the American incursion into Siberia after World War I, professor of political science, former president of the University of California—and a vehement, fanatical anti-communist.

At 2:00 P.M., from the San Francisco Armory, Col. R. E. Mittelstaedt, commanding officer of the 250th Coast Artillery and commander of the waterfront force, announced the imminent occupation. By 5:00 P.M., San Francisco units, steel-helmeted, bayonets fixed, machine guns at ready, began to take over the San Francisco waterfront. Through the evening they were joined by other units from Oakland, Berkeley, and Gilroy. (Automobile ferries from Oakland were "seized" by the Guard for the movement from Oakland "and the trip was made without confusion or mishap.") As the troops were deployed, Colonel Mittelstaedt warned: "In view of the fact that we are equipped with rifles, bayonets, automatic rifles and machine guns, which are all high powered weapons, the Embarcadero will not be a safe place for persons whose reasons for being there are not sufficient to run the risk of serious injury." By midnight, troops were posted in front of every dock from Fishermen's Wharf to Islais Creek on San Francisco's—actually, the State of California's—waterfront.[12]

Silence and peace settled over the battleground. Not the least reason was Bridges's conviction that violence by strikers would alienate public opinion, that retaliation to police violence or to the Guard would be suicidal. Bridges later recalled an earlier inspection of pickets: "I stood there, with guards, and all of the men were rolled, every single man in our union, to see if they had guns. We found a few, maybe, and they were thrown in the safe." Now he said, "We can't stand up against police machine guns and National Guard bayonets." The Guard noted later, the "only weapons used by the strikers, were chalk and flowers," a reference to the chalked memorial to the two dead men at Mission and Steuart streets, surrounded by flowers and a quiet guard of longshoremen.

From Washington to vacationing President Roosevelt, Marvin McIntyre, his confidential secretary, wired:

> Authorities in San Francisco today forced picket lines back by troops without real need, injuring two or three people. Perkins ought to, I told her, take the mail away and John Lang ought to threaten to put the shipowners under [the NRA] code and refuse clearance papers to firms which did not come under the code and live up to it. The attorney general is afraid of the legality but the federal government is given control over foreign shipping by the Constitution and in the past for very trivial reasons clearance has been refused. They need a hard jolt to frighten them, I think, or they will fan flames into life again. The patience and the forbearance of the longshoremen, whom I was violently prejudiced against at the start, has been amazing to me. I hope you will back any effort decided upon to put the fear of God into the shipowners and get the strike situation cleared up. Perkins agrees and I am convinced that on the theory that union labor has not prepared to carry the general strike through, the shipowners deliberately planned to force a general strike throughout the country and in this way they hoped they could crush the labor movement.[13]

14.

PROLOGUE

ON THE MORNING of July 6 fifteen hundred National Guardsmen were stationed along the docks on the Embarcadero. Machine guns atop the pierheads aimed across a no-man's land at scattered pickets along its uptown edge. For the third day, the strikebreaking trucks rumbled to and from the King Street warehouse. The Belt Line busily shunted freight cars—some two hundred, it reported—along the front, in and out of the docks. The stunning violence of the day before was spread across the city's front pages, spotlighting "riots" and "strikers," proclaiming the protection the Guard offered for "property and lives." The coverage, the display, and the reporting dramatized in bold type and pages of pictures the Industrial Association's rationale for opening the port. They graphically underscored the employers' claimed right to operate the trucks with full police protection, regardless of consequences. They plainly placed full responsibility for the "riots" on the "attackers" and "mobs" of strikers and sympathizers. If there was point or reason to the strikers' dissent or their protesting presence the newspapers ignored it.[1]

The National Longshoremen's Board's proposal to move into quick and early arbitration collapsed as both the longshoremen and the shipowners tied unacceptable conditions to their responses. In still another attempt to move the union and employers from their inflexible stands, the board scheduled public hearings to start July 9.

Even as the board acted, events were speeding toward an even farther-reaching confrontation. The regular Friday night session (July 6) of the San Francisco Labor Council packed the tiny auditorium in the Labor Temple; hundreds more spectators jammed the halls and overflowed onto 16th Street. A growing demand for a general strike was inevitably its focus. Fourteen unions had taken action supporting a general walkout. Other unions were planning action. The teamsters had scheduled a special meeting for Sunday (July 8). Delegates from unions attached to the Joint Marine Strike Committee had brought in a resolution calling for a general strike. As a substitute measure, Council President Edward H. Vandeleur and Secretary-treasurer John O'Connell proposed to meet the crisis with a Strike Strategy Committee.

Before the council took up these measures, though, Harry Bridges asked immediate action on an ILA resolution underscoring the ILA position that the question of union hiring halls "cannot possibly be submitted to arbitration." It was approved without dissent. So was a second resolution condemning Governor Merriam for calling out the state militia. The action was "unprecedented and ill-considered;" police "within the bounds of law and reason" could have handled the situation. It led to "rioting and bloodshed," its partiality aroused the "deep resentment and the just indignation in the breast of every laboring man and woman." The resolution urged a peace based on "simple justice and not military force." (The governor replied that the "rioting and bloodshed" had taken place before the Guard was sent to the scene.)

The officers' proposal of a Strike Strategy Committee protested the "indiscriminate shooting down of strikers and innocent bystanders," then blaming "this deplorable situation" on the strikers. It condemned the shipowners and "their notorious strikebreaking agency" for their "vicious and unwarranted attacks" on a "substantial" part of the council's membership. The proposed committee would investigate the waterfront strike and formulate with the officials of the striking unions "a joint and common program for the guidance . . . of the labor movement." The committee was also charged with investigating the "irresponsible propaganda" that the longshoremen and marine unions were not sympathetic to the AFL and to answer "these slanderous innuendoes and vicious attacks." Debate was heated and prolonged but the proposal carried 165 to 8.

Vandeleur promptly named to the committee, in addition to himself and O'Connell, Daniel P. Haggerty, past president of the California State Federation of Labor; Milton S. Maxwell, president of the California State Federation of Butchers; George Kidwell, secretary-treasurer of the Bakery Wagon Drivers; Frank Brown, business representative of the Molders; and Charles Derry, a printer and editor of the *Labor Clarion*. Notably missing was any representative of the striking waterfront unions.

"GENERAL WALKOUT BLOCKED," The *New York Times* headlined the council's action and its interpretation was echoed by most local copy desks. The *Times*'s story, however, was more cautious: the council "adopted a 'go slow' policy," it said, calling it a victory for "conservative leaders." Left wing voices loudly protested the committee as a device to frustrate and circumvent popular demand for a general walkout. That night, though, in a "secret" meeting, Bridges agreed with the "conservative" Labor Council officers that the citywide meeting the next day—called by the Joint Marine Strike Committee to talk about a general strike—would hold off on a final call until the Strike Strategy Committee had an opportunity to act. Delegates the next day concurred (though it seems unlikely they were told of the meeting the night before).[2]

The next day's ILA Strike Bulletin said: "The newspapers carry big headlines: 'SF LABOR COUNCIL BLOCKS GENERAL STRIKE.' The San Francisco Labor Council has not blocked a general strike. The Council has set up a committee to make plans for a strike that will stop every industry in the city." The bulletin noted, too, that the council had endorsed the ILA's refusal to arbitrate the closed shop. Bridges declared, "This is no longer the ILA's fight alone. Thursday's bloody rioting has crystallized labor's attention on the conditions under which the ILA works and labor is demanding concerted action. The Labor Council is definitely behind the marine strike."

George Kidwell, head of the Bakery Wagon Drivers' Union, a member of the committee, and a highly regarded union tactician, told Henry Melnikow that the committee "was the only way of taking over the situation which was slowly putting everybody out of work." Melnikow described Kidwell as "doubtless the brain of the Labor Council during the Twenties and into the Thirties." He was, Eliel said, "generally recognized as one of the most astute of the San Francisco labor union officials." Kidwell knew what had happened in Seattle [in 1919]," Sam Kagel remembered, "when the general strike blew up in the face of the trade unionists. He kept telling me, 'in a general strike situation, you've got to end it fast.' "[3] With a committee, Kidwell told Melnikow, "you could control the situation and you could work out a solution." Kidwell said Mike Casey had agreed to go along. "The whole idea was to get it out of the hands of the individual unions, particularly the longshore, and get it into the hands of the Labor Council."[4] Kidwell reportedly told the delegates: "A general strike would not succeed unless we have a general agency which has the loyalty of the people involved."

Events in recent days had focused tightly on San Francisco but the pressure of the stalemate was being felt in other ports as well. In Portland, almost simultaneously with San Francisco developments, business agents of the city's unions set up a committee to consider a general strike call; it was expected by Monday to come up with a plan for a sympathetic walkout. The next day, strikers blocked the movement of freight cars into a municipal terminal with cargo for intercoastal vessels. In Tacoma, ships for Alaska were being loaded, forcing temporary postponement of an attempt to open the port by force in Seattle. A coroner's jury found that the death of Shelby Daffron, who had been shot by a guard in a clash with strikers, was the result of "criminal means." The guard was taken into custody.

In San Francisco the next morning, the Strike Strategy Committee of seven met with the Joint Marine Strike Committee. Vandeleur emphasized afterward that there was no danger of a general strike; they were "trying to go in there and adjust this thing."

"Are you willing to work under present conditions?" a printed ballot asked some fifteen hundred teamsters who jammed Dreamland Auditorium Sunday. The wording was somewhat vague and indirect but the intent was plain. They voted no, 1220 to 271. They also decided they would no longer work under those conditions starting Thursday morning (July 12) unless the strike was definitely settled or was on the way to a settlement. They would meet again Wednesday evening to confirm their strike vote.

You have no grievances of your own, Mike Casey had told the teamsters. Your contract with your employers runs to next May, and you will probably lose the $10 a week strike benefits usually paid by the international union. Afterward, Casey said, "the men feel very strongly about the final demands of the marine strikers, for the control of hiring halls and the recognition of certain of the unions, and also about strikebreaking truck drivers being used to break the deadlock." He added: "In all my thirty years of leading these men, I have never seen them so worked up, so determined to walk out. I don't believe any power on earth can prevent their going on strike unless the marine strike is settled by Thursday.[5]

In Oakland, Alameda County truck drivers voted, 369 to 54, to take similar action. Three San Francisco butchers' unions voted to cooperate in any plans of the Strike Strategy Committee. The San Francisco Labor Council advised the Santa Clara County Building Trades Council to hold off on a general strike pending the findings of the strategy committee. "We do not want a disorganized general strike, but if such a course be forced upon us, it must be a unified and intelligently directed strike."[6]

"SITUATION VERY TENSE," Assistant Secretary McGrady wired Labor Secretary Perkins Monday (July 9) morning. Teamsters will walk out unless an agreement is reached by Wednesday night, he said. Maritime unions were insisting on coastwide agreements. Shipowners claimed the law calls for collective bargaining by each employer with his employees. The Labor Department had advised the National Longshoreman's Board it could not insist on industry-wide votes. The board was schedule to open its public hearings that morning. Seemingly still determined, McGrady added, "We will work closely with the [Labor Council] committee to aid in securing an agreement."

Paul Scharrenberg, speaking for the three district unions of the International Seamen's Union (ISU), led the parade of witnesses when the board opened three days of hearings in a crowded federal courtroom. One after another—for the first time in some cases—spokesmen for the seagoing unions aired their grievances. Scharrenberg, onetime Sailors' Union officer, longtime secretary-treasurer of the California State Federation of Labor, occasional political officeholder, and an official of the ISU, sketched the deterioration of the seamen's wages and working conditions since union relations in shipping had been disrupted in 1921. Most of all, though, he underscored the repeated and futile efforts of the seamen over some nine months to bargain with the shipowners. (Later, McGrady asked Plant whether he had replied to any of the seamen's letters. Plant replied that he had not. "It was an act of discourtesy on my part not to have done so," he explained, but the letters were "just" notice that the men would be "called out until certain demands were met.") Scharrenberg objected, too, to the shipowners' renewed insistence that bargaining for seamen would have to be on a company-by-company basis. Shipowners, he pointed out, are organized in anticipation of a National Recovery Administration code to maintain hiring halls, "discipline and blacklists" of seamen, and a Washington lobby for subsidies and other prerogatives. However shipowners could not be required as a group to meet with the representatives of the organized seamen. Scharrenberg admitted there are "reds" in the waterfront unions but there are reds among the shipowners, "just as unreasonable and a little more arrogant than the wildest red we have in our ranks." If, he advised the board, "you can prevail on the shipowners to be reasonable and talk to all the men on strike, instead of insisting that the major part must be left out on the street, you can settle the strike on very short notice."

E. B. O'Grady and Oscar E. Rolstad put on the record the masters' and mates' grievances against the American Shipmasters' Association. It was, they charged, a company union that required every licensed officer to forswear any connection with the American Federation of Labor. Under its domination, wages were reduced, overtime rates cut virtually "to extinction," and allowances for subsistence reduced. Requests by their union for negotiations on wages and conditions, like the seamen's, were ignored. In the case of licensed marine engineers, Sam Kagel told the board, the company union was the American Society of Marine Engineers, organized during the 1921 strike at the behest of the shipowners. They used it as a hiring hall, compelling men to pay tribute to obtain jobs, and as a means of "cutting wages, lengthening hours and making peons out of the marine engineers."

The board heard, too, Harry Jackson, representing the Marine Workers Industrial Union—"fiery and intense," an observer described him, pleading in "words and gestures alike picturesque."[7] Seamen's wages have dropped below the level of "Chinese coolies," with men working as one-cent-a-month "workaways" for board and room. They are forced to pay $5 and up for jobs paying $25 a month through shoreside boarding houses. The "rotten food," he said, puts many in the Marine Hospital. (A witness for the Marine Cooks and Stewards, a second cook on the *Monterey*, chronicled the deterioration of wages and working conditions in the stewards' department but denied emphatically he had ever served swill to seamen.) John J. Finnegan, representing the ship clerks in the ILA, described their "modest requests:" recognition and a preferential agreement as on the Atlantic Coast.

Twice, the eighty-year-old Andrew Furuseth—"eyes half-closed, shoulders drooping and a general air of despondency," the *Times* reported—interrupted the proceedings to demand the board use its power of subpoena to get at the facts. "There is an agreement between the banks and the Industrial Association and the shipowners," Furuseth charged, urging the board to "go to the bottom of this thing." Near the end of the morning, McGrady told the audience, "The Board is thinking of adjourning now because we understand that a great many people here would like to go to a funeral."[8]

As the morning waned, crowds began gathering at the ILA hall on Steuart Street, where the bodies of Howard Sperry and Nick Bordoise had been lying in state, and where at 11:00 A.M. funeral services for the two victims of Bloody Thursday would be held. Alex Walthers, who had been a longshoreman in the 1919 strike and whose brother was working on the waterfront, spoke a simple sermon. In the distance the bell of a Belt Line locomotive could be heard. Bridges, asked if he would say something, shook his head, a reporter noted, "too distraught to utter his feelings." After the brief ceremony, the caskets were placed on black-draped flatbed trucks, and flowers were loaded on three more trucks. As the trucks moved along Steuart Street, then turned into Market Street, thousands—

strikers and strike leaders, honor guard, families, sympathizers—followed to the slow step of a funeral march. "That strange, silent march," as George Hedley described it, a march without banners but with a profound moral surge powerfully impressed a city still deeply shaken by the bloody violence of July 3 and 5 and the occupation of the waterfront by the National Guard. It heated the angers of many, reinforced the sympathies of the sympathizers, and converted the sympathies of many more. It put the "riots" and the "mobs" of the port opening, the tortured turns of the strike, as pictured in the daily press, in a different light. Events had made a general protest likely; now this grim, silent parade made it inevitable.

On the second day of the hearings, "Bridges made an extraordinary presentation before the Board," Paul Eliel wrote, "speaking without notes and extemporaneously. He showed not only unusual command of the subject matter but of the English language as well. Employers were able for the first time to understand something of the hold which he had been able to establish over the strikers both in his own union and in the other maritime crafts."[9]

After giving his name—"H. R. Bridges"—and identification—"chairman of the strike committee"—Bridges with barely a breath launched into a wide-ranging, detailed, and comprehensive affirmation of the longshoremen's stand. Though he was chairman of the strike committee "for this port," he wanted it understood that "we deal as a district and we want this thing settled as a district." He insisted: "The shipowners have shown in all their activity, publicity, and maneuvers only one objective, and that is to destroy the right of labor to organize into its own unions." He described the "so-called joint hiring hall" as the equivalent of "the obnoxious 'fink' hall which has been operating for years in San Francisco." Archbishop Hanna interrupted. "Why the word 'fink?' I don't understand it." Bridges replied, "It is just a colloquial expression . . . amongst the workers in the maritime industry. I can assure you they know what it is."

Bridges angrily denounced the "reign of terror" loosed on the strikers by city and state officials. Bloody Thursday was no battle, "it was an attack by armed men against unarmed peaceful pickets.

It was a massacre of workers by the shipowners through the police," he said. Bridges offered the board a letter written by Thomas Plant upbraiding San Pedro employers for spending money for armed guards when protection should have been supplied them without cost by the city government.

Cushing asked him if a union hiring hall means a closed shop. Bridges's discursive answer added up to an argument for preferential hiring for ILA members. But he conceded, given the membership of the union and the amount of work, it would result in assignment of union men only.

On the third and final day, Plant once again restated the shipowners' case. Two agreements and one proposal had been repudiated by the men "under the domination of radicals and communists." Picketing by "longshoremen, sailors, and Communists" practically closed the ports of Portland and Seattle; intimidation and threats of teamsters had blockaded San Francisco, although loading and unloading cargo on the docks and by freight car were handled readily. Plant listed the violence that had resulted. The employers offered to agree to a jointly controlled hiring hall, to hire only registered men, and to spread work through job distribution. They would even accept government supervision of the halls. But a union hall and union dispatcher would not only mean a closed shop (contrary to law), they would also end the employer's right to select his own employees.

McGrady asked Plant about a coastwide agreement for seamen. It is complicated and does not seem feasible, Plant replied. The only conclusion was the employers' suggestion that the representation elections be held company by company. McGrady had a further question: the Waterfront Employers had long had a closed shop agreement with the "independent" longshoremen's union, until it was challenged under the NRA. It was the ILA, Plant replied, who had challenged the arrangement. "The strange thing is that they now want the same arrangement which last year they contended was illegal." But now, he added, the employers, too, "think that is the law."[10]

McCann-Erickson reported the *Examiner* had promised eight thousand words the next day on Plant's testimony, the *Chronicle* "a very full play." The *News* gave it ten thousand words, the memo reported, the *Call-Bulletin* page one banner, picture, and five columns—"by far greater than anything given to individual spokesmen on the other side . . . as much as anyone can reasonably hope to get." Clarence Lindner, the *Examiner*'s publisher, sent word that the Waterfront Employers' Union ads were being reported as spot news on the Hearst radio station KYA.

As the board picked its way through the fine print of grievances and defenses, events moved relentlessly. The Alameda County Central Labor Council asked its seventy-nine affiliated unions to vote on a general walkout in support of the longshoremen. It, too, created a committee of seven, charging it to develop "an effective strike" in the event that the affiliated unions authorized a general walkout. It promised cooperation with San Francisco's committee.

From Washington, William Green, president of the American Federation of Labor, deplored Governor Merriam's use of troops. It means "the substitution of force for reasons and justice," placing the power of the state "on the side of the employers and against the workers. . . . I protest." He protested, too, to Mayor Rossi that his use of the police is "intentionally or unintentionally aiding unreasonable employers to compel striking workers to accept their terms." Rossi replied that the riots and violence started when "removal of merchandise from wharves to warehouses was undertaken." These "lawless acts" were largely "the result of communist activity." Governor Merriam replied that the Guard represented no effort to settle the strike; it was called out only after strike leaders had refused to let the Belt Line operate, to end the defiance, by intimidation, violence, or force of numbers, of the authority of the state.

Even as the board listened to the witnesses in the crowded courtroom, it was seeking ways to avert the growing certainty of a general strike. On Wednesday (July 11), it asked the parties to submit all issues in dispute to arbitration by the board. It asked for replies the next day. Meantime, it spent long hours in session with the shipowners and the Strike Strategy Committee—a development interpreted by some as displacing the Bridges leadership. It also met with teamster leaders in an effort to delay the strike scheduled for

Thursday morning, but John P. McLaughlin said that night's meeting would go on as scheduled unless something "tangible" emerged from the board's sessions.

The next day, as newspaper ads defended the record of the waterfront employers over the months of the prolonged dispute, the WEU took two major steps toward reconciliation. Over the signatures of waterfront employers in San Francisco, Seattle, Portland, and Los Angeles, the WEU told the Board the employers were now prepared to submit all issues, without condition, to arbitration by the board. It removed the longshore employers' last pre-condition to arbitration—their insistence on the open shop—though by no means were they abandoning their demand. It also moved to eliminate a no less serious stumbling block: the WEU said it had communicated with thirty-nine steamship companies who sign on crews in Pacific Coast ports and they had agreed to meet the representatives of their seafaring employees in collective bargaining as soon as elections determined who those representatives would be.

William Lewis, the ILA Pacific Coast district president, said the officers could not answer the board's proposal—that decision rests with the members—but it would submit the proposal to arbitrate all issues to a referendum vote. Archbishop Hanna told reporters he was encouraged, adding "I am going to say my prayers while we wait." Bridges told the *News*, "You can't arbitrate the question of hiring halls. It's got to be a closed shop or an open shop." O'Connell thought the employers' acceptance of arbitration "should make a big difference. It is a great deal more than we expected." But then, still another issue delayed the longshoremen's vote. The shipowners' offer made no provision for resolving a deadlock in negotiations with the seafaring unions. An ILA committee composed of Bridges, A. H. Petersen, and John Finnegan told the board no vote would be taken until the shipowners committed themselves to binding arbitration.

Hundreds of longshoremen, Bridges included, waited outside the hall when the teamsters went into session that Wednesday night (July 11). Mike Casey, O'Connell, and Kidwell backed a plea from the board to delay their walkout until Monday, at least. A noisy and determined audience listened impatiently, clamoring insistently to hear Bridges. When he was finally brought in, the teamsters gave him a rousing ovation. Casey introduced him: "I give you the man of the hour." Bridges reminded the men of past defeats and warned, "The entire labor movement faces collapse if we maritime workers are defeated. If you fellows join us, you will double our power." Casey asked for questions. Had he (Bridges) been run out of Australia, identified with a red organization there? If he had, Bridges replied, he would have been found out long ago. What about arbitration? He personally opposed it, but the members will vote on it. When Casey called for the yes votes, thousands of hands went up; only a few responded to the call for no votes. John O'Connell announced the vote: "The ayes have it and the no's know it." Casey told the teamsters: "You'll go out like gentlemen with nothing to be ashamed of. Of course, you'll be allowed to do the decent thing. Don't worry, the children can eat and have their milk. Retail food deliveries won't be affected. And bless you, San Francisco may have its beer. The brewery drivers are a separate group." Casey later told Eliel that the union "was out of control," blaming it on communists unsympathetic with the traditional labor viewpoint, some wanting a change in leadership, some who saw it as a lark.[11]

In the East Bay, teamsters walked out at midnight, though a few retail deliveries continued until 7:00 A.M.; in San Francisco, they left their jobs at 7:00 A.M. the next morning.

15.

GENERAL STRIKE

THE TEAMSTERS' WALKOUT on Thursday morning (July 12) marked the real start of San Francisco's general strike. The Strike Strategy Committee had made no report, proposed no plans, nor had the San Francisco Labor Council yet acted. But one local union after another followed the teamsters on strike, set dates to strike, or authorized a strike when and if the council or committee called for it. Sympathy, anger, and the determination to join the fight boiled up, finding unmistakable voice in the workers' many and independent decisions to act, with leaders or committees or without them. The general strike was clearly on and rapidly becoming more general, hour by hour.[1]

Joining some 25,000 maritime workers on strike that morning were San Francisco and East Bay teamsters, numbering together over 4,000. Nearly 200 wholesale butchers on both sides of the bay had quit work; they would be joined the next morning by 1,500 retail and jobbing butchers, and on Sunday morning by 2,600 laundry drivers and workers and unknown numbers of culinary workers. Twenty-five San Francisco and six East Bay unions had voted to walk out if the Strike Strategy Committee recommended joint action. Thirteen unions were in the process of voting; the Building Trades Council was collecting the vote of forty-eight building trades locals. Cleaners and dyers walked out on behalf of their own demands. Boilermakers left their jobs in sixty shops. Labor Council

President Vandeleur refused to comment on what actions the Strike Strategy Committee might take at its meeting that afternoon, but he did say: "Do you fellows have to see a hay-stack in the air before you can see which way the straws are blowing?"[2]

Hanging heavily over the committee's deliberations were accelerated preparations for a general strike. Police Chief Quinn reorganized his forces. He ordered all firearms and other weapons removed from the windows of sporting goods stores and pawnshops. Gathering of "mobs" would not be permitted anywhere. Guns, gas of all kinds, and other weapons had been stockpiled. With the California National Guard in place, Quinn redeployed men who had been stationed on the waterfront to downtown and other industrial areas. He would shortly ask the mayor for additional men and equipment.

Teamsters posted picket lines at the city's southern limits, its only vehicular entry. East Bay drivers also posted pickets. Nonunion drivers were turned back; newspapers reported some nonunion truckers had been "threatened," "some" trucks overturned. Food supplies from within a one hundred-mile radius were sharply curtailed; estimates that supplies on hand could not supply the area for the week were prominently displayed. Teamsters' locals began issuing emergency "permits" for deliveries of food and fuel to hospitals, fire stations, and other necessary services.

Asked if the teamsters planned to stop deliveries to the entire city, including their own members, John P. McLaughlin told the *Examiner* they did not intend to repeat the mistake of the English general strike by helping to starve its own strikers into submission. Said another teamster: "Well, we won't starve our own women and children. What do we care about the rich?" The reporter commented: "The rich are moving their families out of town and that only those who can't leave are staying, but there was no further comment forthcoming."[3]

Fifteen oil companies, banded together in the Petroleum Emergency Committee, cut off deliveries to retail outlets and business establishments and arranged to supply hospitals, police, fire departments, and other emergency services. The companies refused, the committee said, to ask their drivers to take the physical risks of continuing fuel deliveries. Service stations began closing down as rapidly as suppliers ran out. Pacific Gas & Electric Co. officials complained to Mayor Angelo Rossi that their drivers and repairmen were being driven from the streets by "threats." Rossi promised full protection; Mike Casey said the men would not be bothered by teamster pickets. The company nevertheless pulled its trucks off the street and held them off through the general strike.

Shoppers rushed grocery stores and butcher shops, where long lines waited in some cases into the night. Grocers rationed food-stuffs they expected would be impossible to replenish—flour and sugar among the first. Shelves were cleared. Meat supplies vanished rapidly in anticipation of the butchers' walkout. Fresh fruit and veg-etables, with out-of-city supplies curtailed, were in short supply. Chickens in Petaluma, "egg basket of the west," kept right on lay-ing but their output could not be delivered. Growers complained they were being forced to leave fruit hanging on trees and crops unharvested. When people learned the U.S. mails were going through, they heaped parcels on the service until the load threat-ened to exceed even the Christmas rush. Signs appeared in shop windows: "Closed. Out of supplies." Hundreds—nobody really knew how many—were fleeing the city. Newspaper reports painted pictures of lines at the railroad stations and outgoing highways "black with cars during the day."

To the Labor Council meeting behind closed doors Friday af-ternoon (July 13), the Strike Strategy Committee proposed creation of a General Strike Committee, made up of five delegates from each of the city's American Federation of Labor (AFL) unions. Such a committee, its report indicated, could coordinate and direct the ac-tivities of the unions in ways, it felt, that were denied the Labor Council itself. AFL President William Green had already reminded the council that AFL rules prohibited, under severe penalities, a central labor body from ordering a strike by any local union without the sanction of its international union. The council finally decided to call the General Strike Committee into session at 10:00 Saturday (July 14). Maritime strikers and their supporters, angry and frus-trated, called it another delay. Vandeleur told reporters afterward that the general strike could be averted if the employers granted the

ILA "the right to conduct its own union headquarters in the same manner in which other unions are conducted" and if the shipowners agree to submit unresolved issues (in negotiations with seafaring unions) to arbitration. Their refusal puts "responsibility for a general strike . . . on their shoulders."

When the new General Strike Committee convened the next morning, it promptly ejected a delegation from the Marine Workers Industrial Union, since it was not affiliated with the AFL. The committee then voted to create an appointed executive committee of twenty-five (later fifty). Vandeleur was elected chairman by acclamation; Clyde W. Deal of the Ferryboatmen defeated Bridges for the vice chairman's post. After Bridges declined a nomination for secretary, Kidwell was chosen. The committee turned down by voice vote a move to defer a decision until Monday as well as a motion "to join in a General Strike immediately." It finally approved a motion asking "all unions that have voted in favor of a general strike to walk out Monday, July 16th at 8 a.m., and that all other unions which have not voted be asked to hold meetings immediately and take action." Roll call recorded 63 unions, voting as units (315 delegates), for the amendment, 3 (15 delegates) against (including the teamsters' 5 votes, cast by Casey, some said to protect the local against discipline by its international union; others saw it as his last-ditch stand against a general strike). Forty-nine unions (245 delegates) were recorded as not authorized to vote. "Radicals in Full Sway," the *New York Times* portrayed the decision. It was taken, the *Chronicle* reported, not without its usual slant, "amid scenes of wildest conditions, with hundreds of delegates shouting and scores of others in a condition approaching hysteria." It also reported that conservative labor leaders fought for four hours to avert the mass walkout, though their opposition was not reflected in the final vote. What seems clear is that the debate was focused less on averting a general strike, more on how to call it. Clearly, neither the "radicals" nor the "conservatives" were in full sway, but rather a broad, cross-section of the unions, left, right, and center, moved into action.

If the atmosphere around the Labor Temple that morning was confused and hysterical, it was nothing compared to the panic and confusion that welled up in the newspapers. The *Chronicle* reported that "While the rest of the city may go hungry, suffering privation and cold, every family of every man on strike in San Francisco will be provided with food, clothing, gasoline, and other necessities of life." It printed a one-sentence denial by "John F. Schelly" (actually Shelley, later head of the Labor Council and State Federation and San Francisco's congressman and mayor). Not until Monday did the *Chronicle* print (on an inside page) Vandeleur's and Kidwell's full-scale denial. To their denial, however, the *Chronicle* added it "DOES NOT" retract its original story. The *Chronicle* also reported that martial law would be invoked "within an hour after a general strike goes into effect." The Ninth Army Corps at the Presidio promptly denied it but the *Chronicle* insisted that "those claiming to know the facts" asserted plans were ready. Clarence S. Morrill, chief of the State Bureau of Identification, put a message on state-wide teletype that "radical strikers and Communists were preparing to throw kerosene bombs on trucks carrying food." It was the *Chronicle*, too, that warned of a "communist army marching on San Francisco from the northwest." The "army" planned to destroy railroads and highways, paralyze transportation and communication. The invaders were reported near the state's northern border. In fact, neither martial law and bombs nor the army materialized.

In the East Bay, some 30,000 union members were reported ready "automatically" to join the general strike. Mayors of East Bay cities were said to be "working out plans" for voluntary deliveries of food and supplies to homes. The Alameda County Central Labor Council asked the Board of Supervisors to join a labor committee in providing commodities to homes with children and invalids. East Bay businessmen had no decisive involvement in the waterfront strikes, according to J. Paul St. Sure, but they wanted to know what was going on and to protect themselves against whatever might be happening. They employed St. Sure as "a kind of liaison guy" between the public authorities, the waterfront employers, and the East Bay businessmen. St. Sure, son of a federal judge, served as a deputy under Earl Warren, and later became a major figure in Bay Area labor relations and president of the Pacific Maritime Association (successor to the Waterfront Employers Union). His group of businessmen, St. Sure recalled, on telephone notice "would rush down to the Oakland Hotel ballroom and listen to someone make a speech about what was happening . . . and how the revolution was at hand and the Communists were on the march. It was almost an hysterical type of atmosphere." St. Sure was convinced Oakland labor wanted to avoid violence. He asked Charlie Real of the teamsters and Bill Spooner of the Central Labor Council, if they had a problem, to give him a chance to see what he could do to avoid conflict. "I don't think there was a plot to create a revolution," he said afterward. "I think they were simply carried away and swept into this thing, which could well have broken into open conflict."[4]

At the same time, in response to reports received by Warren (who later became attorney general and governor of California and chief justice of the United States Supreme Court), a newspaper reported that East Bay union men were joining the police "in an effort to halt terrorizing of merchants, storekeepers and farmers in East Bay cities and Alameda county, by gangs of men, believed to be communists." The *News* noted: "Persons in all walks of life . . . became victims of the strikers' reign of terror," stretching from the countryside where truck traffic was reportedly blocked and restaurants invaded and ordered to close, to neighborhoods where private homes were entered and occupants threatened.

Newspaper coverage was enhanced by the Industrial Association's network of reporters set up early in the strike. Under James Carr, described as director of the association's American Plan Promotion, it scoured police reports, emergency hospital records, and radio broadcasts for acts of "violence;" its men rode with police in patrol cars and haunted the district stations. By phone and hand delivery, it supplied a running and detailed report of any incidents that might be, in whatever way, strike-related. Investigators for the American Civil Liberties Union found the association's "Strike Violence memos" contained "all sorts of information, and a number of [its reports] referred to matters not dealing with police or hospital records." It was plain, too, that some of its reports attributing violence to the strike or strikers often bore little relations to them. Senator Boynton told the investigators that the Association wanted the papers to get all the strike violence news possible, and that they wanted a lot of such information direct and quick." It grew directly from the association's intent from the outset to fix blame for violence on the strikers as a companion-piece to its attack on "radical and Communist" leadership. Some substantial, but immeasurable, part of the violence reported in the press, as a result, was probably less the product of increased violence than of intensified and creative reporting.[5]

With the rising tempo of developments, San Francisco Mayor Rossi called together his department heads and members of the Board of Freeholders (who had written the city's 1932 charter) in an anxious search for emergency powers. The results appeared the next day in a proclamation of a state of emergency and a clenched-jaw radio speech. It is, his proclamation said, "the most serious situation which has beset us since the [earthquake and fire] of 1906." He had, therefore, armed himself with all the powers provided by the charter and the laws of the state. Calling on his "fellow citizens" to preserve the peace, he echoed the Industrial Association theme that responsibility for the violence, as for the strikes themselves, lay on the strikers, without even an intimation that employer oppression and intransigence might have had a part in creating the crisis. Acts of violence will not be tolerated, he proclaimed. Lives and property will be protected. The police chief will be given the additional men and equipment he has requested to handle the situation. "Let there be no hysterical action," he asked. That night, in his radio talk, the mayor added that the general strike has been fomented "by those who seek to prolong our troubles rather than to end them." They "will be dealt with by every force of law and order." He considered it his "obligation" to "use every effort to solve this crisis." Keep cool, he advised, and "go about [your] business in a normal manner as far as [you] are able to do so." Messages backing his stand and volunteering for public service began pouring in moments after he concluded his talk, along with numerous suggestions of a citizens' or vigilante committee.

In Washington, Marvin H. McIntyre, assistant secretary to the president, and Secretary of Labor Perkins kept close watch on the developing situation while the president was vacationing aboard the cruiser *Houston* in the Pacific thousands of miles away. In a late night phone call from San Francisco, James Moffett, representing the Department of Commerce, told McIntyre of the chilling talk he had held with Kenneth Kingsbury, president of Standard Oil of California. Kingsbury told Moffett he could not "impress upon me the seriousness of the situation; that they are Communists and reds and they are out against the government." Kingsbury said that 950 police, 2,000 Guardsmen on duty and 2,000 on call, and something like 500 troops at the Presidio "will not be able to cope with the situation." Kingsbury said he expected the long-planned "thing" to move to Portland, Seattle, even Los Angeles. Six pickets are posted at the [Pacific] Union Club, he said, all transportation is out, no taxicabs are available, they have shut off all food, and he is compelled to walk to his office. "There is no question but that there will have to be Federal troops to feed the people or they will be up against it." Moffett added, "My guess is that the leading citizens of San Francisco probably have their wives out of town, and some of them are penned up in the Club which is up on [Nob] Hill."[6]

Shipowner Roger Lapham found a call from banker Herbert Fleishhacker awaiting him at his Atherton home that same Saturday afternoon. Fleishhacker had had a call from McIntyre wanting to know "all about it." Telling Fleishhacker that he was "going to lay it on the line," Lapham called McIntyre. The stage was set for violence, he told McIntyre; " 'we'd done everything we could.' McIntyre replied, 'There's one more thing you might do.' 'What's that?' 'Give them the closed shop.' " Lapham told him they had done everything the [National Longshoremen's] board had asked; it has the power to give it if it wants to. He would consult his group. McIntyre asked if he would talk to "Madam" Perkins. She called soon after and they talked for forty-five minutes. She asked what the shipowners would do about the seamen; if negotiations failed, would they agree to arbitrate? Lapham said, "That's a different picture. We haven't any issues with the seamen's union; I can't speak for the crowd." But he would speak with his associates.[7]

Secretary Perkins described the situation in a long telegram to the vacationing president:

The officers of the unions have been swept off their feet by the strength of the rank and file movement toward these strikes Stop It is a surprise to them and they are for the most part opposed . . . Stop There is an unusual mass movement unusual solidarity and unity Stop . . . There has been relatively little disorder until the time when the police were put on the docks with orders to shoot if necessary and even now there has been surprisingly little considering the number of people involved and the strength of the feeling Stop It is doubtful if a general strike is really called on Monday morning Stop

Perkins added that after a long conversation with Lapham and Fleishhacker, "they have agreed to try to get the shipowners to agree" to arbitrate any points about which they cannot agree in negotiations. "The shipowners are doubtful of the ability of the present board to understand the problems of life and work aboard ship and I have assured them that if they will agree publicly to the arbitration then when any such arbitration is called for that you will see to it that persons are added to that board who are experienced in seafaring matters and therefore competent to make decisions about conditions of work aboard ships Stop." Perkins's telegram concluded: "The situation is serious but not yet hopeless."[8]

John Francis Neylan, along with Bartley Crum, a young associate who functioned as a kind of administrative aide, moved into the Palace Hotel where other employer figures had taken rooms. From there Neylan called together the newspaper publishers in what Paul C. Smith, the *Chronicle*'s bright, young, soon-to-be editor, called an "editorial cabal."[9] Neylan also dealt himself a major role in the chaotic efforts to avert, then end both the general and waterfront strikes. He held credential for both jobs. He was an old friend of Mike Casey. Years before, Casey had threatened several times to throw Neylan, as a young reporter, out of his office; Neylan's resulting, and accurate, story launched a lifelong friendship.[10] Neylan had served William Randolph Hearst as publisher of the *San Francisco Call*. He had held political office under Governor Hiram Johnson. As a lawyer, he defended Anita Whitney in the historic criminal syndicalism trials, counseled banker A. P. Giannini, and worked with Hearst as general counsel and confidante. Before the week of the general strike was over he was widely recognized as spokesman for Mayor Rossi. "His great frame and craggy face were topped by a shock of white hair," an interviewer recorded. "His voice boomed and resounded."[11] (Lapham, oddly, recalled his voice as "high-pitched.") In his wide-ranging experience he had at times been seen as friendly to organized labor and suspicious of red-baiting. But he could also be a sharp-tongued critic, who saw (along with Hearst) the New Deal increasingly as radical, even revolutionary, and who vigorously opposed the militant leadership in the waterfront strike. He found no justification whatever for the general strike.

As part of his plan to protect the community against communists, Neylan promptly arranged identical editorials to appear in the Monday (July 16) editions of the four newspapers, much as they had done on two occasions in June.[12] To Smith, "the newspapers had done such a poor job of reporting the nature and the depth of the long-standing dock strike that even their own editors and publishers seemed incredulous when the general strike suddenly spread over the entire Bay Region." Smith, a brash twenty-six, lived part-time with former President Herbert Hoover and with close friends muckraker Lincoln Steffens and radical writer Ella Winter. He was also a favorite of the *Chronicle*'s ruling chiefs. That summer he was financial editor; in the following year he was made its first executive editor.

Smith told *Chronicle* publisher George Cameron that he thought Neylan's "cabal" was "disgraceful." Cameron explained, as Smith reported it, that "the press had to be unified in its fight against the Communists on the waterfront." The strike would be resolved when they got rid of an agitator by the name of Harry Bridges. Though it was outside the ken of the paper's financial department, the strike intrigued Smith and he spent some time seeking out Bridges and frequenting waterfront haunts and picket lines. He reported back to Cameron that the rank and file was loyal to Bridges, that the strike would not end without the word of Bridges. Cameron said he would so advise spokesmen for the employers; later he reported "they" said Smith did not know what he was talking about.[13]

Archbishop Hanna, too, appealed on radio and in a board statement to let reason rule, citing some of the main difficulties: the steamship companies had agreed to meet the seamen's representatives when they were chosen, but were unwilling to agree in advance to arbitrate deadlocked issues—unknown demands from unknown representatives, they said. Arbitration of the longshoremen's dispute was held up by the union's insistence on pre-conditions and by failure to resolve the seamen's dispute. But now, public interest is paramount, the archbishop said. Failing a speedy determination, the board would report formally to the president, placing responsibility where it thinks it belongs.

Roger Lapham drove into San Francisco from the Peninsula Sunday (July 15) morning. "The town was deserted; never seen the produce market as empty as it was."[14] The rapidly spreading general strike, though not set formally to start until the next morning, had already stripped the city of much of even its low-level Sunday activity. The National Guard patrolled a deserted Embarcadero. Most street and cable cars had stopped running; the four parallel pairs of track stretching up Market Street lay shiny and abandoned. Employees of the privately owned Market Street Railway had left cars in the barns. Municipal Railway employees were expected to join the strike later. Taxi drivers had quit at 5:00 that morning. Few private automobiles had gas to operate. In the East Bay, Key Route trainmen had voted to walk out Tuesday morning, which would shut down many of the trans-bay ferryboats. Grocery stores were closed; signs in their windows told customers they were out of stock, "closed till the boys win," or "closed for the duration."

Electrical workers had voted to defer a decision on joining the general strike. An official said its action was intended to avert the "widespread catastrophe" that would result from interruption of service. International Typographical Union President Charles P. Howard arrived to take part in the printers' last-minute negotiations with the publishers. A year earlier—in the spring of 1933—the publishers had demanded a 10 percent wage cut from the printers. Publishers had reinforced their demand with three hundred professional strikebreakers, supplied by the American Newspaper Publishers' Association's open shop department, and even then lounging around the corner in the posh Palace Hotel. Now, with the general strike due to start the next morning, the publishers quickly offered to restore the cut and make it effective at once. Howard carried the offer to the printers' meeting. Despite vigorous opposition, it was adopted by a three-to-one vote. The question of joining the general strike was not specifically raised but the new contract effectively insured uninterrupted publication of the Bay Area dailies.

The General Strike Committee announced that nineteen restaurants would remain open Monday—some 3,600 seats for a city of 700,000. Union permits would allow suppliers to provide food to them. At the same time, it said, it was planning a special police force intended to prevent violence and cooperate with regular police. Permits would be issued to continue milk and bread deliveries. Bridges proposed the committee establish food distribution depots throughout the city. Strikers would prevent profiteering, regulate distribution, and prevent hardship. "If the people can't get food, the maritime workers and longshoremen will lose the strike," Bridges said. At the same time, he warned attempts to run picket lines with nonunion food trucks would "create disorder and violence." "If the trucks try to move, the men will try to stop them—I can tell you that." In the East Bay, Charlie Real, head of the teamsters, said trucks operating with union permits would furnish supplies to East Bay Commission houses; the public would be expected to obtain their supplies at these distribution points. Mayors of Bay Area cities in a joint declaration announced that their people must be fed; if the strikers did not make arrangements to do so, they would.

Robert H. Hinckley, representing the Federal Emergency Relief Administration, arrived in the city, declaring, "Nobody is going to suffer from lack of food in San Francisco. The United States Government will see to that. . . . If a dire situation develops, we will do something and do it quick." In the food-growing areas, state highway patrol officers, deputy sheriffs, and volunteers vowed to protect food shipments into the Bay region "at any cost." Physicians and surgeons, properly identified, would be supplied gas at designated service stations.

Police Chief Quinn was preparing to swear in eighty-six "special emergency policemen" and two telephone operators, authorized in an 8:00 A.M "special emergency" session of the Police Commission. They were the first of five hundred authorized by Mayor Rossi. Mounted police were equipped with new long-range firearms and protective helmets, along with additional tear and nauseating gas equipment. Their horses, too, were being fitted with special goggles to protect them from gas. At the same time, Quinn activated a new "anti-radical and crime prevention bureau." Directed by officers who know communist and other extremist movements, Quinn said, the new bureau would focus on violence and sabotage during the general strike.

From his office, Lapham called Secretary Perkins to report that the shipowners would discuss nothing until the general strike is called off. On his way into town that morning, Lapham had stopped off at Neylan's home. "You tell the Secretary," Neylan advised, "you can't talk about a plugged nickel as long as this general strike is on." In his office, Lapham met Herman Phleger, Albert Boynton, and John Forbes who "of course agreed to back the general proposition." Lapham called the secretary—with four or five others on the line—and told her just that. Any further concession would only fuel the flames and justify the general strike. "She couldn't understand it," Lapham remembered; "we were a group of naughty boys fighting." The temper of the conversation quickly escalated. Perkins scolded Lapham when he asserted the situation was revolutionary. Such talk, she thought, might put ideas in the strikers' heads. "We can cure this thing best by bloodshed," Lapham told her. "We have got to have bloodshed to stop it. It is the best thing to do." Perkins replied, "Isn't that a pretty dangerous outlook and a pretty dangerous thing to rely on?" Lapham replied, "I think it is the best thing that could happen, and the best way out for us all." In the end, the Secretary suggested she would be glad to receive any ideas he might have on how she could be helpful.[15]

That weekend, too, the secretary, whom Roosevelt had left in charge of the problem, was summoned to Secretary of State (and "acting president") Cordell Hull's office. She found him huddled with Attorney General Homer S. Cummings over a stack of law books. In their opinion—based on a thirty-year-old article by an elderly gentleman [P. Tecumseh Sherman] who had once been

Commissioner of Labor Statistics in the State of New York—the situation in San Francisco was legally a general strike and called for drastic action under both federal and state law. Perkins protested. A general strike, she argued, was "a strike of a large body of workers planned and coordinated in advance to force the government to take a position on some matter of interest to them." She said Hull and Cummings both thought the National Guard and the U.S. Army should be used to put down the "general strike." She told them the situation was in no way "alarming," that the likelihood was remote that it would go beyond a brief strike of delivery and transportation services, and that it seemed "unwise to begin the Roosevelt administration by shooting it out with working people who were only exercising their rights, under our Constitution and law, to organize and demand collective bargaining." She insisted, in any case, before anything is done, the president must be consulted. From the *Houston*, the president thanked her for her "estimate of the situation." He suggested an offer of arbitration in his name; he also, confidentially and diplomatically, Perkins thought, suggested consulting with Hull and Cummings as to "our authority to maintain food supply and traffic in the affected areas." The president's formula blithely ignored the several boobytraps that had already brought down several other arbitration proposals. Whatever the reason, the secretary noted, the offer was not made.[16]

But U.S. Senator from California Hiram Johnson, a Republican, was concerned that Washington "doesn't understand a general strike" and he wanted "somebody in Washington" to know "what is happening in the unknown and forgotten land of the Pacific Coast." He chose Secretary of the Interior Harold L. Ickes:

> Unless a miracle happens Monday will bring discomfort, possible disaster and actual want. Pictures closed, groceries meat shops barred, gasoline exhausted, laundries no longer working, cessation of street car and all means of transportation doubtful, continuance of power plants, water supplies threatened, every luxury of living gone, every comfort either lost or endangered and most necessities denied and you have what San Francisco is now suffering or faces. . . . It could have been averted once by the intervention of just one man. . . . I would be glad if the Secretary of Labor were advised.[17]

In the day's presidential traffic, Presidential Secretary Louis Howe also reflected on Roosevelt's role:

Think only danger San Francisco strike is that mayor is badly frightened and his fear has infected entire city and vicinity. There is possibility of panic spreading nationally. Any suggestion of your curtailing trip or returning at this time will be very dangerous and might start the very panic it is necessary to avoid. A few calming radio words might be advisable, but have hunch situation will improve by middle of the week. . . . San Francisco Mayor has made country a little nervous by foolishly going on national hook-up last night giving situation undue importance.[18]

In San Francisco, the gum-chewing, rope-spinning philosopher and columnist Will Rogers thought perhaps the president should interrupt his vacation to come to San Francisco and stop the strike: "It looks like he is the only man that can do it. . . . I never saw a man that had to do so many things himself."[19] In the light of Howe's message, though, the president radioed "I am inclined to think . . . it is at present best for me not to consider change my itinerary." He later recalled: "A lot of people completely lost their heads and telegraphed me, 'For God's sake, turn the ship around.' . . . Everybody demanded that I sail into San Francisco Bay, all flags flying and guns double-shotted, and end the strike. They went completely off the handle."[20]

That evening, Mayor Rossi summoned Lapham and Phleger to his office. He had issued a second proclamation of emergency, assuming a broad array of municipal powers. As Lapham remembered the conversation, the mayor was hoping there was some way it could be settled, even at the last moment, perhaps by conceding the hiring hall. " 'Do you realize what you're asking, Mr. Mayor?,' Phleger responded. 'You're the mayor of this town. A general strike is against the city government and all government. It would be a disgrace in the face of a general strike if we conceded anything.' Rossi in effect shrugged, 'All right, whatever you think.' "[21]

Vandeleur and Kidwell issued an eleventh hour statement, drafted by Henry Melnikow and Ray McClung, a newspaperman and associate, and approved only hours before by the General Strike

Committee, defending labor's actions and arguing that the strike was called "purely for the enforcement of trade union policy." The employers were "dead wrong" in trying to portray the general strike as the culmination of communist and radical upheaval, Melnikow said. The statement ran in one edition of the *News*, in none of the other papers. "The newspaper and the powers that be in San Francisco did not want the world to know that this was an economic strike . . . not a political revolution," Melnikow commented.[22] In a letter to the mayor, Vandeleur and Kidwell for the General Strike Committee declared that labor had no intent to paralyze production or distribution or overthrow government. It is simply defending itself "from an anti-labor crusade . . . an un-American attack on principles of organization and collective bargaining." The men who helped to build the city and to develop the high standards of the labor movement "are now prepared to make further sacrifices to preserve these standards." They are acting out of "loyalty to their principles as working men."[23]

16.

THE FIRST DAY

THE SPECIAL CORRESPONDENT for the *New York Times* arrived at
San Francisco's diminutive airport, Mills Field, at 5:15 Monday
morning (July 16). He and his fellow passengers had been warned
there would be no transportation from the airport into the city, so
they hitched rides with friends meeting two of the passengers. On
the way in, through deserted streets and empty streetcar tracks, they
saw two bakery wagons bearing permits from the General Strike
Committee to deliver bread to hospitals. Gas stations displayed
signs: "No Gas, Due to the Strike." They drove past National
Guardsmen on duty at bridges and terminals. At the hotel, they
were asked to be "conservative" in their use of towels since their
laundry service had been discontinued until the strike was settled.
The hotel's restaurants were closed and so were most others, except
nineteen exempted by the General Strike Committee; by 8:00 A.M,
long lines already waited at those. Some hotels, their restaurants
closed to the public, issued identification cards to insure that no
one but guests was served.

Streets usually crowded with streetcars, taxis, and private automobiles were now crowded with pedestrians. Thousands walked to
office or shop, often using the middle of the empty streets. Bicy-
clists were frequent; a few made their commute on roller skates.
Many carried brown paper bag lunches or working-class lunch-
boxes. Others paused to pick up a candy bar or two to carry them

182

through a lunchless day—"probably more milk chocolate sold here today than at any comparable period in history," the *Times* noted. Department stores were open; their managers met later in the day and decided they would remain open, but customer traffic was light. Barber shops were closed; cigar stores, running low on supplies, were limiting smokers to one pack at a time. In the nineteen open restaurants—in a city of some three thousand eating and drinking places—hungry customers lined up behind the lucky ones who had seats and lines straggling from their doors, not without some jostling, lost tempers, even, the *Times* guessed, violence. Fresh supplies were hauled in—under strike committee permits—but not until late in the day did the lines slack off. The General Strike Committee quickly authorized an additional thirty-one restaurants to open for business Tuesday.

Paul Smith, writing as the *Chronicle*'s financial editor, found business activity "slowly throbbing like a waning pulse to an almost lifeless standstill." Business leaders rushed plans for emergency operations, markets were dull. Elevator operators and janitors— "unorganized and intimidated" was Smith's gratuitous comment— responded to the general strike call. Some businessmen munched canned sardines, hunks of cheese, and stale buns "on polished mahogany desks, over which fortunes in currency have passed and repassed," the *Chronicle* said. Many went without. An ILA committee urged liquor stores and bars to close for the duration of the strike. (A newspaper report said a Mission street beer tavern had boarded up its smashed windows and posted a sign saying "Done by mistake—union place.") The six hundred-strong Chinese Laundry Workers Union came out on strike. Non-organized teamsters and truck drivers in Marin County joined the walkout and were waiting to be organized. Employees of Liggett and Myers, a major cigarette distributor, sent a delegation to the Labor Temple looking for a union organizer.

Movie houses closed down, legitimate theaters and night clubs were dark. Radio stations broadcast without interruption, except where union musicians were required. The San Francisco Seals called off their customary night games in favor of daylight baseball. Crews halted work on both the San Francisco-Oakland and Golden

Gate bridges, not yet spanning the Bay. At the Commercial Club "leading citizens," under the direction of the president of the Pacific National Bank, ran the dining room, their wives in the kitchen. The Joint Marine Strike Committee's bulletin listed what, because of the general strike, "you can't do: go to the movies, call a taxicab, get your trousers pressed, buy gasoline, eat in a hotel dining room, get a shave or haircut, buy fresh vegetables, have your automobile repaired, board a boat for Tahiti or even Los Angeles, move your household goods, get your shirt washed, go to a night club." Beyond the obvious services that directly and immediately affected consumers, much of the business and industrial life of the city slowed or came to a standstill. Factories and shops were shut down—often because their employees spontaneously joined the strike. Little moved except "by permission of the General Strike Committee." Some businesses continued operations, but customers were scarce.

Employees of the city's major streetcar line, the privately owned Market Street Railway, had walked out at 2:00 A.M. Sunday for their own demands rather than in sympathy with the general strike. Carmen on the Municipal Railway met, then without the formality of a vote, simply failed to show up for work. As city employees with civil service status and pensions, they faced a special problem. Edward Vandeleur, who headed the Muni carmen's local as well as the San Francisco Labor Council, had tried to keep the cars in the barns without strike action. Vandeleur had appealed to Utilities Manager Edward G. Cahill to withdraw service because of the intimidation and violence that threatened the men if they took out the cars. Cahill refused.

Instead, a special, early morning, two-hour meeting of the Public Utilities Commission (PUC) (in the home of a sick member) instructed Cahill to resume operations immediately and to forfeit the civil service status and pensions of employees who failed to return to work. The General Strike Committee proposed the cars, on returning to service, carry a sign saying they were operated by the committee's permission. The PUC refused. The committee yielded, sending the Muni carmen back to work with its thanks "for their sympathy and assistance."[1] It was the first of the committee's efforts—expanding food supplies, providing gas, opening additional restaurants—to cushion the impact of the general walkout on the public (or, some militants said, to liquidate the general strike).

An estimated 15,000 building tradesmen in the East Bay had laid down their tools; now they were joined by some 27,000 workers affiliated with Central Labor Council local unions. The East Bay's street car system and the Key System ferries halted operations; commuters who flocked to the still-operating Southern Pacific (SP) lines to get to San Francisco were angered when the SP refused to honor the Key System's commute tickets. Employers were especially upset, J. Paul St. Sure recalled, when the Key System's employees' strike resolution called for the employees "and the workers of the community to take over the transportation system for working people." St. Sure said he and several businessmen, "frightened" by the prospect of "an actual class struggle," had asked Governor Merriam to send the National Guard into Oakland.[2]

The National Guard, now established at various East Bay points, put into action six mobile patrols, armed with machine guns. Union officials arranged to continue the flow of fruit and vegetables into the commission districts and to some retail outlets. Ice, milk, and bakery trucks also continued to work. Twenty-three restaurants were serving with strike committee permission. Law enforcement officers were organizing special citizens' forces. Several thousand, most with military experience, one newspaper reported, registered at Oakland City Hall and in other East Bay cities—a total of twenty-five thousand, said the *Chronicle*.

"No one went to work," Robert S. Ash, later secretary of the Alameda County Central Labor Council, recalled; "or very few people tried to go to work; there wasn't anybody on the streets. The streets were clear in Oakland, at least. . . . You'd look down Broadway to the Estuary and see nobody, no cars on the street."[3] The council had asked union members to report to their local unions and to report violence; it barred mass assemblages, violence, and solicitations. Secretary William Spooner questioned the need for troops. He was certain union people would be peaceful and police could handle the situation, but the newspapers continued to report incidents.

From Washington came word that U.S. Senator Robert F. Wagner of New York, chairman of the National Labor Relations Board (or former National Labor Board), was flying to Portland in an eleventh-hour attempt to avert a general walkout there. The Portland unions' strategy board amended its plans to include a mass meeting of its twenty-five thousand members to hear the senator. The unionists already had pledged that the community would be given twenty-four hours' notice of a walkout. With the scheduled mass meeting, the earliest possible time for action was Wednesday, perhaps Thursday. Labor groups outside Portland, and even some nonunion groups, were promising their support to the general strike movement. Some observers heavily discounted reports of a general strike, since Portland workers, like those in other Pacific Coast ports, were awaiting developments in San Francisco. Other reports from Portland told of shoppers flooding into stores, families trucking away heavy loads of groceries, and stores hastily replenishing stocks. An acute shortage of gasoline and oil fuel, the *New York Times* said, had restricted fuel for private cars. Millions of gallons of gasoline and fuel oil were cut off by strike conditions. Dwindling supplies cut short hot water in hotels and apartment buildings. Some industries said they faced shutdowns within a few days.

In Seattle, spasmodic clashes continued among strikers, strikebreakers, and police. A tugboat used by a citizens' committee to haul lumber to ships being loaded by strikebreakers was mysteriously sunk. A central labor council official said that workers in the area would join a general walkout; others said what happens in Seattle depends on what is done at San Francisco. J. C. Bjorklund, district secretary of the International Longshoremen's Association, predicted that, if the waterfront strike was not settled soon, the San Francisco strike would spread all over the coast. Reports said Seattle, too, was beginning to feel the pinch of the fuel shortage. Supplies imported by tank car were insufficient to replace supplies usually brought in by sea. At San Pedro, attention was also turned toward the "crucial battle" at San Francisco.

All through Sunday night and well into the day Monday, additional National Guardsmen reported in for duty in the Bay area strike zone. In all, some three thousand were brought in by truck and train, raising the total on duty and standing by to six thousand. With food supplies arriving in increasing quantities, the Guard threw up barricades around the commission areas that abutted the Embarcadero north of Market street. Reinforcements of the Guard had been requested by Mayor Angelo Rossi in anticipation of "the inability of constituted authorities to cope with the situation . . . when the normal business life of San Francisco is attempted to be resumed." The situation is "largely," the mayor said, the work of Communists; the troops are necessary "to prevent lawlessness and disorder."[4]

Rossi also announced the formations of the Citizens Committee of Five Hundred. A prominent attorney and president of the San Francisco Bar Association, Florence McAuliffe, headed the group, made up of business and professional men. Its job, McAuliffe promptly declared, would be to "safeguard" proper distribution of food and restore transportation for persons and goods, notably gasoline. He ordered the committee into session the next day. "It was generally believed," the *New York Times* reported, "that the Committee of 500 would be a new 'vigilantes' organization which would be ready, if necessary, to emulate the action of prominent Englishmen in driving and guarding trucks loaded with milk and other foodstuffs during the general strike in London in 1926."

That general strike, too, figured in the initial barrage by the "coordinated" dailies (again the *News* excepted). They—this time including the *New York Times*—gave prominent display to a story describing the purported role of angry citizens in crushing the British strike. William Randolph Hearst had telephoned Clarence Lindner, publisher of the *Examiner*, telling him the story was being cabled. The *Chronicle's* headline said: "Citizen Army Broke Mass British Strike." The story said the San Francisco general strike "recalled to Americans in Great Britain measures taken by the public at the time of the great strike [in Britain] in 1926." It emphasized government intervention and direct action by groups of citizens.

The British general strike story was one of the early coordinated efforts of John Neylan's publishers' "cabal" intended, *Editor & Publisher* said, "to keep the public informed . . . so as to dispel the dark cloud of false rumors which were adding to public fear and uncertainty." The papers had made wide-ranging preparations to sustain their self-appointed role. They laid in stores of newsprint, hastily settled their contract with the printers, and won assurances the other printing crafts would stay on the job. The *Examiner* served 362 meals to employees at its own expense on the first day in the Classic Grill next door, which it had leased for the duration. In other newspaper offices, married employees brought large lunches and shared with their single colleagues. The National Guard and police provided credentials to reporters and photographers and the General Strike Committee permitted circulation trucks to move without hindrance.

The *Examiner*, *Chronicle*, and *Call-Bulletin* "vigorously championed the cause of the general public," *Editor & Publisher* said, "while the *News* followed the traditional Scripps-Howard policy of being liberal to organized labor." Local reporters were quickly joined by a small army of correspondents from London and Paris as well as major dailies from the east. The London *Sunday Graphic* spent $546 to ask Mayor Rossi whether people were still fleeing the city, was anybody starving, and how many had been killed. (He replied none, nobody, and two on July 5.) The dailies held a tight-fisted near-monopoly, excepting the minimal competition of radio's rudimentary news services, on the issues, the personalities, the developments of the waterfront walkout, and the general strike. Circulation jumped—"extras" sparked huge increases in street sales.

Through the willing collaboration of the publishers, the Industrial Association, Waterfront Employers Union, and Chamber of Commerce dominated the news. Coverage was heavily skewed against the maritime strikers and the general strike. Heavy-handed, often loaded, and sometimes simply false accounts underscored the negative aspects of every phase of the strike, emphasizing reports intended to discredit, divide, and discourage the strikers and alienate other workers and the general public. Stories of violence, criminal acts, radical plots, alien leaders and philosophies, real or imagined divisions in the strikers' ranks or leadership, and suppression of the "real" views of "real" leaders and "real" rank and file, all of it freely attributed to the strikers and their leaders, were exploited to create the picture the public was given. The strikers' positions on the issues and their views of events were minimized where they were not simply ignored. The publishers gratuitously reinforced these heavily slanted views with unabashed editorial (and frequently, editorialized news) support. The *News* alone sought—it did not always succeed—balance in the news. The undiluted stream of employer-slanted news and editorial comment was momentarily slowed by the naked violence of Bloody Thursday and by the awesome funeral for its victims. For a brief time, public sympathies seemed to shift toward the strikers, even as they moved toward a general strike, until the press (the *News* again largely excepted) could renew the flow with fresh cries of radicals and revolution, of riots and blood in the streets.

San Francisco's troubles provided an abundance of grist for the mills of the pundits and editorial writers, who turned out virtually instant volumes of exegesis and explanation, counsel and condemnation. In the main, they ignored the view of the general strike as basically a sympathetic protest. Rather they clung to the image of a political strike with serious revolutionary intent. To columnist Walter Lippmann the general strike, "a political weapon," could succeed only if it paralyzed the whole life of the community. The leaders of the San Francisco strike appear unwilling, he thought, to make it really general. That they are unwilling to starve the public only means they will incur all the disadvantages of angering the public without achieving its only possible success—that is, replacing the government. The unwillingness of these "ordinary American trade unionists" to use it as it can only be used insures its increasing ineffectiveness and ultimate defeat.[5]

Harold J. Laski, the eminent British political scientist, read the intention of the strikers as enforcement of Section 7(a), their right to collective bargaining. Government might be expected to throw its weight behind the law, rather than behind those who refused to accept the law. But [state and city] government is using "all the implements of modern warfare" to nullify the efforts of the strikers to achieve their lawful rights, to protect what government called "the community." The British general strike failed when it confronted the British government. The San Francisco strike is no revolutionary act; it is a challenge to law and order under the rules of a capitalist society which require government to come to the aid of the right of the capitalist to do "what he wills with his own.[6]

It occurred to Merryle S. Rukeyser, a Hearst columnist, that the National Recovery Act fans "the flames for the agitator." Good wages and working conditions are the best insurance against labor troubles, but perhaps, while unemployment persists, it would be well to abridge the right to strike.[7] David Lawrence contended the Roosevelt administration was unwilling to use its powers under the NRA against labor, but only against employers. The situation, he thought, may have gone beyond "round table discussion;" compulsion may be necessary to wring a settlement from the Pacific Coast situation.[8]

Several thousand miles distant, the London *Morning Post* saw the general strike as an effort

> to reduce San Francisco to terms by starvation . . . as cruel and criminal a device as can be imagined. They intend, however, to make arrangements to feed their own people, having heard that the general strike in England failed because the strikers were in the way of starving themselves with the rest of the population. We do not know how this lie got abroad; the truth . . . is that the conspiracy was defeated by the British nation which rose up and did its own work.[9]

Across the channel, Paris *Temps* blamed the grant of power under the NRA for allowing "the revolutionary forces" to gain the upper hand—not only in San Francisco but in Texas and Alabama and threatening in the industrial East. Other editorial writers and commentators saw it as the result of President Roosevelt's interference with the natural workings of the economy.[10]

Heywood Broun, Scripps-Howard columnist and founder of The Newspaper Guild, observed, "the lawless employers should be restrained, and if they don't like it here I see no possible objection to sending them back where they came from." The *News* which carried Broun's column in San Francisco, pulled it after one edition. It was replaced by a gentle piece about children by Mrs. Franklin

D. Roosevelt.[11] In the usually friendlier pages of the *News*, too, columnist John D. Barry said the strike leaders "did not know what they were doing." Their actions, he feared, might undo "a large part of what labor has gained through generations of struggle.[12]

Broun apart, almost nobody seemed ready to accept the strikers' own evaluation; certainly the newspapers gave it short shrift. The workers' stand, strike committee chairman Vandeleur said, echoing an earlier letter to the mayor, was a result of "loyalty to their principles as workingmen." The refusal of the shipowners to concede "two reasonable demands" left "organized labor in San Francisco no alternative but to support the ideals that they have built up through years of hard and intelligent work."[13]

17.

THE SECOND DAY (PART 1)

THE MORNING OF the second day of the general strike in San Francisco—Tuesday, July 17—found National Guardsmen, armed with rifles and a machine gun, manning a barricade at Jackson and Drumm streets, targeting the traffic in the first block of Jackson Street at number 65 where the Marine Workers Industrial Union (MWIU) had its office. Word of possible trouble had barely reached the MWIU office when a gang of men crashed through the front door. Some wore police badges; some were in plain clothes. An eyewitness recognized one as "Captain Malloy," presumably the same man soon identified in newspaper reports as the police officer who led the "posse" in several of the daylong series of "Police raids on Radical Meeting places." The raiders smashed typewriters on the floor; demolished desks; grabbed piles of stationery, receipt books, or whatever objects lay within reach; and looted the seamen's baggage room. The *Examiner* said the posse captured an "arsenal" of razors, axes, knives, and clubs, along with piles of "inflammatory literature." At the point of guns, men who were threatened by blackjacks and cursed—"you red son of bitches," "get the dirty bastards"—were held in a back room until the patrol wagon arrived. Nearly a hundred, under National Guard guns, were loaded in the wagon and taken to Harbor police station.

Still more raids followed the attack on the MWIU headquarters. Every known "red" center was on the list of targets for a day of what the newspapers called simultaneous though "independent" raids, carried out by the police and unidentified vigilantes, reinforced in at least two instances by the rifles of the National Guard. Occupants of the raided premises, presumed radicals, were often brutalized and manhandled; hundreds were arrested and jailed. Offices and office equipment, files, libraries, literature, and furnishings were devastated.[1]

"Something had to be done to justify the militant "patriotism of officials and employers," Quin explained in his history of the strike. Eliel, in his detailed chronology, implied the raids were an aspect of efforts—by the employer, the mayor, and the press—to mobilize public opinion to crush the general strike and to extend military control of the waterfront to martial law in the entire city. Joyce Maxine Clements, in her study of the strikes, saw the raids as plainly a violent exercise in "the dynamics of repression." William F. Dunne, a prominent Communist and union organizer, labeled them a "reign of terror." Sam Darcy, leader of the Communist party in California, described them as "an effort to decapitate the leadership of the strike."[2] Others argued that the employers and government officials' anti-red fulminations were simply a propaganda ploy, designed to win public opinion to their side. And some contended they were the rationale for the employers' effort to break the strike and smash the unions.

Their accounts, as do others, illuminate facets of the raids, but they do not explain adequately their whole purpose. What emerges from the record is that the anti-red forces—employers, government, and press—must have come finally to believe their own widely proclaimed propaganda: that the Communist party and its supporting structure were seeking revolutionary goals; that they were, for ulterior purposes, deliberately prolonging the strikes; and that dismantling the Communist apparatus would end them. The anti-red forces apparently saw images of revolutionary leadership and influences that they insistently attributed to (and were sometimes claimed by) the "Communists and radicals." They blinded themselves to the non-revolutionary, even traditional union goals that were at the core of the rank-and-file leadership and the strikes.

They attacked the leadership they had envisioned in their propaganda. It was the wrong target.

Word of the raids had gone out during the morning. The Industrial Association, the employers' strikebreaking command, notified by its "violence" scouts, clearly knew of the raids in advance. Kenneth Howell, a seaman and a victim of the MWIU raid that morning, said later a warning had reached the longshoremen's strike headquarters only moments before the raiders struck. In a noontime speech that day, Charles Wheeler, vice president of the McCormick Steamship Line, told the Rotary Club the raids, already in progress, would start soon. He intimated some form of government approval had been obtained. In Berkeley's Greek Theater, even as the raids were going on, General Hugh S. Johnson, the controversial administrator of the National Recovery Administration, declared he knew San Francisco well enough to know that its people "would act to wipe out this subversive element as you clean off a chalk mark on a blackboard with a wet sponge." The general, who had injected himself into the dispute as a mediator, had prefaced his words with a denunciation of the shipowners for failing to recognize the union rights of the strikers. Then he called on "responsible" labor organizations to "run these subversive influences out from its ranks like rats."[3]

From Jackson Street, the posse swooped down on the longshoremen's strike kitchen at 84 Embarcadero. Ten (or twelve) radicals were recognized and "weeded out" as "soldiers squinted down the barrels of their guns." At 765 Howard Street, a lot used by the Ex-Service Men's League and described by the next morning's *Chronicle* as "a supposed outdoor meeting place for communists," police arrested seventy-four while the crowd "cheered them on." The police reported they carted away, as evidence, stacks of "pamphlets, books, banners, and cards, all relating to the Soviet Union of Russia." Five cars, carrying twenty-five unidentified vigilantes, pulled up at the offices of the *Western Worker*, the radical newspaper that also published the longshoremen's official strike bulletin, at 37 Grove Street. The raiders threw stones through the windows, stormed inside to demolish everything in sight, then vanished. Moments later, the police arrived to find only the wreckage and, the

Chronicle reported the next morning, "the opposite plaza crowded with grinning spectators." Eyewitnesses, though, told Evelyn Seeley, who reported it in the *New Republic*, a different story when she arrived at the scene only moments after the vigilantes. One car—not five—of vigilantes smashed the downstairs plate glass windows, then drove off. Seeley went inside, found nothing else smashed. She emerged as four carloads of police, sirens wailing, drove up. In the offices, they smashed typewriters, furniture, windows. Seeley reported: "They hustled a little man named Lord in from the street; we heard them say, 'Get the hell in there!' He came out with his head bleeding all over the place, wiping the blood from his eyes and saying over and over, 'I didn't do nothin'.' We asked the cops who smashed the things and they said, 'It must have been the hoodlums.' The spectators across the street were not grinning."[4]

Headquarters for the International Labor Defense, a workers' school, and a number of other Communist and radical organizations at 121 Haight Street was also a target, but it is not at all clear what happened. Police went there, said the *Call-Bulletin*, in pursuit of the raiders who, meantime, turned up at still another radical meeting place. At Haight Street, however, the *Chronicle* reported, vigilantes broke windows in the two-story building and threw typewriters, furniture, and Communist literature into the alley below. Several "Communists" escaped attack by leaping from second floor windows. Another "mob," said the *Examiner*, followed the raiders, tore down pictures of Lenin and Stalin. Mike Quin reported later that caretaker David Merihew, saber in one hand and bayonet in the other, met the raiders on the staircase. The raiders retreated but Merihew gave himself up on condition he would not be turned over to the vigilantes.[5]

The Mission Workers Neighborhood House at 741 Valencia Street was hit, the *Examiner* noted, by the "biggest, most savage mob, many of them women and children" after the "raiders" left. "Police kept clear and an hour later the screaming, yelling throng was still in an orgy of destruction." The *Chronicle*, though, said "the same group of unidentified civilians [that had attacked 121 Haight Street] destroyed all records and files found in the offices, damaged the interior beyond repair, and splintered the speaker's platform like kindling wood." At 1223 Fillmore Street, identified as the Workers' Open forum, according to the *Chronicle*, civilian raiders dragged out three men "whom they soundly trounced. Police arrived just in time to take the injured to Central Emergency Hospital." The *Examiner* described a battle royal between raiders and "communists" who "slugged, kicked, bit, clawed and hammered each other," while a mob outside yelled approval. The place was raided again the next day, the raiders leaving "wreckage so complete that even hardened police view it with awe."[6] A meeting at Dolores Park was attacked, the Associated Press reported, in "another civilian demonstration against radicalism." Several who resisted "were reported to have been beaten."[7] Industrial Association news scouts, riding with the police, twice reported raids that never took place on the headquarters of Upton Sinclair, the Socialist muckraker running for governor as a Democrat, though Sinclair's campaign had no connection with the Communist movement, and though he, himself, was the target of an anti-red attack.[8]

By the end of the vengeful day, anywhere from 270 to 450—the count varies widely—prisoners were crammed into cells, corridors, every available space in a jail intended to hold only 150. Most of them were booked as "vagrants"; some—the more prominent radicals, presumably considered the more dangerous—were held as "$1,000 vags," that is, as vagrants under $1,000 cash bail.[9]

The next morning's *Chronicle* found the day's work hilarious. "REDS TURN BLACK AND BLUE," read a cutline under one of its photographs of the destruction. "This was a communists' meeting-place, a neighborhood where the radicals dropped in for a cozy chat about the impending revolution. It came sooner than they expected when angry unionists swept down on the place." Another caption read: "First step of beating the swords of San Francisco's strife into plowshares takes the form of beating Communists' furniture into matchsticks. "PARALYSIS OF THE JOINTS," said another. "There's a checkerboard on the floor and it's the Communists' next move. There was a piano in the room and they laughed when a husky teamster sat down to it—with an ax. The rendition was presented with tympanic accompaniment of fists on the persons of radicals who, today, are even more inflamed."[10]

The anti-red hysteria, typified in the day's carefully orchestrated raids, was not confined, either in timing, violence, or geography, to San Francisco. Vigilantes, police, and private armies had been active in agricultural strikes that had flashed across California's fields earlier in the year. In Brawley, gatherings of migratory workers were attacked, a meeting hall was wrecked, furniture was destroyed, and the building flooded. Hundreds were arrested. An American Civil Liberties Union lawyer, A. L. Wirin, was kidnapped and beaten, his automobile driven over an enbankment. In many areas law enforcement officers were jumpy over the threat of new agricultural strikes. Meetings and demonstrations in the Los Angeles area were frequent targets of "red squads."[11]

In San Jose, a posse, variously estimated at from thirty to three hundred, armed with pick handles with rawhide grips, rounded up thirteen San Jose residents in a series of raids on private homes. The San Jose *Mercury-Herald* described the raids: "Armed with bright new pick-handles, their faces grim, eyes shining with steady purpose, a large band of 'vigilantes,' composed of irate citizens, including many war veterans, smashed their way into three communist 'hotspots' here last night, seized a mass of red literature and severely beat asserted radicals." The prisoners were passed, then, from Santa Clara County to the sheriff of San Benito County, winding up in the Salinas jail in Montery County charged as vagrants. They were released the next morning on the condition they would not return to Monterey County for a year. Deputies escorted them again to the county line and passed them on through at least two other southern counties. Observers could not refrain from comparing the episode to the lynching of two men that had taken place in San Jose the previous fall under the eyes of some six thousand men, women and children.[12]

In Berkeley, vigilantes raided Finnish Hall, smashed windows, destroyed furniture, ripped out plumbing, and wrecked a grand piano. The *Call-Bulletin* aped the *Chronicle's* wisecracking style in describing the raid: "Where work-roughened hands once played the 'Internationale' Berkeley citizen raiders with baseball bats reduced a grand piano far beyond the 'Unfinished Symphony' or the 'Lost Chord.'" (The owners of the hall were later awarded $4,742.40 in damages plus costs.) Flying squadrons toured the city, throwing rocks through windows of suspected Communists, threatening drastic action if they did not leave the community. A Richmond photographer was twice the victim of raids on his home and warned not to associate with radicals. (He, too, later collected damages.) Raiders on Communist headquarters in Hayward dragged furniture and desks into the street and set them on fire. In Hayward, too, a scaffold was erected facing the city hall, with a large knotted noose and a sign warning "Reds beware." The police chief of Piedmont later regaled a convention of peace officers with his report on organizing an army of 750 volunteers to stave off an expected effort to sack the homes of shipowners living in the well-off East Bay neighborhood.[13] The attack never came.

The anti-red tactics, though, reached their highest levels in carefully timed, skillfully orchestrated, and far more devastating raids in San Francisco. Responsibility for organizing and coordinating the raids has never been admitted or established; nor has the identity of the vigilantes. But some group or individual laid out the underlying strategy; authorized, planned, coordinated, and directed the organized violence against property and persons; identified the targets; ordered the hundreds of arrests; secured National Guard support—its presence, the *Chronicle* noted the next morning, "ostensibly through coincidence"; organized and equipped the vigilante squads; coordinated the police and vigilante actions; and supplied the newspapers their central message.

Wednesday morning papers offered explanations. "Conservative union labor moved swiftly yesterday to purge it[s] ranks of Communists," the *Chronicle* declared. "Aroused by the discovery that Communist groups had been parading as union strikers and flaunting banners and placards completely at variance with union tenets, conservatives quickly took the situation into their own hands." The "thirty-five" squads of vigilantes, it said, were made up chiefly of teamsters. The *Examiner* explained that the raiders were "rumored" to be members of the Teamsters' Union, angered because men said to be communists—traced back to one of the places raided—interfered with trucks operating under union permits. The union denied involvement, though its denial found no prominent place in the press. Neither explanation survived long. But it seems more than coincidence that the newspapers as well as General Johnson pointed to disgruntled unionists as the actual or potential raiders. It seems not at all unlikely that it was a propaganda brainchild of the closely knit committee of newspaper publishers—the Scripps-Howard *Daily News* excepted—organized by John Francis Neylan, attorney for William Randolph Hearst, his collaborator in other anti-red attitudes. Neylan, too, already a major mover in civic affairs, was now emerging as a principal figure in efforts to end the general strike.[14]

The *New York Times* noted the Chronicle version but added: "At first general opinion was that [the vigilantes] were connected with the Committee of 500 organized by prominent citizens yesterday at the behest of Mayor Angelo J. Rossi." The mayor, the *Call-Bulletin* said, urged "spontaneous action" to bring the committee of young business people and white-collar executives into action but, within hours of its organization, it boasted it had escorted about thirty food trucks to secret destinations in the city that morning.[15] It had been a similar group of young, socially prominent businessmen who had manned the strikebreaking trucks that rolled out of Pier 38 in early July.[16] George West, "editorial" correspondent of the *New York Times*, was still puzzling over it more than a week later. "The opinion prevails," he wrote, "that [the vigilantes] were of the white-collar class and represented the coming together of individuals affiliated with the business community but not sponsored by any responsible organization." But little or no evidence supports that view.

The waterfront employers had brought strikebreakers from San Pedro to help move cargo during the forced opening of the port. Now, the head of the San Francisco Labor Council charged, the Industrial Association was preparing to put strikebreaker-manned trucks into moving cargo. The Industrial Association denied any responsibility for the raids; top officials continued to espouse the seeming fiction that they were started and pushed by union men in opposition to the radical elements in their unions. Association scouts rode with the police, filing a stream of reports on those arrested, even providing in an instance or two advance information of intended raids. The association's managing director later insisted that these activities had been no more than part of the association's determination to provide the newspapers with full and immediate word of strike-connected violence. The philosophy underlying the raids, though, was closely enough related to the association's own that suspicion of a more intimate connection is difficult to avoid.[17]

From New York, the "king of strikebreakers, Pearl L. Bergoff, announced he had sent a hundred strikebreakers from Chicago to San Francisco by airplane and train and that day would be sending another hundred "key men." If the general strike lasted a week, he said he would have 1,500 men on the scene. No records indicate any ever arrived; the *Call-Bulletin* printed the wire report July 17 without comment. Bergoff's biographer dismissed it as another of the strikebreaker king's elaborately rigged publicity ploys.[18] By Wednesday, however, the newspapers dropped the pretense that the vigilantes were teamsters or disgruntled conservative unionists, identifying them only as raiders or as vigilantes. But other sources were apparent.

Even while the raids were in progress, a banner headline in the *Call-Bulletin* credited the action to the police's newly formed "anti-radical detail." The *News* referred to the events simply as "police raids." The police, plainly, are the logical candidate for the guiding hand that organized the raids. Police, after all, made some three hundred (or more) arrests during the day. They were present, at one time or another, at all the raids, though they denied any part in wrecking radical headquarters. (A police spokesman later told investigators, "for all I know, maybe the Communists staged the raids themselves for publicity." His remark was apparently sarcastic but it would not have been the first serious suggestion that they represented the Communists' efforts to claim attention.)[19] The police department daily was swearing in scores of special officers. Its "extra" force had reached three hundred only the day before. "All are immediately armed and assigned to duty," the report said. (Women volunteers, it added, were rejected.)[20] Only a few days before the department had initiated its anti-radical and crime prevention detail, which had been at the core of Tuesday's raids.[21] Too, the day's events fitted comfortably with Chief Quinn's vehement anti-communist philosophy; he fervently believed that the "riots in San Francisco" were programmed by the communists who had grasped control over the powerless and well-intended "conservative labor men" to further their revolutionary ends.[22] But it seems unlikely that even Chief Quinn, whose philosophy so clearly accommodated the raids, would initiate an action of such scope without the consent, if not the command, of higher authority—and only Mayor Rossi could give the necessary consent. Mayor Rossi himself was under massive and unrelenting pressure generated by the anti-red drive of the waterfront employers and shipowners, their political allies and business associates, and the press. In this climate, the raids were conceived, sanctioned, and carried out.

Participants and observers differed widely on the ultimate goals of the raids. Robert Cantwell in the *New Republic* insisted the anti-red attacks were curtain-raisers to some kind of settlement that somehow must be imposed on the strikers and force their return to work—a settlement so unsatisfactory as to require silencing "all articulate critics" to insure its acceptance. Cantwell cited the May 28 and June 16 "agreements;" now, arbitration was to be the imposed settlement. In an editorial, the *New Republic* pictured the raids as a major weapon in a climactic offensive against labor and particularly against its militant leaders.[23] Miriam Allen De Ford, in the *Nation*, depicts the Communists as the welcome scapegoat in a situation tight with distrust and suspicion. They served effectively as the target for the open shop ambitions of the Industrial Association and shipowners, politicians running for office, law enforcement officers fearful of renewed strikes, the American Legion in its anti-Communist drive, and even for conservative unionists convinced they had been fooled by the radical minority.[24] Historian Mike Quin doubted that "higher-bracket" employers believed the strikes were a revolution. In a showdown between capital and labor on the open shop, he believed, the employers labeled it a revolution to win "less informed sections of public opinion to their side."[25] Mayor Angelo Rossi reiterated the familiar charge that the communists "have no regard for our American form of government and are desirous of breaking down and destroying law observance."[26]

The raids occurred in a climate of bitter anti-red invective propagated week after week in the press against the "Communists and radicals," who, in the interests of a violent overthrow of government, had "seized" leadership of the strikes and refused to end them. The raids were an assault on those supposed enemies identified repeatedly and vigorously by the employers, the Chamber of Commerce, business interests, and the press, with Mayor Rossi as their sometimes reluctant leader and the police as their shock troops. They were persuaded by their own propaganda, coming to believe their own repeated assertions that these widely assorted "red" centers and Communist Party adjuncts were in fact the "Communist and radical" leadership they had charged and that they were organically and decisively related to—if not in fact—the leadership and conduct of the strikes.

Still, after a day of wide-ranging raids on the Communist and radical centers and hundreds of arrests, the key strike leadership, longshore and seagoing, was untouched; "articulate critics" were no less outspoken than before; debates in the General Strike Committee no less heated, no less vigorous. Leaders of the general strike and of the waterfront unions pursued their strike-related ways. Spokesmen for the Communist Party said later party activities were not seriously affected. Penetration of the rank and file of strikers by the implied message of the raids is impossible to measure. It may have impressed them and their leaders, but the chances are that their impressions were no more profound than those of the general public. The raids—and their implied message—most likely simply confirmed their already fixed antagonism to police and employers.

Strategically or tactically, the raids had no discernible impact on the dispute or its settlement. It quickly became clear that the Communist apparatus, real and alleged, had no organic relationship to the waterfront or general strikes, their leadership, or, for that matter, the rank and file. The raids did nothing to deflect the course of either the waterfront or general strikes or to influence their ultimate resolution, which was well in motion before and during the raids and continued unaffected afterward. The leadership of the

General Strike Committee, even as the red centers were being hit, was formulating—and had pretty well fixed—its prescription for ending the general strike. The ultimate pattern for settling the waterfront strikes was already foreshadowed in ongoing discussions among General Johnson, Neylan (speaking for the mayor), the shipowners and waterfront employers, and general strike union leaders. These formulas emerged within hours, with no indication that the raids had affected any change in timing or substance.

When their place in the overall dispute is fixed, the raids seem almost pointless, except as a violent response to the instigators' perceptions of "radicals" and "revolution." The red scare, then, was not merely a propaganda device; it was a response to a movement that was perceived as a serious threat. The raiders' conviction that "Communists and radicals" were threatening to overthrow the government and unnecessarily and stubbornly prolonging the strikes to that end totally obscured the trade union issues at the heart of the dispute and the commitment of strike leaders to trade union goals. Only such self-deception would have allowed the employers' high command to consent to, if not order, the raids. In that light, the raids seem to have been a violent exercise in self-induced hysteria.

18.

THE SECOND DAY (PART 2)

HUGH S. JOHNSON's first trip to San Francisco in 1906 found the city in smoldering ruins, its people camping in the parks. As a "shavetail" lieutenant of cavalry with the United States Army relief force, he plunged into the job of bringing aid to the victims of the earthquake and fire. He returned later to earn a law degree at the University of California in Berkeley. "He was a most remarkable student," a law professor said, "probably the most brilliant we have ever had."[1] Now, he was returning as the colorful, controversial administrator of the National Recovery Administration on a tour of inspection of the NRA organization on the Pacific Coast. This "florid-faced, big-jowled" ex-cavalry officer had the job of putting American industry under the codes of fair competition and fair labor standards that were the keystones of the New Deal's initial design for economic recovery. Historian Arthur M. Schlesinger, Jr., described his style: "This emotional, pungent, truculent figure saw life as a melodrama slightly streaked with farce; he was forever rescuing the virtuous, foiling the villainous, chewing the carpet . . . and mingling it all with a fusillade of insults, wisecracks, and picturesque phrases."[2]

The Army plane from Portland put him down at Oakland, as it happened, on the first day of the general strike—pure coincidence, the general insisted. In the first day of his NRA command, his disastrous experiences as a mediator had left him "plainly unhappy and bewildered," an observer wrote, "determined to have nothing more to do with strikes." The new labor relations disputes act had further removed labor troubles from his official ken. In Portland he had said he would have nothing to do with this strike. His tour of inspection had long been fixed. The San Francisco date had been set to accommodate the award to him of a Phi Beta Kappa key by the chapter at his alma mater at Berkeley. Nevertheless, he told reporters, he would, if called on, be glad to do what he could. It quickly became apparent, however, that the general had not the faintest intention of keeping hands off.

Kenneth Dawson, head of the States Steamship Company in Portland, phoned Roger Lapham that General Johnson wanted to meet with John Francis Neylan, the Hearst lawyer who was now emerging as a key player in the dispute. "I don't know if I'll meet that bird or not," Neylan told Lapham. Only a month before, Neylan had referred to him as "that howling military economist, who ought to have his pet blue buzzard [the Blue Eagle, the NRA symbol] embalmed before the Board of Health takes action." But Neylan was persuaded. When he returned after an hour in the general's suite on the floor above his own in the Palace Hotel, Neylan reported to the assembled employers and others: "Well, we had the ball down on the one-yard line ready for Johnson to shove it over. But now it's way back in the middle of the field." The general "arrived here drunk," Neylan said later.[3] One report—Neylan seems a likely source—said the general proposed conceding the union hiring hall before discussing arbitration. Later, Neylan recalled Johnson had wanted "to work out a political compromise. I told him no, that you couldn't compromise with civil war." As Johnson recalled it, "he and I had a beautiful fight at our first conference but I left that place with a great respect for that man [though Johnson remembered him as John P. Neyland] and we were in perfect agreement."[4]

Neylan's strategy aimed tightly at cutting off any further discussion of strike issues or settlement until the general strike was ended. General Johnson's speech at Berkeley offered a highly visible and influential opportunity to swing "all the authority of the U.S. government" behind Neylan's stand, but University officials had canceled it and General Johnson had failed to win its reinstatement. Neylan, though, a regent of the University, succeeded.

Neylan had no trouble convincing General Johnson to denounce the general strike. Johnson recalled (not without some dramatic license) that he had been "physically" shocked by his introduction to the general strike—transportation paralyzed, food supply "practically shut off," "the economic life of the city was being strangled. There was fear that the power, light and water supply would be shut off. A foreign enemy could scarcely threaten more than that." But Johnson also insisted, apparently as a result of his talks with some of the general strike leaders, on including a vigorous defense of the workers' rights to collective bargaining, and specifically in the shipping industry.

Labor is entitled to bargain collectively, he told the "almost full" Greek Theatre audience Tuesday afternoon; "the employer who denies or even obstructs that right is anti-social." In the shipping industry, he went on, "the right has not been justly accorded." "These things" cannot be evaded by "legal cavil. They are necessary to humanity in this age and they will prevail. The whole force of American opinion is behind them. . . . If the shipping industry does not fully and freely accord these rights, then on its head will lie every ounce of responsibility for whatever may happen here. I think that their personal position is extreme and unreasonable and must be tempered if we are to have peace."[5]

Newspaper reports buried the general's indictment of the shipowners in the tag-end paragraphs, often jumped to another page deep in the paper. But they gave page one headlines and unmistakable endorsement to "another and worse side to this story"—the general strike. "It is a threat to the community. It is a menace to government. It is civil war," Johnson said. One side in a dispute can no more use the weapon of "economic strangulation" than "it could go into the street and shoot innocent bystanders down in cold blood with machine guns." Responsible labor organizations must "purge themselves of this blight immediately" or bear the blame for setting back the clock of labor organization ten years. "This ugly thing is a blow at the flag of our common country and it has got to stop." (In a curious semantic leap, "this ugly thing"—the general strike—

became, particularly in newspaper reports, "this subversive element"—the Communists, as the *Times* explicitly noted—and, probably, as General Johnson intended.) If the federal government did not act, the general said, he knew San Francisco well enough to know that her people would. . . . Responsible labor organization" has a duty, he said, to "run these subversive influences out from its ranks like rats." (Even as he spoke, San Francisco police and their anonymous vigilantes were smashing their way through the headquarters of virtually ever identifiable radical group in the city. The coincidence strongly suggests Neylan as a likely source of the initial attempt to pin responsibility for the vigilante raids on disgruntled unionists, perhaps for the motivation of the raids themselves.)

The situation, Johnson concluded, "is made to order for a just settlement." The distance between the "extreme" positions of both sides is "a trader's paradise." But the people would not tolerate "insurrection"—"it would be safer for a cotton-tail rabbit to slap a wildcat."

His intervention was not entirely welcome, the general later recalled. The new labor disputes act gave him no status; as administrator of the NRA he was no longer officially involved. Administration sources (though Johnson may not have been fully aware of this) wanted to keep him out. Neylan questioned his official standing. Nevertheless, after consulting the members of the National Longshoremen's Board, the general phoned the president's secretary, Marvin McIntyre, at the White House who, the general said, "authorized" him to speak for the board. Johnson spoke to Secretary Perkins, as well. "I did not understand her even to intimate the slightest objection," the general wrote in his memoirs.[6]

From the moment he established himself in the Palace Hotel, the general was caught up in a frenzy of negotiation, fourteen to sixteen hours a day. Not only the general, but Neylan, too, and a steady stream of strike figures met in Palace Hotel suites, in the City Hall or board offices. They involved the general strike leaders—Edward Vandeleur, George Kidwell, Mike Casey, and executive committee of the General Strike Committee (but not Harry Bridges); the mayor; shipowners and Industrial Association figures; and newspaper publishers. General Johnson urged Governor Merriam to hold off declaration of martial law. Arrangements were made for Johnson to serve a formal demand to end the general strike on John P. McLaughlin, Mike Casey's number two man in the teamsters, and through him to assure labor that Johnson would use the best offices of government to resolve all issues. The script called for McLaughlin to promise to call on all good union people to end the strike. But, J. Paul St. Sure remembered, the general was so drunk he forgot his part and instead delivered a denunciation of labor. McLaughlin, St. Sure said, was "flabbergasted." The story was quickly squelched.[7] But "by Wednesday morning," said a Washington correspondent, "[General Johnson] had made himself, after Bridges, the most conspicuous figure of the strike drama."[8]

Few useful recollections and even fewer records remain of those marathon conversations but, extrapolated from events and recall, something like a meeting of the minds plainly emerged. It was never reduced to writing; it may not have been voiced as such; it may have been no more than the parties' educated estimates of what was in the other parties' minds. It bore some resemblance to the patterns of settlements sometimes engineered in local labor relations. It paralleled the good faith relationship that existed between Mike Casey and Neylan, or between other labor representatives and some San Francisco businessmen. However the consensus came about, its elements included an end to the general strike; arbitration of all issues (including the hiring halls) by the longshoremen; an agreement by the shipowners to deal with the unions chosen by the seamen in representation elections; and, not least of all, agreement by the shipowners to arbitrate all unresolved issues if bargaining with the seafaring unions deadlocked. It did not materialize in one piece but unfolded in a series of steps. However it came about, that is how it was finally resolved.

Afterward, Neylan gave credit to businessman Athol McBean, Mike Casey, and others. The role of McBean, a major figure in the Industrial Association, remains a mystery; only Neylan refers to his role. On Casey's death in 1937, though, Neylan wrote to his widow:

> What a pity it is that, in the present disturbed conditions, it is probably not wise to publish yet what I think was the greatest achievement

of his career. I don't know whether you fully realize it or not, but Old Michael was the greatest single force in 1934, in saving organized labor and winning for the longshoremen the award they got that year.

The general strike in San Francisco had infuriated the whole community. Martial law was almost a certainty and a terrible drive on organized labor was already underway. The steps which he took and the faith men in key positions had in his word were all that saved San Francisco from civil war.[9]

In another letter, Neylan said the community owed a debt to "reputable labor leaders" who "at a time of hysteria within their own ranks" had "lived up to the full requirement of American citizenship." Their "courageous and intelligent action" prevented "an extremely complicated situation, leading to bloodshed and the spread of the general strike idea to other communities."[10] William Storie, then on the staff of the Industrial Association, credited Vandeleur and his committee as "the most instrumental" in ending the general strike. Storie believed that they obtained a commitment from Bridges that the general strike had made his point but had to be limited.[11]

The General Strike Committee at its Tuesday (July 17) session had increased the number of operating permits for restaurants to fifty. It had voted, too, to permit Pacific Gas & Electric Co. emergency trucks to continue their troubleshooting. Then it turned to a resolution introduced by George Kidwell, calling on all employers and unions to submit all "unsolved" issues to binding arbitration by the National Longshoremen's Board. It was contingent, however, on acceptance "by the employers of each group of the employees involved in the dispute." It urged the governors of California, Oregon, and Washington and the mayors of the port cities to ask President Roosevelt to act "in this emergency to [that] end." It was, in all probability, a reflection (not yet complete) of the "courageous and intelligent" action to which Neylan later referred. The committee, after a heated debate, sent the resolution to the executive committee, asking for a prompt recommendation. The executive committee returned at 3:55 P.M. with a recommendation to adopt the resolution. After more, and still heated, debate, now stretching to seven hours, the resolution was adopted by a rising vote of 207 to 180.

Bridges told the *Examiner*, "You can be damned sure the long-shoremen will never consent to arbitration of the hiring halls. If necessary we'll cut loose from the other unions and carry on our own strike alone. . . . They packed the meeting. When it came to a final standing vote it was so close that a roll call was demanded. The chairman refused . . . and adjourned the meeting. They railroaded it through on us." Kidwell, however, insisted that precautions had been taken to insure regularity in the balloting. Vandeleur said it was now up to the shipowners. "If they show the same cooperative spirit which has been shown by the labor unions, business activities in San Francisco should resume their normal status promptly."[12]

Kidwell promptly sent copies of the resolution to General John-son and Neylan. Neylan was blunt: "In light of the existing condi-tions, I desire to avoid any unnecessary formality but may I say that General Johnson has no authority to [meet] either persons or groups in a state of insurrection against the United States or its subsidiaries. I shall file your communication." General Johnson praised the resolution—"an example in labor disputes which will appeal to the whole country," he told Kidwell. "There is just one fly remaining in the ointment. I refer to the general strike. The Federal government cannot take part in this situation while this wholly unauthorized and improper threat remains," said Johnson. Arbitration, though, could proceed "at once . . . if you will meet tomorrow and call off the general strike."[13] Neylan also blocked a statement by Mayor Rossi calling on all parties to arbitrate all is-sues, again insisting the general strike must be ended before further steps were taken.

On board the USS *Houston* at sea, President Roosevelt watched as the *Houston* and its accompanying warship, the *New Orleans*, en-gaged in long-range gunnery and range-finding practice. He was looking forward to some deep-sea fishing as the *Houston* continued on course to Hawaii. Secretary McIntyre's overnight summary told him of the General Strike Committee's action in calling for arbitra-tion of all points at issue. But McIntyre added, "Confidentially this was done under slight misapprehension that operators had agreed to same thing." McIntyre affirmed General Johnson's place in the situation, noting that the general and the board were constantly in touch with the shipowners in an effort to have them adopt the board's proposals. McIntyre added, "trouble between armed citizens committee and citizens seems less acute and for present martial law which seemed imminent is postponed." Secretary Perkins had replied to Governor Merriam's telegram regarding deportation of communist aliens, indicating no action was contemplated to deport Bridges. "Using all sources here bring pressure on individual ship operators to arbitrate and on individuals in citizens committee keep cool and avoid trouble," McIntyre concluded.[14] From Honolulu came word that FDR had advised Governor Poindexter that he planned to make a radio address to the people of the territory on July 28 as planned. FDR clearly had no intention of returning to the Pacific Coast to intervene directly in the strike.

19.

T HE T HIRD D AY

UNDER INTENSE PRESSURE and in the face of vigorous opposition
and prolonged debate, the General Strike Committee moved still
further on the third day (Wednesday, July 18) to ease the crunch of
the strike. The executive committee authorized all union restaurants and butcher shops to reopen. Hugo Ernst, head of the culinary workers, voted against reopening the restaurants, he said, but,
if the committee ordered it, they would return to work. Hotels that
had closed their restaurants to all but guests announced they were
again open to the public. Butchers returned to work and meat deliveries began almost at once. The strike embargo on gasoline and oil
was lifted. C. T. Dixon, representing the taxi drivers, resigned his
vice chairmanship, saying he was absolutely against raising it. He
did not want to "to tell his men to go back to work; he did not want
to be crucified."[1] The oil companies, organized into an emergency
committee, had announced earlier they would reject union permits
and operate under police protection. They claimed only some forty
deliveries in the preceding week but now, full service allowed service stations to reopen. Samuel Kahn, president of the Market
Street Railway, with a vice president as conductor, took out the first
of a string of four cars in defiance of the striking carmen. He promised more cars the next day and restoration of night runs soon. The
strikers, though, renewed their demand for arbitration. Normal ser-

vice did not return until the following week when the company reluctantly agreed.[2]

"San Francisco business has suffered a 65 per cent loss on account of the general strike," the *Chronicle* reported. Department stores were empty, it said; restaurants and shops, closed because of the strike, took "staggering" losses. "San Francisco was in no shopping mood." "Lady Teazle" reported in the *Chronicle* that "society" had been "staying at home and being very, very quiet." Some "lucky ones" have gone traveling, but at home "entertaining has ceased. . . . no matinees, no afternoon teas . . . going places and doing things have been suspended for a lack of places to go and things to do." The municipal golf course, though, reported lines of golfers waiting to tee off. Attendance at Pacific Coast League baseball games jumped. Sporting goods stores reported brisk sales.[3]

R. Stanley Dollar radioed his company's ships at sea "to lay a course for San Francisco." William P. Roth said Matson, too, was bringing back its ships—"The citizens of San Francisco have again shown us a city that knows how." Roth also announced a fleet of "the most modern trucking equipment," would replace the "six elderly trucks" that had been moving cargo. Annie Laurie, the *Examiner*'s lachrymose columnist, too, thought the city knew how: "The idea that any one should believe for one minute that the good, honest, intelligent working people of San Francisco would go whispering and plotting and trying to tear down by any way whatsoever the prosperity and peace of our own dear city."[4]

Newspapers predicted an early end to the general strike. "UNION EMBARGO SMASHED," the *Chronicle* shouted. "STRIKE NOW COLLAPSING" said the *New York Times* on page one, "STRIKE NEARS END" on the page two jump. "I have reason to believe that the general strike will be called off within a few hours," Mayor Angelo Rossi said at the end of the day. Harry Bridges was quoted as saying "The strike has failed because of mismanagement, but the spirit of the longshoremen will continue." Later, Bridges contradicted the statement, saying the longshoremen's strike will continue, adding: "No one should kid himself that the general strike is over." Banker William H. Crocker summed it up for the New York *Daily News:*

This strike is the best thing that ever happened to San Francisco. It's costing us money, certainly. We've lost millions on the waterfront in the last few months. But it's a good investment, a marvelous investment. It's solving the labor problem for years to come.

Mark my words. When this nonsense is out of the way and the men have been driven back to their jobs, we won't have to worry about them any more. They'll have learned their lesson. Not only do I believe we'll never have another general strike, but I don't think we'll have a strike of any kind in San Francisco during this generation. Labor is licked."[5]

Major General David Prescott Barrows, announcing a full-dress "retreat" for his National Guard troops, said, "No seditious mob can make a dent in this force we have assembled to defend the Embarcadero." His forces now numbered 4,500 troops, including two bands, three tanks (with four more available)—"they can break up anything that can form on Market street"—one hundred twenty machine guns, twenty 37-mm cannon, and twenty trench mortars.[6]

From New York, Joe Ryan, president of the International Longshoremen's Association (ILA), promised there would be no sympathy strike by East Coast longshoremen. "Our boys are smart enough to know that the radical elements want us to get out so they can take control of the situation as they did in San Francisco," Ryan said. From Chicago, the American Federation of Labor's William Green once again disowned the general strike which was, he said, "local in character." The AFL had neither ordered nor authorized it; San Francisco strikers had not consulted with the federation or asked for its services. But Green added that labor understands the risks of a sympathetic strike. "When working people are engaged in an economic life-or-death struggle it does not seem appropriate for their friends to engage in comment which might be used against them by their enemies." Instead, he said, an equitable and honorable settlement should be of "supreme concern."[7]

Machine-gun squads continued to patrol the East Bay waterfront and industrial areas; armed guards convoyed food and gas trucks in mounting numbers. Some two hundred food trucks reached the Oakland commission district. Gas trucks brought supplies to Piedmont and Hayward. National Guard units took over guard duties at major docks, releasing Oakland police to speed the process. Oakland Mayor MacCracken said thousands of volunteers had signed up as citizen vigilantes. Through district headquarters, they were working to expedite the reopening of closed restaurants, shops, and service stations. In Alameda they patrolled the streets where shops had reopened. Canneries in San Leandro, closed for several days, announced that eight hundred workers had returned to their jobs. In Piedmont citizens armed with shotguns guarded service stations with replenished stocks of gas.

The East Bay strike strategy committee decided to ask striking unions to vote the next night—July 19—on returning to work. The labor unions of Alameda County originally took action, the committee said, "to be helpful" in achieving the objectives sought by the maritime organizations. "In view of the developments in San Francisco wherein the general strike committee has permitted certain organizations of labor to return to work," the committee concluded that "it will be unfair to the unions of this district to continue the strike."[8]

In Portland, special guards suddenly opened fire on U.S. Senator Robert F. Wagner and a party of union officials while they were inspecting an embattled pier. It had been the scene, the *Times* reported, of strikebreaking activities and of clashes between police and striking longshoremen. Ten shots were fired by the guards who claimed they fired only when the party failed to heed their challenge; members of the party denied hearing any such demand. Four guards were placed under arrest.

Senator Wagner had come to Portland, representing the National Labor Relations Board, in an effort to head off the threatened general strike. Initial plans for the walkout had been delayed to hear the senator, and he continued to meet in long sessions with the unions' strategy committee, with Governor Meier, and employer representatives. Newspaper reports said that the committee was sharply divided. Sentiment for a general strike seemed to be wilting, deterred in part by developments in the San Francisco general strike and a "cooling down" among union members.[9]

Judge Charles A. Reynolds, regional labor board chairman at Seattle, saw no likelihood of a general strike there, though the question was on the local central labor council's agenda for Thursday night. Meantime, though, Seattle strikers were locked in a rock and tear gas battle at a dock where strikebreakers were working. Strikers and sympathizers twice shattered police lines at the dock but police held them back from reaching the strikebreakers by tear gas and, finally, by hand-to-hand fighting. The strikers, nevertheless, regained picketing territory from which they had been ousted several weeks before under orders from Mayor Charles Smith.

City officials charged the battle was provoked by "radical agitators" in an effort to influence the unions' decision on a general strike. The mayor had said he would drive all known communists out of Seattle. The confrontation at the pier came, the mayor said, at the moment the police were organizing a squad for that purpose. Police, he told the *Times*, have a list of 250 "known Communists" as targets for their hunt. In Portland, police arrested thirty-five "alleged" radicals in raids on "Communist headquarters."[10]

To a San Francisco courtroom, jam-packed with victims of the previous day's raids and guarded by officers bearing shotguns and revolvers, Judge George J. Steiger delivered a grim homily:

> This condition requires immediate and drastic action. This strike is no longer a controversy between employers and employees, but rather between legally constituted authority and a band of agitators and communists who have no regard for our institutions or our human laws; it is a conflict between the government of our city, state and nation and a band of undesirable, irresponsible destroyers who would tear down all that is sacred.
>
> No man or woman, however humble his or her occupation, will countenance terrorism, violence, or open and overt acts against the government of the United States. Law and order must prevail to the last drop of blood in my veins. I will not sidestep my duty.[11]

District Attorney Matthew Brady asked the court's help in tracing the backgrounds of the arrested men. Every American, he thought, has the right to advocate change by lawful and peaceful means, but not by force and violence. If the communists went beyond their rights as American citizens, they might be asked to "return to the land from which [they] came and there assist in carrying out the principles [they] advocate." The threat of deportation, Brady said, "will calm down the average communist." Judge Steiger promised to dig into "their activities, their police records, their intentions, and their agitations . . . with a view to helping to send them back where they came from."

In another courtroom, Attorney George Andersen appeared on behalf of another group of raid victims before Judge Sylvain Lazarus. The men pleaded not guilty, he told the judge, and requested trial by jury. At the same time, he protested the $1,000 cash bail under which some were being held. "Ridiculous," the judge replied to Andersen's request for jury trials. They should be tried at once and by the trial judge. If they do not like the verdicts, they can appeal. Andersen protested the men had been arrested while following "peaceful pursuits;" a mass trial would be illegal unless all had been arrested at the same time. Lazarus had his own homily for the prisoners:

> Stepping out of my judicial role, I say these men are probably acting to further disturb the industry of the city. They are undesirable citizens, ready to pounce down in time of storm. I recognize we are existing in a time of public peril and I am going to keep that in mind. These men are enemies of the state and government.

Addressing Andersen, he added, "and if you talk too much, you will be in contempt of court."[12]

Some of the raid victims—members of the Marine Workers Industrial Union, many identified as communists, and many who asked for jury trials—were held as "$1,000 vags." The vagrancy charge and inordinate bail, used by police for "tough" cases—drug peddlers and addicts, hardened professional criminals, and habitual criminals—had been invoked frequently during the strike against those the police identified as "radicals and Communists." Bail for vagrancy cases was usually $20. An Industrial Association attorney said the $1,000 bail was intended as a deterrent to requests for jury trials, since, to virtually penniless defendants, the bail meant they would have to await their jury trials in jail. Defendants were held, in lieu of bail, from three to four days to several weeks, as Andersen's attempts to have bail reduced were repeatedly rebuffed, as in Judge Steiger's court.

Two more raids picked up where the police had left off the day before. Wreckage at the Open Forum Club, 1223 Fillmore street, was absolute, and raiders "tore into little pieces" the headquarters of the "International" (probably, Industrial) Workers of the World—a tiny remnant of the once militant Wobblies. (A jury later awarded the IWW $175 and costs for property damage.)

The same day's *Chronicle* (and the *New York Times*) carried the copyrighted revelation that "the Communist high command in New York planned nearly a year ago to shake the maritime cities of America by strikes" such as those in Pacific Coast cities. The source was *The Party Organizer*, for October 1933. Intended for Communist Party workers, the so-called "guidebook" urged organizing party nuclei on "key" docks to develop "some kind of a struggle on the dock. . . . any small action on any section of the waterfront would spread like fire." (Early issues of the *Waterfront Worker* had urged a similar course.) The dock strike on the Pacific Coast and the general strike, over the opposition of conservative labor men, the newspaper report claimed, demonstrate the "thoroughness" of the Communist strategy."[13]

General Johnson, now publicly identified as the official spokesman for the National Longshoremen's Board, was spearheading the drive in San Francisco to end the strikes. He had wholly adopted Neylan's strategy of first ending the general strike, then meeting with the shipowners to end the maritime strike and moving to have the National Guard withdrawn. The Kidwell resolution, adopted by the General Strike Committee the day before, calling on all parties to arbitrate all issues, had only a few, and not always the expected, defenders. Mike Casey called it "a great victory for conservatism and sanity," but the WEU's Thomas Plant noted there could be no arbitration until the board determined who represents the various maritime workers. Shipowner Roger Lapham asked, "Why should the employers arbitrate with the seamen's unions?" The Industrial Association's Albert Boynton said the resolution settled nothing. "Let the unions go back to work, then talk about arbitration," he said. A representative of the International Seamen's Union said its members would not accept the terms of the resolution.[14] Bridges was widely quoted as challenging the fairness and accuracy of the vote and the chairman's handling of it. The ILA's publicity chairman, Ralph Mallen, protested that the resolution contradicted the San Francisco Labor Council's action only a week before endorsing the ILA's refusal to arbitrate the control of the hiring hall. In the General Strike Committee, the Cooks' Union, Local 44, called the resolution "a tremendous defeat" both for the workers involved and for all organized labor, a contradiction of "the fundamental issue" for which labor is striking.[15]

Now General Johnson called in the executive committee of the General Strike Committee. Bridges declined the invitation. The general apparently was greatly encouraged by his conclusion that the "conservative leaders" had been opposed to the strike all along. He reiterated his now-familiar stand that he would give no help to arbitration of the longshoremen's and seamen's disputes until the general strike was called off. Afterward, assuming the full mantle of the federal government, he said he was here to do what it could do to settle this trouble. But the government could not act "under the continuing coercion of a general strike." Until it is ended, "I have nothing to offer." Mayor Rossi echoed his stand: "In the presence of the general strike nothing can be accomplished."

The National Longshoremen's Board again called on the ILA to agree "now", as the employers had agreed, to arbitrate all issues. A letter from the ILA had said it was ready to vote on arbitration pending resolution of two issues: disposition of the question of the control of the hiring hall—the letter did not say how the hiring hall issue should be "disposed of, but merely says it shall be disposed of"—and the shipowners' agreement to arbitration with the seamen. The board then called on the shipowners to agree to arbitrate disputed issues remaining after thirty days of negotiations with the elected representatives of the seafaring unions. Until now, shipowners had agreed to collective bargaining but had not accepted arbitration in the event of a deadlock. Finally, the board proposed all strikes would be ended and the men return to work.

From Washington, Secretary of Labor Perkins transmitted the latest word from the vacationing President Roosevelt: "You may say that I have expressed to you and to the public my confidence that common sense and good order will prevail on all sides of this controversy and that I have full confidence in the Board and its agencies to arrive at a reasonable solution." The secretary added that the possibility had been discussed of exerting pressure on the shipowners to accept arbitration by altering existing mail contracts, but nothing was being done about it. "I have no indications that I can discuss," she said, "that employers are prepared to arbitrate."[16]

20.

THE FOURTH DAY

ON THE FOURTH day (Thursday, July 20), the General Strike Committee voted to end the general walkout. Through more than seventy hours of the general strike, the unending, day-and-night, round-robin of talks had gone on. Repeatedly and emphatically the union leaders were told the general strike must be called off before settlement of the underlying disputes could be seriously discussed, even though a clear pattern for settlement was, by now, in plain sight. Both the General Strike Committee and the National Longshoremen's Board had proposed arbitration of all issues by all parties—longshoremen and seamen, longshore employers and shipowners. But the general walkout had to be ended before the proposals could be put to work and the threat of martial law ended. The efforts to persuade Mayor Rossi to ask Governor Merriam for martial law appeared intended less to insure public order than to crush the general walkout and force labor into a broad retreat. The governor was willing but the mayor was stubbornly resisting. Edward Vandeleur and the strike committee leaders were faced with the insistent demand to end the general strike that barred the way to a settlement of the waterfront strikes.

To the committee session Thursday morning, George Kidwell brought a second resolution reflecting the emerging consensus (as well as his conviction that an early end to the general strike was necessary). It linked immediate termination of the general strike to acceptance of arbitration by the shipowners employing maritime labor and to the willingness of the longshoremen to arbitrate the hiring hall. Will the employers accept arbitration?, a delegate asked Vandeleur. The general strike must be called off, Vandeleur replied, before the government authorities would talk about the board's—and the committee's—proposal. "The delegate can take it for what it is worth," he said, "that all government agencies . . . will do everything in their power to compel the employers of the maritime workers and the longshoremen to accept the terms for arbitration that this General Strike Committee has proposed."[1]

Delegate Charles Derry of the Typographical Union, however, proposed an even more direct end: the General Strike Committee would simply advise those unions on strike in sympathy with the maritime workers and longshoremen "to immediately resume work" and pledge "every resource, moral and financial," to end successfully the longshoremen's and maritime strikes. This advice, Derry said bluntly, was contingent on nothing—the committee at the start had had only the power to recommend a general strike; it now had only the power to recommend ending it. The delegates adopted the Derry amendment 191 to 174, then the amended resolution itself by voice vote. Before adjourning, the delegates added two codas: one, the General Strike Committee would be recalled if the president deemed it necessary to organized labor and its interests; the second, the National Guard should be removed without delay. So, at 1:15 P.M., on Thursday, July 19, the general strike ended.[2]

The first word of the committee's action came from Mayor Rossi, echoed almost instantly on radio and in the "extras" that quickly hit the streets. Within minutes, it seemed, taxis appeared. Private cars quickly jammed the streets, the numbers even greater than usual since streetcar service had not yet been fully restored. Service stations started pumping gas. Downtown movie houses opened their box offices and restaurants reopened as rapidly as supplies permitted. Business houses opened their doors. Matson reported its liner *Lurline* would arrive Saturday. Dollar liner *President Lincoln* was reported due early next week. "As we understand it," said the Dollar line president, "San Francisco has answered the threat of insurrection."[3]

Trucks reappeared almost at once. Though the teamsters had not yet formally ended their walkout, many union drivers returned to their jobs, working on the waterfront under military guard. Mike Casey phoned the Industrial Association to say the men were returning to work, were in fact already hauling strikebound cargo from the docks. He assured association officers, too, that they would handle all freight without discrimination, including the strikebreaking cargo in the Atlas Trucking Company warehouse. Even though the teamsters had effectively ended their strike, formal action would not be taken until the union's membership meeting that evening. Until then, too, employers suffered "a period of extreme anxiety," Paul Eliel said, before they could know that their troubles were in fact over. That certainty would come only when the teamsters had agreed to return to work and to haul all cargo without discrimination as to origin or mark. Strong and vociferous objections surfaced among the teamsters. Though Casey felt the officers could have forced through a vote to return to work, they ducked a showdown and ordered an all-day secret ballot vote at the union hall the next day.

Market Street Railway carmen, in the face of a muscular show of the company's strikebreaking strength, stayed out. The first car left the barn at 10:01 that morning, followed by another three minutes later. Thirty policemen guarded the carbarn, thirty-eight more were stationed along the route. Three squad cars, carrying heavily armed police, led the way, convoyed by two motorcycle policemen. In all, four cars made the trip, fifty to one hundred yards apart, eight police cars in between.

East Bay workers that day ended their general strike. Workers streamed back to their jobs as stores, shops, and businesses of every sort reopened. That evening, union representatives formalized the end of the strike as the Strike Strategy Committee had proposed the night before. Key System workers voted to resume work Friday morning. Teamsters decided they would return to work early the following week. Unions of laundry drivers and cleaners and dyers stayed out, pressing their own independent strikes. Novelist Elenore Meherin sampled East Bay opinion. An "irate lady" told her: "What's the matter with us that we sat dumbly by and allowed this little boys' fight . . . to reach such savage proportions?" A quiet, fifty-year-old worker: "The strike is labor's only weapon. We'd still be working sixteen hours a day and for starvation wages if we waited until capital volunteered us any chance. They'd bottle up the sun and the air if they could and make us pay for it." A small, union shopkeeper: "I'm glad labor is putting that interloper [Bridges] in his place. I don't believe the rank and file workers ever wanted this general strike."[4] In Berkeley, vigilantes, identified as members of the Berkeley Nationals (Major General David Barrows of the National Guard was said to be one of its organizers), were patrolling the streets, encouraging shopkeepers to reopen. An American Legion group in Carmel, the *Oakland Tribune* reported, launched a drive to oust reds, citing particularly the John Reed Club, headed by Ella Winter, wife of muckraker Lincoln Steffens. In Monterey, reports said, the posh Hotel Del Monte has been filled to capacity. In Hayward, "police searched that city for agitators last night," the paper said, "but were unable to find any." A sign erected near the city line warned "reds" to beware of Hayward. San Jose vigilantes were searching for a Communist candidate for county supervisor to urge his departure. Communist leaders are hurriedly leaving the city, a "government official" told the *Chronicle.*

Police broke in on what the *Chronicle* said was "a secret Communist meeting," arrested the "so-called big shots," and seized important documents. Four of the defendants were Elaine Black and Joseph Wilson, officials of the International Labor Defense (ILD), and Harry Jackson and John Rogers, both of the Marine Workers Industrial Union (MWIU). The Communist Party-sponsored ILD had been active throughout the strike in providing legal defense for arrested strikers; most of its efforts, the Resner report said, had been devoted to the defense of alleged radicals. (The International Longshoremen's Association had its own defense committee which worked energetically to retrieve its members from the law.) Black had been reported to have made "inflammatory speeches along the docks," urging strikers to pack courtrooms where strikers were being tried. On one occasion Judge George Steiger ejected her from his courtroom, saying: "This woman can't come in here. She is a vagrant without visible means of support." Arrested without warrant, the defendants were ordered booked as "vags and enroute." Judge Steiger, too, sent a list of "red" defendants to relief authorities. "It is my purpose to see that agitators and communists are not going to be fed and housed by the city," he said.[5]

As the general strike ended in San Francisco, hostilities broke out in Seattle. Mayor Charles Smith directed a force of three hundred police, under a barrage of tear and nausea gas, in driving some two thousand pickets from the city's pier at Smith's Cove. In a fifteen-minute battle, scores were gassed and countless pickets and police were bruised and battered by police clubs, stones, and clubs. Once the union men had been routed, railroad crews began moving freight cars in and out, resuming the strikebreaking operations that had been interrupted by the strikers' picket lines.

The Seattle chief of police had resigned the night before, because he did not favor the drastic police action the mayor wanted; the mayor took charge. About five hundred pickets had maintained their lines through the night; they were joined at dawn by new arrivals from Tacoma, Everett, and other Puget Sound ports. The mayor's forces moved in soon after, but the pickets ignored police warnings to leave. Commands of "let 'er go" from a bridge overlooking the pier launched the gas barrage, followed by the police attack.

The next day, the sailing of the Dollar liner *President Grant* ran into difficulty when the collector of customs in Seattle refused clearance. The ship was crewed, the collector said, mostly by men who could not, "by any stretch of the imagination or by the most liberal construction," be considered qualified seamen. And that day, too, Seattle teamsters announced they would handle all merchandise as they had prior to the start of the strike.

In Portland, with National Guard troops encamped some eight miles from the waterfront, a convoy of trucks, heavily guarded by police, broke through picket lines and opened the way to resume cargo handling in the strikebound port. Governor Julius Meier's orders the day before, putting the Guard on standby duty, had been promptly and wrathfully answered by a renewed threat of a general strike. His action, too, brought regrets from U.S. Senator Robert Wagner who had won a commitment from the General Strike Committee that it would not set the day and hour for a general walkout until peace efforts in San Francisco had been exhausted. The governor's "monstrous" order, the committee said, freed it from its promise to the senator.

Earlier, the governor had telegraphed President Roosevelt aboard the *Houston*, asking authority for General Hugh Johnson "to prevent insurrection which if not checked will develop into civil war." (An annoyed Roosevelt instructed his staff to tell Governor Meier to keep his telegram private and "to communicate with me hereafter through the White House.") Shipowners gave notice that they intended to start loading ships—they were weary of waiting, they said, and had little faith that mediation efforts could end the deadlock. If such an attempt came, Portland Mayor Joseph Carson and county authorities declared their present forces could not protect life and property. Nevertheless, the governor put the Guard on standby. Senator Wagner spent the night and day apparently in an effort to dissuade the shipowners from their plan to work cargo. He boarded a plane for San Francisco, expressing disappointment that the opening should have been attempted and the Guard mobilized. Pickets from the Textile Workers and Waitresses unions paraded at the Meier and Frank department store (the governor was joint owner of the store) to protest his mobilization of the Guard. The picketing was intended to launch a boycott of businesses and persons shipping or importing merchandise by way of struck ships. With peace seemingly near at San Francisco, though, Portland labor temporized. It set a meeting the next day (July 21) to act on its suspended plans for a general walkout.[6]

The tide of San Francisco's general strike ebbed rapidly: People returned to their everyday pursuits, normalcy was speedily restored, and traces of the general walkout were obliterated almost overnight. General Johnson wired President Roosevelt:

GENERAL STRIKE CALLED OFF BY SPLENDID PATRIOTIC ATTITUDE OF REGULAR LABOR LEADERS PERIOD FULL SITUATION SHOULD BE SETTLED WITHIN TWENTY FOUR HOURS PERIOD HOORAY FOR ROOSEVELT[7]

(The file copy carries a note: "NOT RELAYED.") Vandeleur sent a congratulatory message to Mayor Rossi, appreciating his part in "this adjustment" and citing the absence of violence in the general strike as proof that "the rank and file of union labor are law-abiding citizens and good Americans." Mayor Rossi, for his part, congratulated the "real leaders" of the union forces on their decision. San Francisco, he said (in a statement probably drafted by John Francis Neylan), had stamped out "the very real danger of revolt." But, Rossi added, "The crushing of this strike cannot be allowed to be used "to destroy union labor or its rights." He pledged his efforts to "secure justice" and defend "his fellow citizens" against "unfair aggression." To the Committee of Five Hundred he pledged: "I will, to the full extent of my authority, run out of San Francisco every communistic agitator."

As the dust of the general strike cleared, though, it was plain that the strikes of the longshoremen and the seamen were still in place, frustrating any expectations that they would immediately turn and run. The *Joint Marine Journal*, even while the General Strike Committee was voting, declared "we intend to REMAIN on strike until we get a fair and just settlement." The ILA publicity committee's daily strike bulletin, though, called the committee's action a betrayal of the longshoremen's and the seamen's fight, accused the "labor traitors" of joining the union-fighting employers and their allies—the Industrial Association and Chamber of Commerce, the police and the National Guard—and of supporting "the open shop and compulsory arbitration." It was an extreme statement of a not uncommon view that the general strike had failed, and that the retreat of the teamsters and a looming decision on arbitration spelled not merely a speedy end to the waterfront strikes but defeat for the workers. On the other hand, it soon came clear that the leaders of the general strike had accomplished pretty much what they set out to do: impose a compromise on the striking unions and their employers that, as they saw it, maintained basic rights of the workers, preserved their unions, and locked the employers into the collective bargaining process. The General Strike Committee forced both union and employers into arbitration. "That was the face saver and also a device to end it," Sam Kagel remembered. "Otherwise it was in dead center."[8] Bridges commented, "And in going out on general strike the unions of San Francisco proved that they would not stand by and see the maritime unions crushed."[9] Some years later, the International Longshoremen's & Warehousemen's Union, successor to the ILA Pacific Coast District, called it "the first successful general strike in American history."[10]

From Washington, fears were expressed that the shipowners' refusal to accept arbitration could upset the emerging settlement. Secretary of Labor Frances Perkins indicated her feeling—not yet a "command"—that the shipowners would accept the National Longshoremen's Board, saying "it shouldn't be necessary to coerce anybody." Meantime, Postmaster General James Farley, on a speaking tour, was being diverted to San Francisco, and Senator Wagner was already on his way from Portland. They would join government mediators in their efforts to work out a satisfactory agreement.

In the next morning's *Chronicle*, Royce Brier and the copy desk produced a near-lyrical obituary of the general strike: "SF Stirs, Blinks and Then Smiles as Clatter Drowns Silence," said the headline. Beneath it, Brier wrote:

> An imperial city, one of the great communities of men in this world, heir to the gay and lusty Dons and Forty-niners, arose from a staggering sickness yesterday. Like a giant stirring after a knockout potion, it stretched its mighty limbs, blinked and murmured "Wotahell?" Then through the street swept the multitude, as water through a broken dam. . . . What happened yesterday perhaps never happened in just such a pattern before. No communal machine of such magnitude had ever been so stricken.

That day, too, Neylan "invited all the shipping magnates down to [his] place in the country, and we had an ice-water lunch, no cocktails or anything of that kind." They were joined by the newspaper publishers and representatives of the Waterfront Employers Union and Industrial Association. This was to be Neylan's all-out drive to clear away one of the two remaining obstacles to a general settlement. "And then I took them down in the open air," Neylan recalled, "where all the orators could blow off steam and so on, and we read the riot act to them: that they had played right into the hands of the radicals by their atrocious neglect of the legitimate interests of labor down there; that they had to get on to themselves, and get in line and help us out on this thing. That went on all afternoon down there."[11] Opinions were strong and divergent. J. Paul St. Sure remembered being told that Neylan, speaking for the publishers, was prepared, without authority from the employers' side, to announce the shipowners had agreed to arbitration. Let them deny it, Neylan said.[12] Herman Phleger, representing a number of the steamship companies, vigorously objected that the shipowners were not agreeing to arbitration, that any such statement would be not only gratuitous but a disservice to the steamship industry. Phleger himself recalled the session only as an effort to maintain the shipowners' united front which was threatening rapidly to disintegrate.[13] The session, nevertheless, early that evening, produced a statement saying the steamship owners had agreed to submit to arbitration any issues unresolved in negotiations with the seafaring unions, provided the longshoremen would agree, too, to submit all issues to arbitration. Shipowners who had not been present at the Woodside session, it said, had been solicited by phone and had given their consent as well. Thus, the penultimate piece in the General Strike Committee peace formula dropped into place.

That day, too, a steady stream of teamsters had passed through their union hall to cast ballots on a return to work. "The general strike committee has ordered all men on strike in sympathy with longshoremen to return to work immediately. Are you in favor of returning to work?" the ballot asked. They voted yes, 1138 to 283. In Oakland, the teamsters voted to return to work but to refuse to haul cargo to and from the docks. When word of the San Francisco teamsters' action reached Oakland, the union said it would reconsider and vote on a resolution for an unconditional return to work. Michael Casey said the men would return to their jobs the next morning "and do all work without reservation." J. F. Vizzard, president of the Draymen's Association, saw the men's action as "a blow at Harry Bridges. . . . He has been the fly in the ointment and now he is through."[14]

The resumption of work by the teamsters, on the waterfront as elsewhere in San Francisco, continued without apparent objection by waterfront strikers. The ILA *Strike Bulletin* was more philosophical: although teamsters were now working "alongside the Finks," a year of intensive organization and a "militant and active" strike had accomplished much; it had produced a strong coastwide union and the employers "will never forget the great strike of 1934." A general peace was hurried, too, by the announcement that the National Guard forces would be reduced by three thousand in the first stage of discharging the troops. Some fifteen hundred were left on duty on the city's eastern front.

The San Francisco longshore local agreed at its meeting Saturday night [July 21] to a coastwide referendum on submitting "the issues in dispute" to binding arbitration by the president's National Longshoremen's Board. The action, though stated in broad terms, in reality boiled down to arbitration of the control of the hiring hall, the one issue which, through the long weeks of the strike, the union had held to be non-arbitrable. The action was resisted "bitterly," the *New York Times* reported the next morning, by Harry Bridges "and other radical leaders, but the conservatives carried the day in favor of holding the referendum." That night, too, the board announced its intention to hold an immediate coastwide referendum among the striking longshoremen up and down the coast. Ballots were printed and arrangements made for board supervision of the voting in all Pacific Coast ports where the longshoremen were on strike.

A membership card in the ILA was all a longshoreman needed to vote. Strikers rushed to cast their ballots Monday morning when the polls opened. "Smiling and in apparent good humor," the *Times* correspondent noted in what had become the conventional, if pejorative, journalistic style, "a change from the ugly, snarling men who composed the rock-throwing brigades in the strike riots, hundreds of men milled around in the street near union headquarters. All day long, a steady line of voters filed in and out of the booths to cast their secret ballots." Momentarily, the election was threatened when the ILA complained that the police and National Guard were preventing it from picking up longshoremen along the front to take them to vote. Intervention of the board worked out a truce that opened the way for union patrols. Union leaders—"even the radical leaders," the *Times* again, "who precipitated last week's general strike"—freely predicted they would vote overwhelmingly to put the issue before the board.

They did. The board on Wednesday announced the longshoremen had approved arbitration of all issues, 6,615 to 1,635. One port in Raymond, Washington, turned it down, 37 to 61. The longshoremen's decision cleared a major, but not the only, barrier blocking a general settlement. Still to be resolved was the certification of bargaining agents for the seamen's unions, now that the shipowners had agreed to arbitration. Not the least of the unfinished business was the touchy issue of return to work.

Even as the longshoremen trooped into the voting booths, the city's municipal courts were pressing hard to clear their calendars of some three hundred arrests resulting from the previous week's violent roundup of alleged communists and radicals. "A remarkable spectacle of raids," commented George P. West in the *New York Times* with the benefit of two weeks' hindsight, "in which constitutional rights were either disregarded outright by vigilante bands or lightly brushed aside by the constituted authorities." Since the arrests, mostly on the second day of the general strike, the cases of 110 prisoners had been heard. Five were found to be aliens illegally in the country and were turned over to immigration officials; twenty, usually those with police records, had been sent to county jail for terms of up to ninety days. Prisoners without police records were dismissed, often with a warning to stay away from Communists headquarters. At the beginning of the week, some two hundred prisoners remained in jail awaiting trial and the two municipal courts hearing their cases were planning day and night sessions to dispose of their cases.

George Andersen, defense lawyer for most of the radical prisoners, complained to Judge Sylvain Lazarus that he had been forced to vacate his offices and that his life had been threatened. In a surprising reversal of form, the judge declared that matters had come to a fine pass when an accredited member of the bar could not "defend the cases he wanted to because of interference by such illiberal and un-American groups." The judge went further. Facing a courtroom packed with defendants, he said,

> I am disgusted to think that this good old town should have acted like a pack of mad wolves. I don't know who is responsible, but it should be traced back to its source. Boys never before arrested were thrown into jail and aging men were also subjected to that humiliation. My heart bleeds for them. . . . If it had been the son of a leading financier caught in that Howard street lot there would have been such a stir it would have turned the town upside down.

Some men, he said, wanted to return to jail because they had no place to sleep. To help them find a night's lodging, the judge handed out fifty-cent pieces to many of the men. He vowed he would stay all night rather than see "these unfortunate human beings spend another night in jail." With 101 cases on the docket, the judge dismissed 84, continued 11 for investigation, and set trials for 6 who had asked jury trials.[15] District Attorney Matthew Brady, too, saw affairs from a somewhat different perspective. "Legal penalties should be imposed on Communists who break the law, but free speech should not be restrained even then," he said. On the other hand, Judge Steiger was accused of visiting prisoners in their cells, passing sentence on them without the legal formalities of pleading or a record of their day in court. Superior Court Judge I. M. Golden found records of sentences without pleas, but apparently accepted Judge Steiger's explanation that the pleas had not been recorded in "the confusion of the time." Chamber of Commerce President J. W. Mailliard protested what he called judicial leniency. "Wholesale release of Communists with apologies to them for their arrest supply whatever fresh proof may be needed to convince the public of its duty to suppress radicalism," Mailliard said.

Appellate opinions—in the cases of Harry Jackson, Elaine Black, and others—later underscored the essential illegality of much of the police and court conduct as well as the distorted uses of the "$1,000 vag" charge. Judge Walter Perry Johnson said he could find no evidence that Jackson was a vagrant, though that was the charge against him. Instead, "he was really convicted of communism, notwithstanding the fact that under the law of California communism as a political faith is not made a crime." In the case of Elaine Black, too, the appellate department of the Superior Court noted: "We are led to believe that in rendering the verdict against defendant, the jury was of the opinion that defendant and her associates were engaged in activities subversive of the form of government. That, however, was not the charge against her. . . . The evidence being insufficient to support the charge of vagrancy, the judgement must be reversed."[16]

When the strike finally ended, some 30 defendants were still in jail awaiting trial. They were the last of the 938 arrests during the course of the strike, as tabulated by the Resner report: 176 strikers, 41 strikebreakers, 587 communists, and 210 not stated. Of the more than 900 arrests, more than 600 were dismissed; 150 were sentenced to jail; and 29 "reds" were held for deportation. As of July 31—arrests continued without interruption right up to the day work on the front was resumed—a hundred cases were continued or awaiting jury trials; most of these were subsequently dismissed. The ILA's defense committee, headed by "Dutch" Dietrich and its lawyer, Leo Collins, which had functioned effectively throughout the strike, recorded 402 arrests of the union's members: 346 were dismissed, 4 sentenced to jail, 28 fined (a total of $335), and 24 continued or held for jury trial were later dismissed. Charges ran the gamut from violating anti-picketing or anti-handbill ordinances through disturbing the peace to assault and riot. Of the 300 arrested in the police and vigilante raids, all were charged as vagrants: 211 were dismissed, 41 sentenced to jail, 29 held for deportation; and 19 were continued or held for jury trial.[17]

Voting in the board's election of seamen's bargaining representatives began July 28 in San Francisco, and as rapidly as ballots could be distributed in other ports. The ballots asked the seamen, both licensed and unlicensed, to designate "what person, persons, or organization" do you want to represent you in collective bargaining with your employer. The board intended to restrict the ballot to men who, within a reasonable time, had in fact been employed by one or another of the forty-two steamship companies involved in the proceedings; seamen at sea as well as ashore were to be polled. It would take some time. Meanwhile, the pressure grew to end the strike and get back to work. With the representation vote being taken, and with the seamen's unions meeting to consider their next step, the Shipowners of the Pacific, representing primarily the steam schooner coastwise operations and possessing a long record of union operations, offered to recognize and negotiate with the seamen's unions and to eliminate the employer-controlled hiring hall, the Marine Service Bureau. At almost the last moment, Andy Furuseth—the "grand old man," recently recovered from a breakdown—in a final, and confusing, gesture of independence and defiance, won the sailors' unanimous support when he asked them if they were "willing to stay as you are absolutely until the International Seamen's Union orders you back to work." Their action came after a fervent appeal from Harry Bridges to return to work alongside the longshoremen, however disappointed they may be in the way the strikes were ending.[18] Next day, though, seamen celebrated both the shipowners' gesture and their own newly declared independence with a bonfire of their employment books—the grave of the Fink Hall, a sign said. Furuseth stood proudly by as the burning fink books lit the Embarcadero sky. "God help somebody," a seaman said, "that flashes one of those slave market records around these parts again." And when the day came, the seamen joined the return to work.

The job of organizing the return fell mainly to the National Longshoremen's Board. It was faced not merely with setting the conditions for resuming work, but with coordinating the procedure to accommodate the strikers' determination to return to work together. The Joint Marine Strike Committee early on had resolved that "under no circumstances shall any of the striking groups be left alone, but return to work shall be by all simultaneously."[19] As it became clear that firing the strikebreakers would be a primary condition of the return to work, the strikebreakers began to desert the front. By midweek, estimates of the number of strikebreakers who had abandoned the docks ran as high as 40 percent. The problem, employers began to realize, was no longer in getting freight to and from the docks, but in loading and unloading the ships. The employers told the board that, pending its final and binding decision, conditions should be restored to those existing at the time the strike was called. To that end, the WEU said it would fire all strikebreakers hired after the strike started, except those pre-strike longshoremen who had stayed on the job. Where hiring halls existed, representatives of the board should supervise their operations. The ILA would be entitled to appoint observers to insure fair treatment. Neither union members nor strikers would be discriminated against. Presumably, until the board decided otherwise, San Francisco longshoremen would continue to be hired off the street or pierheads. The shipowners made a similar proposal.

The ILA immediately challenged the employers' good faith in retaining their hiring halls—"they still insist upon being treated as the victor retaining the spoils."[20] It had expected hiring from neutral grounds. The employers promptly supplied good reason for suspicion by placing ads offering longshore work in the next day's newspapers. The WEU promptly denied any intent to "bludgeon the longshoremen," as Eliel put it; it was a response, he said, to the dwindling supply of longshoremen with the desertions of the strikebreakers. The day was marked, too, by the discharge of the last seven hundred National Guardsmen patrolling the waterfront.

A joint meeting of longshoremen under the Joint Marine Strike Committee moved toward setting a firm date for returning to work. It was necessary, Bridges was quoted in the *Chronicle*, "to return to work before the employers issue an ultimatum which might block any further negotiations." The board cut through the confusion with an announcement July 30 that the longshore strike would end the next morning. Men would be returned to work, it said, without discrimination because of union membership or strike activity. Board representatives would supervise the hiring halls; union observers would insure longshoremen and seamen against discrimination. Wage rates when fixed by the board would be paid from the date of returning to work. The board acknowledged the longshoremen's belief that they should not have been required to return to the jobs through the employers' hiring halls, stating "in recognition of public interest in the termination of the strike they have even waived this point." That same night mass meetings of the seamen voted 4,305 to 409 to accept arbitration and end their strike.

21.

AND THEN . . .

THE NEXT MORNING—Tuesday, July 31—some thirty thousand maritime workers returned to their jobs at large ports and small, the length of the Pacific Coast. After eighty-two strikebound days, ports sprang to life, workers swarmed over the docks and ships, cargo moved in and out in a full and swelling flow.

The cost had been high. Seven men were dead, including Howard Sperry, the San Francisco longshoreman, and Nick Bordoise (Counderakis), the uptown cook working in the strike kitchen; two International Longshoremen's Association members in San Pedro, Dick Parker and John Knudsen; and Shelby Daffron of the Seattle ILA. Ole Helland, a Seattle sailor, died in August of police-inflicted wounds; Bruce Lindgren, a nineteen-year-old member of the Sailors' Union, was stabbed to death in Hong Kong by a strikebreaker. Strike battles had hospitalized hundreds of strikers, strikebreakers, and "innocent bystanders." Thousands more privately nursed sore heads and bruises, burning eyes and gas-induced vomiting. Close to a thousand in San Francisco alone were hauled into court, and many were jailed, along with hundreds more in other ports on strike-related charges.

Workers gave up a total of 2.7 million days of work in the eighty-two-day conflict. San Francisco and East Bay union members invested nearly 400,000 days of work in the general strike; maritime workers over the course of the strikes rejected close to 2.3

million workdays.[1] The president of the San Francisco Chamber of Commerce bitterly charged the strike had cost the city of San Francisco $100 million in lost business, salaries, and wages. It was no "lark," he said, the menace of radicalism had not been imaginary. The cleanup of agitators must be completed, lost business recovered. And "never again," he said, can "the repudiation of alien leadership . . . cost us so great a toll."[2]

Arthur Caylor, commentator-columnist in the *News*, reported that "anybody who wants a nice warehouse, a fleet of trucks or a boat can do some smart bargain hunting at the Industrial Association's offices." The association had put out something like $500,000 to outfit the Atlas Trucking Co., he said. "The boat, which cost $2000, probably could be picked up for $1000 by anybody who would rather pick up a boat than $1000." Some of the town's business leaders launched a quiet drive to buy a gift for the National Guard—whether as an appreciation of good citizenship or a tip for strike services was debated. The *Chronicle* awarded staff members gold medals in appreciation of their "efforts and courage." William Randolph Hearst cabled Neylan his pleasure in "watching you in the process of your contribution toward the life of San Francisco and United States of America. Newspapermen are pretty skeptical chaps—they haven't much respect for many people. There are no words to express my respect to you."[3]

Almost from the moment the longshoremen returned to the docks, and without waiting for formal arbitration, they confronted the job conditions that underlay their eighty-two-day walkout. Rank-and-file job action, a ship or a dock at a time, undertook to deal piecemeal with sling loads they considered excessive, manning they considered inadequate, and work practices they considered unsafe—the chief determinants of the pace, the difficulty, and the hazards of their work. Aboard ship, too, crews put rank-and-file job action to work to deal with their grievances and improve their job conditions. The rank-and-file actions on the job—economic at the outset, later mingled with political motives, and ultimately accommodated in their contracts—introduced extensive changes in job conditions and initiated a new era in maritime labor relations. The new era, too, was underscored as the maritime unions, on shore and at sea, welded together a long-sought coastwide alliance, the Maritime Federation of the Pacific, which played a short-lived but vital role in the immediate post-strike labor relations.

Even as these developments began to break out, on the morning of August 8, the National Longshoremen's Board, O. K. Cushing presiding, opened formal arbitration hearings on the disputed issues in the longshore strike. On October 12, after some two months of hearings in the four major ports, scores of witnesses, thousands of pages of testimony and exhibits, it handed down its award. Its formula for governing labor relations on the docks opened new perspectives for the longshoremen and their employers, even while attempting to reconcile the irreconcilable. It fell short of the longshoremen's pre-strike demands, as it did of the employers' proposals. It borrowed generously from earlier unsuccessful attempts to write an agreement and from the innumerable suggestions and proposals that had been bruited about. Its final prescription, though, was of its own compounding. It proposed the machinery for a working relationship, but it also planted contradictions that could—and did—give rise to seemingly interminable disputes.

On what had been the most bitterly contested issue, the award called for jointly operated hiring halls in each of the major ports. Employers originally had insisted on controlling the halls; the ILA had insisted on union control. The board cut the knot by requiring joint control, but allowing the union to select the job dispatcher, who would be required to dispatch all longshoremen "without favoritism or discrimination, regardless of union or non-union membership." (Ironically, this particular proposal had first been publicly suggested by the ILA's totally discredited national president, Joe Ryan.)

The joint hiring halls would be governed by labor relations committees made up of three representatives from each side. They would establish lists of regular longshoremen of the port; no longshoremen not on the list would be dispatched as long as any registered longshoremen was available. The committees would decide questions relating to lists of extra men and casuals, the rotation of gangs, and addition of new men to the registered list. They would also hear and adjust all disputes relating to working conditions and discharges.

Alongside restricted entry to the industry, the board set a six-hour day and a thirty-hour workweek, averaged over a four-week period—essentially, the longshoremen's strike demand. The combination supplied the foundation for a broad-gauged system of equalizing earnings "as nearly as possible" among men and gangs. Subject to these provisions, employers were free to select their men from those eligible and were entitled to the gangs when available which "in their opinion [were] the best qualified to do their work." The men were free to select their jobs, but they were required to work "as ordered by the employer." The employer was given control over work methods as long as they were not harmful to the health and safety of the longshoreman. The employer retained the power of discipline by discharge. In these provisions was the seed-bed for prolonged dispute, numerous job stoppages, and repeated arbitrations until unending conflict ground a new matrix for peaceful relations.[4]

The board gave the longshoremen an increase of 10 cents an hour in their base pay, raising the rate to 95 cents an hour for straight time, $1.40 an hour for overtime (after six hours). The strike demand had been $1 an hour. Not least of all, in force and effect, the award and resulting contract applied coastwide, as the union had insisted from the outset. The resulting contract would run to September 30, 1935.

With the longshore dispute out of the way, the board turned to the problems of the seafaring workers. Steam schooner owners had voluntarily recognized the International Seamen's Union as the strike ended. The board at the same time had launched a representation election among the seamen, on shore and at sea. Early in 1935 the board certified the ISU as the unlicensed seamen's bargaining agent at thirty-six steamship companies. The Masters, Mates & Pilots was chosen to represent licensed deck officers at twenty-nine firms, the Marine Engineers' Beneficial Association as the agent for licensed engine room officers at thirty companies. Soon thereafter the board plunged into arbitration of the seamen's complaints. The board's decision on April 10, 1935, left seamen less than satisfied and set the unions' agenda for the years just ahead. It failed to touch on many issues and allowed hiring from the pierhead or union, as the shipowner pleased. Ordinary seaman's pay was increased to $45 a month, able-bodied seaman's and fireman's to $70. The work day was fixed at eight hours; overtime was payable in time off rather than cash.

Thomas G. Plant, speaking to a meeting of West Coast longshore employers in 1940, unforgivingly remembered the strike's aftermath:

> Most of us heaved a big sigh of relief, and felt that the old peace and order would soon be restored. But the old order had changed. The old union had said to us, "We believe our interests are common with yours; we will cooperate with you in every way; we will produce more work and will try in every way to make your business profitable so you can pay us better wages." . . . The new union was to say to us, "We believe in the class struggle, that there is nothing common between our interests and yours, therefore, we will hamper you at every turn, and will do everything we can to destroy your interests, believing that by doing so we can advance our own.[5]

Looking back, Henry Schmidt, too, recalled the return to work:

> When the fellows went back to work on the last day of July, the employers realized immediately that this was the same group of men, but they were different. And the guys themselves, they didn't immediately realize what power they had.
>
> The gang and walkin' bosses were all very polite, very civil. A few of them got beat up, especially those who stayed in. But it was all to the good, this working class power, after a struggle like that. It was certainly good to see, good to experience.[6]

Afterword

EARLY IN THE developing conflict, the waterfront employers and their allies—other shipowners, uptown employers in the Industrial Association and Chamber of Commerce, the newspapers, and city and state officials—saw the rising unions and the subsequent strike on the waterfront as the evil work of Communists and radicals, engaged in a largely undefined, ambiguous revolution. They looked back on the open-shop days as the good old days of no disagreements and no strikes, efficient, hard-working, "satisfied" workers. In rising and insistent volume, they worked and reworked these themes, concealing their struggle initially to escape coming to terms with the independent unions and demands of the maritime workers, increasingly to frustrate where they could not avoid collective bargaining, and ultimately to rescue as much as possible of their dictatorial job control. In oddly irrelevant ways the red scare set the scene of the conflict, hanging over it like a red cloud behind which the real, unspoken conflict took place.

Ironically, the Communist Party in the person of Sam Darcy, party chief in California, supplied the initial substance for the employers' contentions, until then largely unsupported, repeatedly denied, and widely rejected. "Even in midstream," as Darcy put it in a July 1934 article, it was none too early to discuss "how far [the Party] had gotten" in the West Coast maritime strike.[1] It was perhaps too early for final judgments, he thought, but discussions of

241

the strike developments "will help strengthen revolutionary activity amongst the workers in this strike." So, in his introductory note, as in the article itself, Darcy staked his claim to a leadership role in the maritime strike, as he would later in the general strike. Since his chief concern was with the party's role, his treatment of causes, roots, and background was incidental. Launching of the *Waterfront Worker* by a group consisting of "Communists and other militant elements" led his chronology. The Communists were identified with the Marine Workers Industrial Union (MWIU), the Party's "dual" union in the transport industry. They made errors, he noted, and very little progress toward a "real union." After several years of effort, the MWIU "had not a single worker on the docks." The revival of the old-line ILA local took place in the face of MWIU (and *Waterfront Worker*) opposition. He sketched the February convention of the ILA Pacific Coast District and strike developments. By this time, Darcy was speaking as a strike leader, perhaps *the* strike leader. Problems in the conduct of the strike were "our problems," he wrote. His October sequel focused on the general strike—"the largest single strike in the history of the country," and "the first general strike in which it could be said that our Party participated as a Party." He declared, "There would have been no maritime or general strike except for the work of the Party." Now, the activities of the strikers, union, and strike committees became "our" strikers, "our" pickets. But, he concluded, the failure of the party to work inside the AFL cost it its ability to seize the direction of the general strike from the San Francisco Labor Council leadership—the "fakers," as Darcy labeled them—and to prevent what he considered a betrayal of the general strike.

In 1949, fifteen years later, two years after Mike Quin died, his *The Big Strike* was published.[2] His publisher called it "vivid and dramatic, with painstaking accuracy and historic authenticity." Nearly half a century later, Quin's work appears more "vivid and dramatic" than accurate and authentic. Too often, Quin substitutes the colorful generality for the more specific incident, the more dramatic metaphor for the more prosaic fact, blurring moments of crucial decision. The strikes and strikers became heroic and romantic in the vein of the 1930s proletarian novel; the conflict a great drama on a vast stage, part stagecraft, part harsh reality. Quin offers few clues to his sources and provides no bibliography. In the course of his story, Quin, too, offers an apparent confirmation of the ship-owners' red scare, though it may be no more than a distant echo of the Darcy claims. "The employers," he writes of the founding of the *Waterfront Worker*, "were quick to brand it as communist propaganda. In this they were largely correct." In other ways, too, Quin underscored the contributions of party members: the use of the *Western Worker* to carry the ILA strike bulletins, for example; the role of the International Labor Defense in defending the strikers and others who fell to the arrests of the police.

Charles Larrowe's biography of Harry Bridges, as every history of these episodes must, also paid attention to the founding of the *Waterfront Worker*.[3] Larrowe concluded that the paper, from the start, was intended to promote the Marine Workers Industrial Union as the union for longshoremen and seamen. "The point it was trying to make was the obvious one:" he said, "the right union for the longshoreman was the MWIU." Both Darcy and Bridges agreed the MWIU lit no fires on the docks. People, Bridges commented, "didn't cotton too much to their political views." This became most apparent when, in the face of the *Waterfront Worker*'s opposition, longshoremen in mid-summer, 1933, flooded into the revived ILA. As for party influence, Bridges reiterated frequently that, even when he and the party followed parallel lines, the implicit ideas were not necessarily, nor always, those of the party. He was accustomed to thinking for himself—often after a lot of conversation with a lot of people, but in any case for himself. In the union and its strike, Larrowe finds the basis for half of his subtitle: "the rise and fall of radical unionism."

Bruce Nelson elaborated that theme in his *Workers on the Waterfront*.[4] Nelson traces the roots of the maritime unions' to a confluence of a number of streams: a syndicalist mood which stripped the traditional syndicalism of many of its political trimmings but retained its notions of job action and of resistance at the point of production; "desperate conditions brought on by the Great Depression;" the hope and inspiration of the National Industrial Recovery Act and its Section 7(a); and the brutal oppression and exploitation in the shape-up and on the job. From these sources came what Nelson labeled the "Pentecostal era" that yielded the "rank and file insurgency at the 'point of production,' " that transformed working conditions on dock and ship, heightened class-consciousness, and produced "significant bursts of radical political activity." In these developments he called the Communists "a major force," bringing "a number of disciplined cadres . . . more able and energetic . . . far more in tune with the sentiments and aspirations of the men." Their "main role was to help shape an effective trade union program, sum up and popularize the lessons of strikes and other mass actions, and sharpen and focus . . . the workers' antagonism toward their principal adversaries."

Two reservations are relevant: The maritime strike demands, principally the union hiring hall and coastwide bargaining, arose directly out of West Coast union tradition. Shorter hours and higher wages were spurred by the New Deal drive for recovery from the depression. These were more ambitious goals, more militant, more trade-union conscious than the cautious program put forward by the MWIU-dominated *Waterfront Worker*. These conclusions should be read, too, with the calendar prominently in mind. Many of Nelson's generalizations are founded far more strongly in the post-strike period—fall 1934 to the end of the decade. The pre-strike organizing period showed only a few signs of the militant job activity and none of the political strikes that the maritime workers brought to their jobs afterward and that so dramatically shifted the balance between them and their employers. The strikes, Nelson said, "ushered" in the era.

Labor historian David Brody has concluded that "the labor upsurge of the 1930s must be seen essentially as an extension of the existing trade-union movement," clinging to the "power orientation and narrow job objectives" of the preceding half century.[5] That view brings the 1934 maritime and general strikes into sharp focus.

Perhaps the view is even sharper if the 1934 strikes are seen as an angry and rebellious uprising against the oppression and exploitation that held in thrall the nation's workers generally, the longshoremen and seamen particularly, in the years after World War I. Not often in the nation's economic history has exploitation been more oppressive, or the traditional anti-union open shop more tightly clamped on American workers. Earnings were flat and un-yielding, while all around them the nation and the industry seemed to prosper mightily. When the Great Depression swept across the country, wages started falling and unemployment began rising. Workers and their already-debased living standards were the chief victims. The workers' efforts to recognize (and reorganize) their unions in the first years of the New Deal were a traditional, class-conscious response, molded into an effective answer by the events of the summer of 1934.

NOTES

Chapter 1

1. For day-to-day (often hour-to-hour) details, I have drawn heavily on daily newspapers. None of them provided, by any means, impartial or objective reports—the *Daily News* sometimes an exception. In their display and editorial treatment, the daily newspapers unabashedly reflected the employers' attitudes, as well as served their own anti-union, anti-strike biases. In the employer efforts to indict the strike leadership as "Communist and radical" and the strikes as "revolutionary," the newspapers were willing, enthusiastic, and creative collaborators. They shared the employers' conviction that the radical leadership was responsible for needlessly prolonging the waterfront strike and calling the general strike, and that if the strikes were not literally unlawful, they probably should have been and, in any case, were certainly improper, un-American, and unwise. The papers were, beyond that, a force in their own right, a veritable "fourth estate" in the dispute. Nevertheless, the underlying reports were generously detailed and impressively comprehensive, often corroborated (or corrected) in a variety of eyewitness and oral history accounts. Principally I drew on the San Francisco dailies: the *Chronicle, Call-Bulletin, Daily News,* and *Examiner,* along with the *Oakland Tribune* and the *New York Times.* For corroboration, I have looked to eyewitness accounts, among many, of George Hedley, *The Strike as I Have Seen It,* (San Francisco: Conference for Labor's Civil Rights, 1934); Donald Mackenzie Brown, "Dividends and Stevedores," *Scribner's Magazine,* January 1935, 52; Germain Bulcke, "Longshore Leader and ILWU-PMA Arbitrator," an oral history interview by Estolv Ward (Regional Oral History Office, The Bancroft Library, Berkeley, 1984); Henry Schmidt, "Secondary Leadership in the ILWU, 1933–1936," an oral history interview by Miriam F. Stein and Estolv Ethan Ward (Regional Oral History Office, The Bancroft Library, University of California, Berkeley, 1983); also, the part-eyewitness, part-secondary accounts, among others, of Paul Eliel, *The Waterfront and General Strikes, San Francisco, 1934: A Brief History* (San Francisco: Industrial Association of California, 1934); and Mike Quin [pseud.], *The Big Strike,* (Olema, California: Olema Publishing Co., 1949).

2. *San Francisco Chronicle,* July 10, 1934; Henry Schmidt, "San Francisco Maritime Strike Statements, unpublished, ca. 1935, in ILWU Library, San Francisco.

3. Quoted from several witnesses and the coroner's report in San Francisco *Daily News,* August 2, 1934.

4. Hedley, *As I Have Seen It*, 8.

5. Hedley, *As I Have Seen It*, 8.

6. *Chronicle*, July 10, 1934.

7. *Labor Clarion*, July 13, 1934.

8. Hedley, *As I Have Seen It*, 9.

9. Eliel, *Waterfront Strikes*, 128. Exceptionally useful for its broad collection and verbatim reproduction of news releases, newspaper articles, letters, draft agreements, and other strike-related documents.

10. Bruce Nelson, *Workers on the Waterfront: Seamen, Longshoremen, and Unionism in the 1930s* (Urbana and Chicago: University of Illinois Press, 1988); Charles P. Larrowe, *Harry Bridges: The Rise and Fall of Radical Labor in the United States* (New York and Westport: Lawrence Hill & Co., 1972).

Chapter 2

1. Quoted in International Longshoremen's & Warehousemen's Union, *The ILWU Story: Three Decades of Militant Unionism* (San Francisco: ILWU, ca 1963), 12.

2. See Ira B. Cross, *A History of the Labor Movement in California* (Berkeley: University of California Press, 1935). Cross's work is the principal source for the nineteenth-century history of labor in California and, mainly, San Francisco. Many of the records to which he had access were destroyed in the 1906 earthquake and fire. His account remains the most comprehensive and reliable.

3. Henry P. Melnikow, "Henry Melnikow and the National Labor Bureau," an oral history interview by Corrinne L. Gilb (Institute of Industrial Relations, University of California, Berkeley, 1959), 62.

4. For accounts of the 1901 Teamsters' strike, see Cross, *Labor Movement in California*; Robert Edward Lee Knight, *Industrial Relations in the San Francisco Bay Area* (Berkeley and Los Angeles: University of California Press, 1960); Bernard Cornelius Cronin, *Father Yorke and the Labor Movement in San Francisco* (Washington, D.C.: The Catholic University of America Press, 1943); Robert M. Robinson, "A History of the Teamster's Union in the San Francisco Bay Area, 1850–1950" (Ph.D. diss., University of California, Berkeley, 1951).

5. Thomas G. Plant, "The American-Hawaiian Steamship Co.," an oral history interview (Institute of Industrial Relations, University of California, Berkeley, 1962), 32.

6. Harry F. Grady, "The Open Shop in San Francisco," *The Survey* 37 (November 25, 1916), 192.

7. Principal sources dealing with the 1916 strike include: Plant, "American-Hawaiian"; United States, National Longshoremen's Board, *Proceedings:* July 9–11, August 8 et seq, 1934 (Unpublished, typewritten), Bancroft Library, University of California, Berkeley (cited as NLB, *Proceedings*); San Francisco Chamber of Commerce, "Law and Order in San Francisco: A Beginning" (1916); San Francisco Labor Council, *Papers*, Bancroft Library, University of California, Berkeley; Steven C. Levi, *Committee of Vigilance, The San Francisco Chamber of Commerce Law and Order Committee, 1916–1919* (Jefferson, North Carolina and London: McFarland & Co., 1983). See also Roger Buchanan, *Dock Strike* (Everett, Washington: The Working Press, 1975); Ronald Magden and A. D. Martinson, *The Working Waterfront: The Story of Tacoma's Ships and Men* (Tacoma: International Longshoremen's & Warehousemen's Union, Local 23 and Port of Tacoma, 1982); Louis B. Perry and Richard S. Perry, *A History of the Los Angeles Labor Movement* (Berkeley: University of California Press, 1963); Knight, *Industrial Relations*; Eliel, *Waterfront Strikes*.

8. See, among many, Curt Gentry, *Frame-up* (New York: W. W. Norton & Co., 1967); Richard H. Frost, *The Mooney Case* (Stanford: Stanford University Press, 1968).

9. Schmidt, "Secondary leadership", 106; Thomas G. Plant, *Pacific Coast Longshore History*, pamphlet (Waterfront Employers' Association, 1940).

10. Plant, *Longshore History*.

11. Quoted in ILWU, *Three Decades*, 16.

12. Waterfront Employers Union, *Full and Bye: A Message from the Waterfront Employers Union*, San Francisco, 1921.

13. Quoted in William Martin Camp, *San Francisco: Port of Gold* (Garden City, New York: Doubleday & Co., 1948), 427.

14. Plant, *Longshore History*.

15. The account of the 1919–1921 strikes relies on Waterfront Employers' Union, *Full and Bye*; Giles T. Brown, "The West Coast Phase of the Maritime Strike of 1921," *Pacific Historical Review*, 19 (November 1950), 396; Walter J. Petersen, *Marine Union Labor Leadership* (probably San Francisco: Employment Service Bureau, third edition, June 1925); Hyman Weintraub, *Andrew Furuseth: Emancipator of the Seamen* (Berkeley and Los Angeles: University of California Press, 1959); ILWU, *Three Decades*; NLB, *Proceedings*; Eliel, *Waterfront Strikes*; Plant, *Longshore History*; Plant, "American-Hawaiian".

16. Joyce Maxine Clements, "The San Francisco Maritime and General Strikes of 1934 and the Dynamics of Repression" (D. Crim. diss., University of California, Berkeley, 1975), 17.

17. Frank Foisie in NLB, *Proceedings*, Exhibit II.

18. See NLB, *Proceedings*; Buchanan, *Dock Strike*; Magden & Martinson, *Tacoma Story*.

19. See Stephen Schwartz, *Brotherhood of the Sea: A History of the Sailors' Union of the Pacific* (San Francisco: Sailors' Union of the Pacific, 1985).

20. Brown, "West Coast Phase."

Chapter 3

1. NLB, *Proceedings*, July 10, 1934, 92.

2. *Waterfront Worker*, July 1933.

3. Plant, "American-Hawaiian," 29.

4. NLB, *Proceedings*, Exhibit II.

5. NLB, *Proceedings*, 882.

6. U.S. Bureau of Labor Statistics, Bulletin 552 (Washington, D.C., Government Printing Office, 1932), quoted in Samuel Yellen, *American Labor Struggles* (New York: Harcourt Brace & Co., 1936), 329.

7. *Waterfront Worker*, February, 1934.

8. Bulcke, "Longshore Leader," 36.

9. NLB, *Proceedings*, 224.

10. NLB, *Proceedings*, 224.

11. NLB, *Proceedings*, 171.

12. BLS Bulletin 552, quoted in Yellen, *Labor Struggles*, 328.

13. NLB *Proceedings*, 105; Plant, "American-Hawaiian," 66.

14. NLB, *Proceedings*, 2016.

15. Schmidt, "Secondary Leadership," 33.

16. *Waterfront Worker*, February, 1933.

17. NLB, *Proceedings*, 177.

18. NLB, *Proceedings*, 215.

19. Bulcke, "Longshore Leader," 39.

20. NLB, *Proceedings*, 568.

21. *Waterfront Worker*, February 9, 1934.

22. Schmidt, "Secondary Leadership," 41.

23. NLB, *Proceedings*, 101.

24. NLB, *Proceedings*, Longshoremen's Exhibit 1.

25. NLB, *Proceedings*, 646.

26. NLB, *Proceedings*, 436.

27. NLB, *Proceedings*, 1009.

28. NLB, *Proceedings*, 1101.

29. NLB, *Proceedings*, 1112.

30. Bridges quoted in Larrowe, *Bridges*, 10; Plant, *Longshore History*.

Chapter 4

1. Plant, "American-Hawaiian," 58.

2. Roger Lapham, "An Interview on Shipping, Labor, City Government, and American Foreign Aid," an oral history interview by Corinne L. Gilb (Regional Oral History Office, The Bancroft Library, University of California, Berkeley, 1957), 76.

3. Schmidt, "Secondary Leadership," 113.

4. Plant, "American-Hawaiian," 59.

5. NLB, *Proceedings*, 76.

6. NLB, *Proceedings*, 166.

7. Bulcke, "Longshore Leader," 34.

8. See John A. O'Connell, "Transforming a Company Union," *American Federationist*, January 1930, 61; Sam Kagel, "A Rightwing Dual Union" (1930, unpublished), in author's possession; San Francisco Labor Council, *Records*.

9. Employment Service Bureau, report to Pacific American Steamship Association, Shipowners' Association of the Pacific Coast (unsigned, incomplete), January 15, 1924.

10. Henry P. Melnikow, "Henry Melnikow," 87; NLB, *Proceedings*, Exhibit 55, 2355.

11. Bulcke, "Longshore Leader," 6.

12. NLB, *Proceedings*, 1739.

13. Quoted in Larrowe, *Harry Bridges*, 12.

14. NLB, *Proceedings*, 1823, also 877, Exhibit II.

15. NLB, *Proceedings*, Exhibit II.

16. Quoted in NLB, *Proceedings*, 2276.

17. NLB, *Proceedings*, 1852.

18. NLB, *Proceedings*, 1601.

19. NLB, *Proceedings*, 976.

20. NLB, *Proceedings*, 1913.

21. NLB, *Proceedings*, 2144.

22. Magden & Martinson, *Working Waterfront*, 53, 61; *NLB Proceedings*, 1746.

Chapter 5

1. Irving Bernstein, "Unemployment in the Great Depression," in National Conference on Social Welfare, *Social Welfare Forum, 1959, Official Proceedings*, 86th Annual Forum, San Francisco, May 24–29, 1959, 39.

2. NLB, *Proceedings*, July 11, 1934, 107.

3. NLB, *Proceedings*, 984.

4. NLB, *Proceedings*, Longshoremen's exhibit 8.

5. NLB, *Proceedings*, Employers' exhibit Y.

6. Lapham, "An Interview," 70.

7. Bulcke, "Longshore Leader," 117.

8. *Chronicle*, October 20, 1979.

9. *Waterfront Worker*, October 18, 1933.

10. NLB, *Proceedings*, 229.

11. Ira B. Cross, *California Labor Notes* (The Bancroft Library, University of California, Berkeley).

12. The national mood of crisis is recorded in Arthur M. Schlesinger, Jr., *The Age of Roosevelt: The Crisis of the Old Order* (Boston: Houghton Mifflin Co., 1957), esp. pp. 1–8; and *The Coming of the New Deal* (Boston: Houghton Mifflin Co., 1959).

13. Schlesinger, *Crisis*, 3.

14. Quoted in Larrowe, *Harry Bridges*, 13.

15. *Waterfront Worker*, December 1932.

16. Sam Darcy, "The San Francisco Bay Area General Strike," *The Communist*, 13, October 1934, 665.

17. Schmidt, "Secondary Leadership," 52.

18. ILWU, *Records* (ILWU Library, San Francisco).

19. *Waterfront Worker*, June 1933.

20. *Waterfront Worker*, August 1933.

21. Bulcke, "Longshore Leader," 8.

22. See Sam Darcy, "The San Francisco General Strike," *The Hawsepipe*, (Marine Workers Historical Association), I:6, September–October 1982.

23. *Waterfront Worker*, September 15, 1933.

24. Eliel, *Waterfront Strikes*, 4, 185.

25. ILWU, *Records:* Memo, William Glazer to Telford Taylor, June 22, 1955 (ILWU Library, San Francisco).

26. Quoted in Larrowe, *Harry Bridges*, 21. See also *Waterfront Worker*, September–October, 1933; Eliel, *Waterfront Strikes*, 4, 185; NLB, *Proceedings*, July 11, 1934.

27. Quoted in Larrowe, *Harry Bridges*, 16.

28. Darcy, "The San Francisco Bay Area General Strike," *The Communist*, October, 1934, 665.

29. Darcy, "The San Francisco General Strike," *The Hawsepipe*, September–October, 1982.

30. Robert Cherny, interview of Harry Bridges by Nikki Bridges, tapes 17–18, undated, cited in unpublished manuscript on Harry Bridges.

31. NLB, *Proceedings*, 1573.

32. NLB, *Proceedings*, 1667.

33. Buchanan, *Dock Strike*, 44.

34. Perry and Perry, *Los Angeles*, 364.

35. Magden and Martinson, *Working Waterfront*, 105.

36. Magden and Martinson, *Working Waterfront*, 106.

37. Magden and Martinson, *Working Waterfront*, 106.

38. These developments are drawn from NLB, *Proceedings*, July 10, 1934, 75; July 11, 1934, 108; Larrowe, *Harry Bridges*, 21; ILWU, *Records*, ILA documents.

Chapter 6

1. Quoted in Carey McWilliams, *California: The Great Exception* (Santa Barbara and Salt Lake City: Peregrine Smith, Inc., 1976), 131.

2. The data in this chapter on the economics of the maritime industry are drawn primarily from, among many: NLB, *Proceedings*, 475, 489, 2334, Exhibit II, Employers' Exhibit R, Longshoremen's Exhibit 13; William Addams, "The Shipping Conspiracy," *Nation* 139 (September 5, 1934, 262; September 12, 1934, 295); Clements, "Dynamics"; Quin, *Big Strike*, 20ff.

3. William G. Storie, "Employer Organizations of San Francisco: President of San Francisco Employers' Council," an oral history interview by Corinne L. Gilb (Institute of Industrial Relations, University of California, Berkeley, 1959), 32.

4. Melnikow, "Henry Melnikow," 52.

5. Eliel, *Waterfront Strikes*, 55; Frederic L. Ryan, *Industrial Relations in the San Francisco Building Trades* (Norman: University of Oklahoma Press, 1936), 227.

6. Quoted in Clements, "Dynamics," 143.

7. Lorena Hickok, quoted in Bernstein, *Turbulent Years*, 286.

8. Herman Phleger, "Sixty Years in Law, Public Service, and International Affairs," an oral history interview by Miriam S. Stein (Regional Oral History Office, The Bancroft Library, University of California, Berkeley, 1979), 70.

9. Clements, "Dynamics," 113.

10. Plant, "American-Hawaiian," 11.

11. Melnikow, "Henry Melnikow," 166.

12. Clements, "Dynamics," 130.

13. Clements, "Dynamics," 193.

14. NLB, *Proceedings*, July 10, 1934, 91.

15. U.S. Senate, Subcommittee of the Committee on Education and Labor, Hearings, January 26 and 27, 1940, 21962, 21998.

Chapter 7

1. The account of the convention is drawn from International Longshoremen's Association, Pacific Coast District, *Proceedings of the 27th Annual Convention*, February 25–March 6, 1934.

2. Eliel, *Waterfront Strikes*, 7, 186.

3. Schmidt, "Secondary Leadership," 75.

4. Telegram, George Creel to FDR FORMS OF716, box 8: Pacific Coast longshoremen's strike, 1934.

5. Eliel, *Waterfront Strikes*, 7.

6. Clements, "Dynamics," 161; Larrowe, *Harry Bridges*, 28.

Chapter 8

1. NLB, *Proceedings*, 714.

2. Eliel, *Waterfront Strikes*, 7, 189.

3. San Francisco Labor Council, *Records*, Bancroft Library, University of California, Berkeley.

4. ILWU, *Records*, resolution, letter Holman to Ryan (ILWU Library, San Francisco).

5. Quin, *Big Strike*, 43.

6. ILWU, *Records*, letter, Lewis to Pacific Coast District local unions (ILWU Library, San Francisco).

7. Eliel, *Waterfront Strikes*, 195; NLB, *Proceedings*, 716.

8. Eliel, *Waterfront Strikes*, 11.

9. NLB, *Proceedings*, July 11, 1934, 115.

10. Eliel, *Waterfront Strikes*, 11; Minutes, ILA Strike Committee, May 8, 1934; Plant quoted in Larrowe, *Harry Bridges*, 32G; Lewis quoted in Camp, *San Francisco*, 458.

Chapter 9

1. NLB, *Proceedings*, 726.

2. ILA statement quoted in Eliel, *Waterfront Strikes*, 17.

3. Magden and Martinson, *Working Waterfront*, 111.

4. Quoted in Clements, "Dynamics," 129.

5. Eliel, *Waterfront Strikes*, 200.

6. NLB, *Proceedings*, 745.

7. Theodore Durein, "Scabs' Paradise," *Reader's Digest*, January 1937, 19.

8. Stan Tulledo, "The Least Creditable Performance: How the San Francisco Press Published to Break the 1934 General Strike," *New Labor Review*, No. 6, Spring 1934, 83, quoting interview with Germain Bulcke.

9. Durein, "Scab's Paradise," 20.

10. NLB, *Proceedings*, 2258.

11. Durein, "Scab's Paradise," 21.

12. Samuel Yellen, *American Labor Struggles* (New York: Harcourt Brace & Co., 1936), 334.

13. Durein, "Scab's Paradise," 21.

14. Strike "Bulletin 2," *Western Worker*, May 9, 1934.

15. Herbert Resner, *The Law in Action* (Works Progress Administration Project, 1936), 58.

16. Quoted in Resner, *Law in Action*, 8.

17. Schmidt, "Secondary Leadership," 81.

18. Quoted in Clements, "Dynamics," 195.

19. Schmidt, "Secondary Leadership," 77.

20. The word "radical," as well as "Communist," ought almost always to be preceded by "alleged," but in the course of the dispute these became virtually generic terms. They were used indiscriminately to label longshore and other strike leaders, active sympathizers and supporters, as well as real radicals (how was one to know?) and Communists, officials and representatives, participants, hangers-on, and bystanders at various real and alleged Communist Party and Party group headquarters, halls, offices. (See Chapter 17.) The terms are used in these pages in their broadest, generic meanings.

21. See Resner, *Law in Action*, 1.

22. Eliel, *Waterfront Strikes*, 16.

23. Quoted in Eliel, *Waterfront Strikes*, 19.

24. Eliel, *Waterfront Strikes*, 14; "Bulletin 2," *Western Worker*, May 9, 1934.

25. Eliel, *Waterfront Strikes*, 21.

Chapter 10

1. David F. Selvin, *Sky Full of Storm*, (San Francisco: California Historical Society, revised edition, 1975), 13.

2. See Selvin, *Sky*.

3. Selig Perlman and Philip Taft, *History of Labor in the United States, 1896–1932, Volume IV: Labor Movements* (New York: The Macmillan Co., 1935), 161.

4. Plant, "American-Hawaiian," 56.

5. Paul Eliel, "Labor Problems in Our Steamship Business," *Yale Review* 26: March 1937, 510.

6. Plant, "American-Hawaiian," 56.

7. NLB, *Proceedings*, July 9, 1934, 14.

8. NLB, *Proceedings*, July 9, 1934, 14.

9. Schmidt, "Secondary Leadership," 61.

10. NLB, *Proceedings*, July 9, 1934, 5.

11. Phleger, "Sixty Years," 80.

12. For the Federal account, see U.S. Congress, Senate Committee on Labor and Education. Digest of report: Industrial munitions. U.S. Government Printing Office, 1939; also Larrowe, *Harry Bridges*, 3, 39; Clements, "Dynamics," 200.

13. Schmidt, "Secondary Leadership," 80.

14. Quin, *Big Strike*, 59.

15. Schmidt, "Secondary Leadership," 80; Quin, *Big Strike*, 57; Bridges tapes, No. 8.

16. Quoted in Clements, "Dynamics," 172; Eliel, *Waterfront Strikes*, 26.

17. Quoted in Larrowe, *Harry Bridges*, 45.

18. Eliel, *Waterfront Strikes*, 26.

19. Eliel, *Waterfront Strikes*, 27.

20. See Larrowe, *Harry Bridges*, 47; Lapham, "An Interview," 84; Phleger, "Sixty Years," 83; Bernstein, *Turbulent Years*, 266.

21. Eliel, *Waterfront Strikes*, 31, 32.

22. Ryan quoted in Larrowe, *Harry Bridges;* Lewis in NLB, *Proceedings*, 129.

23. Eliel, *Waterfront Strikes*, 34.

24. See Eliel, *Waterfront Strikes*, 33–40; Quin, *Big Strike*, 61; Schmidt, "Secondary Leadership," 84; Perry & Perry, *A History*, 368; NLB, *Proceedings*, 129, 729; Larrowe, "The Great Maritime Strike of '34," Part I. *Labor History* 11:4 (Fall 1970) 441.

Chapter 11

1. New Economics Group, *Preliminary testimony taken by the San Francisco Committee Against Police Brutality*, pamphlet (San Francisco, 1934).

2. Estolv E. Ward, *Harry Bridges on Trial* (New York: Modern Age Books, 1940), 150.

3. Schmidt, "Secondary Leadership," 85.

4. Eliel, *Waterfront Strikes*, 36.

5. Telegram, WEU to Grady, June 5, 1934; Ryan quoted in Eliel, *Waterfront Strikes*, 216.

6. Schmidt, "Secondary Leadership," 88.

7. Adrien J. Falk, "An Interview with Adrien J. Falk," an oral history interview by Corinne L. Gilb (Regional Oral History Office, The Bancroft Library, University of California, Berkeley, 1955), 65.

8. Melnikow, "Henry Melnikow," 102.

9. Storie, "Employer Organizations," 40.

10. Melnikow, "Henry Melnilow," 102.

11. Eliel, *Waterfront Strikes*, 44.

12. Quoted in Charles P. Larrowe, "The Great Maritime Strike of '34," Part I. *Labor History:* 11:4 (Fall 1970), 443.

13. Kagel, comment to author.

14. Eliel, *Waterfront Strikes*, 42.

15. Eliel, *Waterfront Strikes:* Mailliard letter, 55; ILA reply, 210; Forbes response, 211.

16. Lapham, "An Interview," 86.

17. *News*, June 13, 1934; Eliel, *Waterfront Strikes*, 60.

18. Eliel, *Waterfront Strikes*, 217.

19. U.S. Congress, Senate Committee on Labor and Education. Report: "Employers associations and collective bargaining in California," chapters 1 and 2, 75th Congress, 1939–1941, 121.

20. Eliel, *Waterfront Strikes*, 58.

21. Eliel, *Waterfront Strikes*, 58.

22. NLB, *Proceedings*, 736.

23. Quoted in Eliel, *Waterfront Strikes*, 76.

Chapter 12

1. Bernstein, *Turbulent Years*, 451.

2. U.S. Congress. Senate Committee on Labor and Education, "Employer Associations," 121.

3. NLB, *Proceedings*, 737.

4. Eliel, *Waterfront Strikes*, 220.

5. Eliel, *Waterfront Strikes*, 81; Magden and Martinson, *Working Waterfront*, 114; *Chronicle*, June 18, 1934.

6. *Chronicle*, June 18, 1934.

7. Quoted in Larrowe, "Great Maritime Strike," Part I: 446.

8. NLB, *Proceedings*, July 11, 1934, 127.

9. The letters of the Joint Marine Strike Committee and the Waterfront Employers' Union are published in NLB, *Proceedings*, July 11, 1934, 127.

10. Quoted in Eliel, *Waterfront Strikes*, 222.

11. Letter to San Francisco Labor Council, SFLC *Records*.

12. Darcy, *The Hawsepipe*, (November–December, 1982), 2.

13. Quoted in Clements, "Dynamics," 94.

14. Letter, Machinists, Lodge 68 to San Francisco Labor Council, *Records*.

15. Storie, "Employer Organizations," 41.

16. Quoted in Eliel, *Waterfront Strikes*, 90.

17. Quoted in Eliel, *Waterfront Strikes*, 91.

18. Quoted in Eliel, *Waterfront Strikes*, 85.

19. Eliel, *Waterfront Strikes*, 93.

20. Memorandum, [Charles] Wyzanski to Secretary of Labor, June 22, 1934.

21. Eliel, *Waterfront Strikes*, 95.

22. Melnikow, "Henry Melnikow," 199.

23. Lapham, "An Interview," 226.

24. Lapham, "An Interview," 226.

25. Quin, *Great Strike*, 100.

26. *Call-Bulletin*, June 28, 1934; quoted in Larrowe, *Harry Bridges*, 58.

27. *Call-Bulletin*, June 27, 1934; Eliel, *Waterfront Strikes*, 101.

Chapter 13

1. This account of the opening of the port is drawn from the observations and recollections of eyewitnesses and participants, including principally the daily newspapers; Schmidt, "Secondary Leadership"; Bulcke, "Longshore Leader"; Brown, "Dividends and Stevedores"; Storie, "Employer Organizations"; Phleger, "Sixty Years"; Hedley, *And I Have Seen It*; Eliel, *Waterfront Strikes*; Quin, *Great Strike*; and anonymous eyewitness statements held in the ILWU library, San Francisco.

2. Eliel, *Waterfront Strikes*, 227.

3. Storie, "Employer Organizations," 45.

4. Brown, "Dividends and Stevedores," 52.

5. Schmidt, "Secondary Leadership," 91.

6. *News*, August 2, 1954.

7. Quoted in Larrowe, *Harry Bridges*, 40, 67.

8. Engle's affidavit is reprinted in Clements, *Dynamics*, 210.

9. Quoted in Larrowe, *Harry Bridges*, 34.

10. *Examiner*, July 6, 1934, quoted in Eliel, *Waterfront Strikes*, 114.

11. Eliel, *Waterfront Strikes*, 115.

12. See *California Guardsman*, August 1934, 13; September 1934, 7.

13. Marvin McIntyre to FDR (FDR MS OF407b, box 11, file: Pacific Coast longshoremen's strike, 1934).

Chapter 14

1. The record of the days immediately following Bloody Thursday—the dramatic funeral of its victims on July 9 and the NLB July hearings—is drawn from the National

Longshoremen's Board; SFLC *Records*; ILA Strike Bulletins and leaflets; the *Chronicle*; the *New York Times*; *News*; *Examiner*; and Larrowe, *Harry Bridges*; Quin, *Big Strike*; and Eliel, *Waterfront Strikes*.

2. Sam Darcy (*The Hawsepipe*, November–December, 1982, 4) says that Bridges, in a secret meeting with "Vandeleur and Scharrenberg," agreed the meeting would not issue a general strike call in return for assurance that the Strike Strategy Committee would do so at the Labor Council meeting July 13. In 1934, Darcy had written ("The San Francisco Bay Area General Strike," *The Communist* 13 [October 1934], 991): "Our own leading comrades in the leadership of this conference, in deference to the wishes of this Strategy Committee of Seven, decided not to take final action on that day until the Strategy Committee had the chance to do something."

3. Sam Kagel, "Hotel Strike Series," an oral history interview (Oral History Program, California Historical Society, San Francisco, March 1987).

4. Melnilow, "Henry Melnikow," 182.

5. Quoted in Eliel, *Waterfront Strikes*, 123, 124.

6. Letter, July 8, 1934, SFLC *Records*.

7. Hedley, *As I Have Seen It*, 9.

8. The hearings are reported verbatim in NLB, *Proceedings*, July 9, 10, 11, 1934, and, unlike the arbitration hearings, are cited by date.

9. Eliel, *Waterfront Strikes*, 120.

10. Quoted in Larrowe, *Harry Bridges*, 77.

11. See, among others, Eliel, *Waterfront Strikes*, 131; Larrowe, *Harry Bridges*, 77; Quin, *Big Strike*, 135.

Chapter 15

1. Again, the course of the fast-moving dispute is covered in the full range of sources: the newspapers, union and employer press statements, the more academic studies (Eliel, Larrowe, Clements), minutes of the labor groups, as well as others cited in footnotes below. My account is constructed from the broad sweep of the participants and observers.

2. *Call-Bulletin*, July 13, 1934.

3. *Examiner*, July 13, 1934.

4. Joseph Paul St. Sure, "Comments on Employer Organizations and Collective Bargaining in Northern California Since 1934," an oral history interview (Institute of Industrial Relations, University of California, Berkeley, 1957), 69.

5. See "Who owns the San Francisco Police," August 29, 1934, and "A report on the Industrial Association" and "A denial," October 10, 1934 in the *Nation*.

6. James A. Moffett to Marvin McIntyre, July 14, 1934 (FDR MS OF407b, box 11, file: Pacific Coast longshoremen's strike, 1934).

7. Lapham, "An Interview," 86.

8. Telegram, McIntyre for FDR, July 15, 1934 (FDR MS OF407b, box 11, file: Pacific Coast longshoremen's strike, 1934).

9. Paul C. Smith, *Personal File* (New York: Appleton-Century, 1964), 152.

10. John F. Neylan, "Politics, Law, and the University of California," an oral history interview by Walton E. Bean and Corinne L. Gilb (Regional Oral History Office, The Bancroft Library, University of California, Berkeley, 1954), 145.

11. Neylan, "Politics," introduction.

12. See Earl Burke, "Dailies Help Break General Strike," Editor & Publisher 67: July 28, 1934, 5.

13. Smith, *Personal File*, 152.

14. Lapham, "An Interview," 88.

15. Lapham, "An Interview," 89.

16. Frances Perkins, *The Roosevelt I Knew*, (London: Hammond, Hammond & Co., Ltd., 1947), 253.

17. Telegram, Hiram Johnson to Secretary of the Interior Ickes, July 15, 1934 (FDR MS OF407b, box 11, file: Pacific Coast longshoremen's strike, 1934).

18. Telegram, Louise Howe to President, July 15, 1934 (FDR MS OF407b, box 11, file: Pacific Coast longshoremen's strike, 1934).

19. *Chronicle*, July 15, 1934.

20. President to White House, July 16, 1934 (FDR MS OF407b, box 11, file: Pacific Coast longshoremen's strike, 1934).

21. Lapham, "An Interview," 89.

22. Melnikow, "Henry Melnikow," 186.

23. *Chronicle*, July 16, 1934.

Chapter 16

1. Eliel, *Waterfront Strikes*, 150.

2. St. Sure, "Comments," 72.

3. Robert S. Ash, "Alameda County Central Labour Council During the Warren Years," an oral history interview by Miriam Feingold (Regional Oral History Office, Bancroft Library, University of California, Berkeley, 1972), 13.

4. Mayor Rossi to Governor Merriam, July 16, 1934, in Eliel, *Waterfront Strikes*, 153.

5. Walter Lippmann, *Interpretations: 1933–1935* (New York: The Macmillan Co., 1936), 136.

6. Harold J. Laski, "The Problems of the General Strike," *Nation* 139: August 15, 1934, 179.

7. *Examiner*, July 17, 1934.

8. *Chronicle*, July 17, 1934.

9. Reprinted in *Call-Bulletin*, July 17, 1934.

10. Quoted in the *New York Times*, July 18, 1934.

11. Quoted in Kenneth Stewart, "The Free Press in California," *American Mercury* 34: January 1935.

12. *News*, July 17, 1934.

13. *New York Times*, July 17, 1934.

Chapter 17

1. The account of the July 17 raids draws heavily on newspaper reports even though they were strongly, even viciously, pejorative, and often exaggerated and fanciful. But the reports covered a wide range of events in abundant detail.

2. Eliel, *Waterfront Strikes*, 159; 164; Clements, "Dynamics"; William F. Dunne, *The Great San Francisco General Strike: The Story of the West Coast Strike—The Bay Counties General Strike and the Maritime Workers Strike* (New York: Workers Library Publishers, 1934) 19; Darcy, *The Communist*, October 1934, 998.

3. Hugh S. Johnson, *The Blue Eagle from Egg to Earth* (Garden City, N.Y.: Doubleday, Doran & Co., 1935) 323.

4. Evelyn Seeley, "Journalistic Strikebreakers," *New Republic*, 79: August 1, 1934, 311.

5. Quin, *Big Strike*, 161.

6. *Chronicle*, July 19, 1934.

7. *New York Times*, July 18, 1934.

8. "Report on the Industrial Association," *Nation*, October 10, 1934.

9. Resner, *Law in Action*, 26.

10. *Chronicle*, July 18, 1934.

11. Lew Levenson, "California Casualty List," *Nation*, 139: August 29, 1934, 243–45.

12. John Terry, "The Terror in San Jose," *Nation*, 139: August 8, 1934, 161–62.

13. Quoted in Larrowe, *Harry Bridges*, 34.

14. See Neylan, "Politics."

15. *Call-Bulletin*, July 17, 1934.

16. Phleger, "Sixty Years," 80.

17. "Who Owns the San Francisco Police," *Nation*, August 29, 1934, 228; "A Report on the Industrial Association," *Nation*, October 10, 1934, 410.

18. Edward L. Levenson, *I Break Strikes! The Technique of Pearl L. Bergoff* (New York: Arno & The New York Times, 1969), 290.

19. Resner, *Law in Action*, 44.

20. *Minutes*, San Francisco Board of Police Commissioners, July 1934.

21. Resner, *Law in Action*, 46.

22. Quoted in Larrowe, *Harry Bridges*, 34.

23. Robert Cantwell, "War on the East Coast," *New Republic*, August 1, 1934, 308; Unsigned, *New Republic*, August 1, 1934, 305.

24. Miriam Allen De Ford, "San Francisco: An Autopsy on the General Strike," *Nation* 139: August 1, 1934, 65.

25. Quin, *Big Strike*, 149.

26. *Call-Bulletin*, July 16, 1934.

Chapter 18

1. Dr. Orrin K. McMurray, quoted in *News*, July 17, 1934.

2. Schlesinger, *The Age of Roosevelt*, 105.

3. Lapham, "An Interview," 91.

4. Johnson, *Blue Eagle*, 325.

5. *New York Times*, July 18, 1934.

6. Johnson, *Blue Eagle*, 324.

7. St. Sure, "Comments," 75.

8. TRB, *New Republic*, 79: August 1, 1934.

9. Letter, Neylan to Mrs. Michael Casey, May 7, 1937, in John Francis Neylan, *Papers* (Bancroft Library, University of California, Berkeley).

10. Letter, Neylan to F. C. Atherton, August 16, 1934, in Neylan, *Papers*.

11. Storie, "Employer Organizations," 54.

12. *Chronicle*, July 18, 1934.

13. Quoted in Clements, *Dynamics*, 240, from Neylan, *Papers*.

14. Telegram, [Marvin] McIntyre for the President (FDR MS OF407b, box 11, file: Pacific Coast longshoremen's strike, 1934).

Chapter 19

1. General Strike Committee, *Minutes*, July 18, 1934.

2. Eliel, *Waterfront Strikes*, 166.

3. *Chronicle*, July 18, 1934.

4. *Examiner*, July 18, 1934.

5. *New York Daily News*, July 18, 1934.

6. Oakland *Post-Enquirer*, July 18, 1934.

7. *New York Times*, July 18, 1934.

8. *Chronicle*, July 19, 1934.

9. *New York Times*, July 19, 1934, *et seq.*

10. *New York Times*, July 19, 20, 1934.

11. Oakland *Post-Enquirer*, July 18, 1934.
12. Quoted in Resner, *Law in Action*, 37.
13. *Chronicle, New York Times*, July 18, 1934.
14. *News*, July 18, 1934.
15. General Strike Committee, executive committee, *Minutes*, July 18, 1934.
16. *New York Times*, July 18, 1934.

Chapter 20

1. General Strike Committee, *Minutes*, July 19, 1934.
2. General Strike Committee, *Minutes*, July 19, 1934.
3. Yellen, *American Labor Struggles*, 353.
4. Oakland *Post-Enquirer*, July 19, 1934.
5. See Resner, *Law in Action*; also, *New York Times*, July 19, 23, 29, 1934.
6. See Buchanan, *Dock Strike*; also, *News*, July 18, 1934; Oakland *Tribune*, July 18, 1934; *Chronicle*, July 19, 1934; *New York Times*, July 19, 20, 21, 22, 1934.
7. Telegram, Johnson to FDR (FDR MS OF407b box 5: Strikes).
8. Kagel, *Interview*, 1.
9. Quoted in Larrowe, *Harry Bridges*, 86.
10. ILWU, *Three Decades*, 18.
11. Neylan, "Politics," 78.
12. St. Sure, "Comments," 78.
13. Phleger, "Sixty Years," 85.
14. *New York Times*, July 21, 1934.
15. Quoted in Resner, *Law in Action*, 39.
16. Resner, *Law in Action*, 282.
17. Resner, *Law in Action*, 19.
18. Nelson, *Maritime Unionism*, 254.
19. ILA Strike Bulletin 25, July 23, 1934.
20. Eliel, *Waterfront Strikes*, 180.

Chapter 21

1. *New York Times*, July 21, 1934.
2. *New York Times*, July 21, 1934.
3. Quoted in Clements, "Dynamics," 274.
4. See Herb Mills and David Wellman, "Contractually Sanctioned Job Action and Workers' Control: The Case of the San Francisco Longshoremen," *Labor History*, 28:2 (Spring 1987), 167; also Nelson, *Maritime Unionism*.
5. Plant, *Pacific Coast Longshore History*.
6. Schmidt, "Secondary Leadership," 49.

Afterword

1. See Darcy, *The Communist* 13: July 1934, 664; October 1934, 985; and Sam Darcy, *The Hawsepipe* Vol. I, No. 6 (September–October, 1982); Vol. II, No. 1 (November–December, 1982).
2. Quin, *Big Strike*.
3. Larrowe, *Harry Bridges*.
4. Nelson, *Workers on the Waterfront*.
5. David Brody, *Workers in Industrial America: Essays on the Twentieth Century Struggle* (New York and Oxford: Oxford University Press, 1980), 128.

BIBLIOGRAPHY

AFL Rank & File Committee, *The Lessons of the Bay District 1934 General Strike* (pamphlet, nd), AFL Rank & File Committee of Oakland.

Adamic, Louis, "Harry Bridges: Rank-and-File Leader," *Nation* 142: 6 May 1936, 576.

Adams, William, "The Shipping Conspiracy," *Nation* 139: September 5, 12, 1934.

Ash, Robert S., "Alameda County Central Labor Council During the Warren Years," an oral history interview by Miriam Feingold (Regional Oral History Office, The Bancroft Library, University of California, Berkeley, 1972).

Bartlett, Alan V., "The Great Depression in San Francisco: Financing City Government," revised seminar paper, History 790, San Francisco State University, 1978.

Bernstein, Irving, *The Turbulent Years* (Boston: Houghton Mifflin Co., 1970).

Boyer, Richard and Herbert Morris, *Labor's Untold Story* (New York: Cameron Associates, 1955).

Brecher, Jeremy, *Strike!* (San Francisco: Straight Arrow Books, 1972).

Bridges, Harry, interviewed by Nikki Bridges, undated, cited by Robert Cherny in unpublished manuscript on Harry Bridges.

Bridges, Harry, Defense Committee, *Harry Bridges: Who He Is . . .* (San Francisco: The committee, undated).

Brody, David, *Workers in Industrial America: Essays on the Twentieth Century Struggle* (New York: Oxford University Press, 1980).

Brown, Donald Mackenzie, "Dividends and Stevedores," *Scribner's Magazine:* January, 1935, 52.

Brown, Giles T., "The West Coast Phase of the Maritime Strike of 1921," *Pacific Historical Review:* 19 (November) 1950.

Buchanan, Roger, *Dock Strike* (Everett, Wash.: The Working Press, 1975).

Bulcke, Germain, "A Longshoreman's Observations," an oral history interview by Frank Jones in "Labor Looks at Earl Warren" (Regional Oral History Office, The Bancroft Library, University of California, Berkeley, 1970).

———, "Longshore Leader and ILWU-PMA Arbitrator," an oral history interview by Estolv E. Ward (Regional Oral History Office, The Bancroft Library, University of California, Berkeley, 1984).

Burke, Earl, *Editor & Publisher* 67: July 21, 1934.

——, "Dailies Helped Break General Strike," *Editor & Publisher* 67: July 28, 1934, 5.

California Guardsman, August, September, 1934.

California State Unemployment Commission, *Abstract of Hearings on Unemployment*, April and May, 1932.

Camp, William Martin, *San Francisco: Port of Gold* (Garden City, New York: Doubleday & Co., Inc., 1948).

Cantwell, Robert, "War on the West Coast," *New Republic* 79: August 1, 1934.

——, "San Francisco: Act One," *New Republic* 79: July 25, 1934, 280; *see also* October 10, 1934, 245.

Chaplin, Ralph, *Wobbly* (Chicago: University of Chicago Press, 1948).

Chaudet, Joseph W., "A Printer's View," an oral history interview by Frank Jones in "Labor Looks at Earl Warren," (Regional Oral History Office, Bancroft Library, University of California, Berkeley, 1970).

Chiles, Frederic, "General Strike: San Francisco, 1934—An Historical Compilation Film Storyboard," *Labor History* 22, No. 3 (Summer, 1981), 430.

Clements, Joyce Maxine, "The San Francisco Maritime and General Strikes of 1934 and The Dynamics of Repression," D. Crim. diss., University of California, Berkeley, 1975.

Conboy, William J., "Teamster Life in San Francisco," an oral history interview (Institute of Industrial Relations, University of California, Berkeley, 1957).

Crook, Wilfrid, *Communism and the General Strike* (Hamden, Conn.: Shoestring Press, 1960).

Cross, Ira B., *A History of the Labor Movement in California* (Berkeley: University of California Press, 1935).

——, *California Labor Notes* (1847–1932). The Bancroft Library, University of California, Berkeley).

Crowley, Thomas, "Recollections of the San Francisco Waterfront," an oral history interview by Willa K. Baum and Karl Kortum (Regional Oral History Office, The Bancroft Library, University of California, Berkeley, 1967).

Darcy, Sam, "The Great West Coast Maritime Strike," *The Communist* 13: July, 1934, 664.

——, "The San Francisco Bay Area General Strike," *The Communist* 13: October, 1934, 985.

——, "The San Francisco General Strike," *The Hawsepipe* (Marine Workers Historical Association). Vol. I, No. 6 (September–October, 1982); Vol. II, No. 1 (November–December, 1982).

Darcy, Sam-Robert W. Cherny letters, September 20, 1986 and October 17, 1986, in Professor Cherny's possession.

Deal, Clyde W., "The tide turns," (unpublished autobiography, nd).

De Ford, Miriam Allen, "Labor Bids for Power," *Nation*, 139: July 18, 1934, 65.

——, "San Francisco: An Autopsy on the General Strike," *Nation* 139: August 1, 1934, 121.

Dellums, C. L., "International President of the Brotherhood of Sleeping Car Porters and Civil Rights Leader," an oral history interview by Joyce A. Henderson (Regional Oral History Office, The Bancroft Library, University of California, Berkeley, 1973).

Dunne, William F., *The Great San Francisco General Strike* (New York: Workers Library Publishers, 1934).

Durein, Theodore. "Scabs' Paradise," *Reader's Digest*, January, 1937, 19.

Eliel, Paul, *The Waterfront and General Strikes of San Francisco* (San Francisco: Industrial Association of San Francisco, 1934).

——, "Labor Problems in Our Steamship Business," *Yale Review* 26: March 1937, 510.

Falk, Adrien J., "An Interview with Adrien J. Falk," an oral history interview by Corinne L. Gilb (Regional Oral History Office, The Bancroft Library, University of California, Berkeley, 1955).

Figari, William, "San Francisco Bay and the Waterfront," an oral history interview (Regional Oral History Office, The Bancroft Library, University of California, Berkeley).

Francis, Robert Coleman, A History of Labor on the San Francisco Waterfront, Ph.D. diss., University of California, 1934.

General Strike Committee, Minutes, ILWU Library, San Francisco.

Goldblatt, Louis, "Working Class Leader," an oral history interview by Estolv E. Ward (Regional Oral History Office, The Bancroft Library, University of California, Berkeley, 1980).

Goldbloom, Maurice and others, "The San Francisco General Strike," in *Strikes Under the New Deal*, (New York: League for Industrial Democracy, 1936).

Green, James, "Working Class Militancy in the Depression," *Radical America* 6:6 (November–December 1972), 1.

Hamilton, Iris. "General Strike," *New Masses* 12: July 24, 1934, 9.

Hedley, George P., *The Strike as I Have Seen It* (a pamphlet), San Francisco: Conference for Labor's Civil Rights, 1934.

Heide, Paul, "A Warehouseman's Reminiscences," an oral history interview by Frank Jones, in "Labor Looks at Earl Warren," (Regional Oral History Office, The Bancroft Library, University of California, Berkeley, 1970).

Hopkins, William S., "Employment Exchanges for Seamen," *American Economic Review* 25: June 1935, 250.

Hugo, Karl, "Strange Burial in San Francisco," *The Modern Monthly* 8:7, August, 1934, 396.

Industrial Association of San Francisco, "The American Plan," The Bancroft Library, University of California, Berkeley.

International Longshoremen's Association, Local 38-79, Minutes of general meetings, 1933–July, 1934, International Longshoremen's & Warehousemen's Union Library, San Francisco.

International Longshoremen's Association, Pacific Coast District. *Proceedings of the 27th annual convention*, February 25–March 6, 1934.

International Longshoremen's & Warehousemen's Union, *The ILWU Story: Three Decades of Militant Unionism* (San Francisco: ILWU, ca. 1963).

International Longshoremen's & Warehousemen's Union, Local 38-79, *The truth about the waterfront* (pamphlet), 1934.

International Longshoremen's & Warehousemen's Union, *Case files: Early ILA organization, 1931–1933*, San Francisco: ILWU Library.

International Longshoremen's & Warehousemen's Union, ILWU manuscript collection: "Indices to National Longshoremen's Board Hearings," San Francisco: ILWU Library.

Johnson, Hugh S., Papers, 1914–1934, The Bancroft Library, University of California, Berkeley.

———, *The Blue Eagle from Egg to Earth* (Garden City, New York: Doubleday, Doran & Co., 1935).

Joint Marine Strike Committee, *Joint Marine Journal*, 1934.

Joint Marine Strike Committee, *Minutes*, ILWU Library.

Kagel, John, "The Day The City Stopped," unpublished, in author's possession.

Kagel, Sam, "A Rightwing Dual Union," (1930), unpublished, copy in author's possession.

———, "Hotel Strike Series," oral history interview, (Oral History Program, California Historical Society, San Francisco, March, 1980).

Kimeldorf, Howard, *Reds or Rackets? The Making of Radical and Conservative Unions on the Waterfront* (Berkeley and Los Angeles: University of California Press, 1988).

Knight, Robert Edward Lee, *Industrial Relations in the San Francisco Bay Area* (Berkeley and Los Angeles: University of California Press, 1960).

Lapham, Roger Dearborn, Papers (n.d.) The Bancroft Library, University of California, Berkeley, and the California Historical Society, San Francisco.

————, "An Interview on Shipping, Labor, City Government, and American Foreign Aid," an oral history interview by Corinne L. Gilb (Regional Oral History Office, The Bancroft Library, University of California, Berkeley, 1957).

LaPiere, Richard T., "The General Strike in San Francisco: A Study of the Revolutionary Pattern," *Sociology and Social Research* XIX:4, March–April, 1935, 355.

Larrowe, Charles P., "The Great Maritime Strike of '34," *Labor History*. Part I (11:4): Fall, 1970, 404; Part II (12:1): Winter, 1971, 3.

————, *Harry Bridges: The Rise and Fall of Radical Labor in the United States* (New York and Westport: Lawrence Hill & Co., 1972).

Laski, Harold J., "The Problem of the General Strike," *Nation* 139: August 15, 1934, 179.

Lerner, Tillie, "The Strike," *Partisan Review* 1: September–October, 1934, 3.

Levenson, Lew, "California Casualty List," *Nation* 139: August 29, 1934, 243.

Levi, Steven C., *Committee of Vigilance, the San Francisco Chamber of Commerce Law and Order Committee, 1916–1919* (Jefferson, North Carolina and London: McFarland and Co., 1983).

Levinson, Edward. *I Break Strikes!* (New York: Arno & The New York Times, 1935) (reprint edition, 1969).

Lippmann, Walter, *Interpretations: 1933–1935* (New York: The Macmillan Co., 1936).

Lotchin, Roger W., "John Francis Neylan," unpublished article in Neylan, Papers.

Lynd, Staughton, "The Possibility of Radicalism in the Early 1930s: The Case of Steel," *Radical America* 6:6 (November–December 1972), 37.

Mabon, David White, "The West Coast Waterfront and Sympathy Strikes of 1934," Ph.D. diss. University of California, Berkeley, 1966.

McWilliams, Carey, *California: The Great Exception* (Santa Barbara and Salt Lake City: Peregrine Smith, Inc., 1976).

Magden, Ronald and A. D. Martinson, *The Working Waterfront: The Story of Tacoma's Ships and Men* (Tacoma: International Longshoremen's & Warehousemen's Union, Local 23 and Port of Tacoma, 1982).

Marine Workers Industrial Union, *Four fighting years: a short history of the MWIU*, ca. 1934.

Martin, George, *Madam Secretary* (Boston: Houghton Mifflin Co., 1976).

Matyas, Jennie, "Jennie Matyas and the ILGWU," an oral history interview by Corinne L. Gilb (Regional Oral History Office, The Bancroft Library, University of California, Berkeley, 1957).

Melnikow, Henry P., "Henry Melnikow and the National Labor Bureau," an oral history interview by Corinne L. Gilb (Institute of Industrial Relations, University of California, Berkeley, 1959).

Mettee, Grace, "Zero Hour on the Coast," *Nation* 139: July 23, 1934, 102.

Mills, Herb and David Wellman, "Contractually Sanctioned Job Action and Workers' Control: The Case of the San Francisco Longshoremen," *Labor History* 28: 2 (Spring 1987), 167.

Montgomery, David, *Workers' Control in America* (Cambridge: Cambridge University Press, 1979).

Nation, "Worse than the earthquake," 139: July 25, 1934, 89.

————, Editorial paragraph, 139: August 8, 1934, 141.

————, "Who Owns the San Francisco Police?" and "A Denial," 139: August 29, 1934.

————, "A Report on the Industrial Association," 139: October 10, 1934.

Nelson, Joseph Bruce, "Maritime unionism and working-class consciousness in the 1930s," Ph.D. diss. University of California, Berkeley, 1982.

————, *Workers on the Waterfront: Seamen, Longshoremen, and Unionism in the 1930s* (Urbana and Chicago: University of Illinois Press, 1988).

Neuberger, Richard L., "Bad-man Bridges," *The Forum*, April 1939, 195.

New Economics Group, *Preliminary testimony taken by the San Francisco Committee Against Police Brutality* (pamphlet), San Francisco, 1934.

New Republic, "Crack Down on the General!," 79: August 1, 1934.

———, "The Press as Strikebreaker," 79: August 8, 1934, 333.

Neylan, John F., "Politics, Law and the University of California," an oral history interview by Walton E. Bean and Corinne L. Gilb (Regional Oral History Office, The Bancroft Library, University of California, 1954).

———, Papers (ca. 1911–1960), The Bancroft Library, University of California, Berkeley.

O'Connell, John A., "Transforming a Company Union," *American Federationist*, January 1930, 61.

O'Conner, Larry, "The Facts Behind the San Francisco Strike," *Today*, September 8, 1934.

Pacific Coast Longshoremen's Strike, a collection of pamphlets (Social Sciences Graduate Library, University of California, Berkeley).

Palmer, Dwight L., "Pacific Coast Maritime Labor: A Study in Industrial Relations Before and Under NRA," Ph.D. diss., Stanford University, 1935.

Perkins, Frances, *The Roosevelt I Knew* (London: Hammond, Hammond & Co., Ltd., 1947).

Perlman, Selig and Philip Taft, *History of Labor in the United States 1896–1932*. Vol. IV: *Labor Movements* (New York: The Macmillan Company, 1935).

Perry, Louis B. and Richard S. Perry, *A History of the Los Angeles Labor Movement* (Berkeley: University of California Press, 1963).

Petersen, Walter J., *Marine Labor Union Leadership* (probably San Francisco: Employment Service Bureau, third edition, June 1925).

Phleger, Herman, "Sixty Years in Law, Public Service, and International Affairs," an oral history interview by Miriam S. Stein (Regional Oral History Office, The Bancroft Library, University of California, Berkeley, 1970).

Plant, Thomas G., *Pacific Coast Longshore History*, a speech to the Waterfront Employers Association, February 14, 1940.

———, "The American-Hawaiian Steamship Co.," an oral history interview (unfinished) (Institute of Industrial Relations, University of California, Berkeley, 1962).

Police and Peace Officers' Journal XII: 5, 7 (May, July, 1934).

Preston, William, "Shall This be All? U.S. Historians versus William D. Haywood et al." *Labor History* 12:3 (Summer 1971), 435.

Quin, Mike, *The Big Strike* (Olema, California: Olema Publishing Co., 1949).

Resner, Herbert, *The Law in Action During the San Francisco Longshore and Maritime Strike of 1934* (Works Progress Administration project, sponsored by the Division of Law Enforcement, Department of Industrial Relations, State of California, 1936).

Riesenberg, Felix, Jr., *Golden Gate: The Story of San Francisco Harbor* (New York: Knopf, 1940).

Robinson, Robert McClure, "Maritime Labor in San Francisco, 1933–37," master's thesis, University of California, 1938.

———, "A History of the Teamster's Union in the San Francisco Bay Area, 1850–1950," Ph.D. diss., University of California, Berkeley, 1951.

Rossi, Angelo J., "The Truth About the Maritime Strike," radio broadcast, January 5, 1937.

Ryan, Frederic L., *Industrial Relations in the San Francisco Building Trades* (Norman: University of Oklahoma Press, 1936).

San Francisco Labor Council, *Records*, The Bancroft Library, University of California, Berkeley.

San Francisco Police Commission, *Minutes*, July 16–21, 1934.

San Francisco Waterfront Strikes: 1934, a collection, Social Sciences Graduate Library, University of California, Berkeley.

Scharrenberg, Paul, "Paul Scharrenberg Reminiscences," an oral history interview by Corinne L. Gilb (Regional Oral History Office, The Bancroft Library, University of California, Berkeley, 1954).

———, *Papers* (1893–1960) The Bancroft Library, University of California, Berkeley.

Schlesinger, Arthur M., Jr., *The Age of Roosevelt: The Crisis of the Old Order*, Volume 1. (Boston: Houghton Mifflin Co., 1957)

———, *The Age of Roosevelt: The Coming of the New Deal*, Volume 2. (Boston: Houghton Mifflin Co., 1959).

Schmidt, Henry, "San Francisco Maritime Strike Statements," unpublished, ca. 1935, in ILWU Library, San Francisco.

———, "Secondary Leadership in the ILWU, 1933–1936," an oral history interview by Miriam F. Stein and Estolv Ethan Ward (Regional Oral History Office, The Bancroft Library, University of California, Berkeley, 1983).

Schneider, Betty and Abraham Siegel, *Industrial Relations in the Pacific Coast Longshore Industry* (Institute of Industrial Relations, University of California, Berkeley, 1956).

Schwartz, Harvey, *The March Inland: Origins of the ILWU Warehouse Division* (Los Angeles: Institute of Industrial Relations, University of California, 1978).

———, "Harry Bridges and The Scholars: Looking at History's Verdict," *California History* LIX: No. 1 (Spring, 1980), 66.

Schwartz, Stephen, *Brotherhood of the Sea: A History of the Sailors' Union of the Pacific*, excerpts (San Francisco: Sailors' Union of the Pacific, 1985).

Seeley, Evelyn, "San Francisco's Labor War," *Nation*, 138: June 13, 1934, 672.

———, "Journalistic Strikebreakers," *New Republic* 79: August 1, 1934, 310.

Selvin, David F., *Sky Full of Storm* (San Francisco: California Historical Society, rev. ed 1975).

Slobodek, Mitchell, *A Selective Bibliography of California Labor History* (Institute of Industrial Relations, University of California, Los Angeles, 1964).

Smith, Paul C., *Personal File* (New York: Appleton-Century, 1964).

St. Sure, Joseph Paul, "Comments on Employer Organizations and Collective Bargaining in Northern California Since 1934," an oral history interview (Institute of Industrial Relations, University of California, Berkeley, 1957).

Steffens, Lincoln, *Lincoln Steffens Speaking* (New York: Harcourt Brace, 1936).

Stewart, Kenneth, "The Free Press in California," *American Mercury* 34: January 1935.

Storie, William G., "Employer Organizations in San Francisco: President of San Francisco Employers' Council," an oral history interview by Corinne L. Gilb (Institute of Industrial Relations, University of California, Berkeley, 1959).

Strike Bulletin, Joint Strike Committee of the International Seamen's Union (Pacific Coast District), 1934.

Symes, Lillian, "Thunder over San Francisco," *The Modern Monthly* 8: 7, August 1934.

A symposium on Andrew Furuseth (New Bedford, Mass.: Darwin Press, ca. 1949).

Taylor, Frank J., "Behind the San Francisco Strike," *Nation's Business* 23: March, 1935, 25.

Taylor, Paul S., Materials on Agricultural and Maritime Strikes in California, The Bancroft Library, University of California, Berkeley.

Taylor, Paul S. and Norman Leon Gold, "San Francisco and the General Strike," *Survey Graphic* 23: September, 1934, 405.

Tulledo, Stan, "The Least Creditable Performance: How the San Francisco Press Published to Break the 1934 General Strike," *New Labor Review* 6: Spring 1934, 83.

U.S., Department of Labor, "Longshore Labor Conditions in the United States," *Monthly Labor Review* 31: November, 1930, 19.

U.S., National Longshoremen's Board, *Proceedings: July 9–11, August 8 et seq., 1934* with exhibits, unpublished. The Bancroft Library, University of California, Berkeley.

U.S. Congress, Senate Committee on Education and Labor, *Violations of Free Speech and*

Rights of Labor: Employer Associations and Collective Bargaining in California, chapters 1 and 2., 75th Congress, 1939–1941.

U.S. Congress, Senate Committee on Education and Labor, *Industrial Munitions*, digest of report (U.S. Government Printing Office, 1939).

U.S. Congress, Senate Committee on Education and Labor, *Violations of Free Speech and Rights of Labor*, hearings, San Francisco, January 26–27, 1940.

Vernon, Ernest H., "A Machinist's Recollection," in "Labor Looks at Earl Warren," an oral history interview by Frank Jones (Regional Oral History Office, The Bancroft Library, University of California, Berkeley, 1970).

Walsh, Victor Anthony, *The International Longshoremen's Association: The Rebirth of a Union*, master's thesis, San Francisco State College, 1971.

Ward, Estolv E., *Harry Bridges on Trial*, (New York: Modern Age Books, 1940).

Waterfront Employers Union of San Francisco, circulars and releases 1934–1937 (Social Sciences Graduate Library, University of California, Berkeley).

Waterfront Worker, 1932–1933 (Library, International Longshoremen's & Warehousemen's Union, San Francisco).

Waterfront Workers' Federation, *The Longshoremen's Strike* (San Francisco: Waterfront Workers' Federation, August 23, 1916).

Watkins, T. H. and R. R. Olmsted, *Mirror of the Dream* (San Francisco: Scrimshaw Press, 1976).

Weintraub, Hyman, *Andrew Furuseth: Emancipator of the Seamen* (Berkeley and Los Angeles: University of California Press, 1959).

Wilson, Walter, "Lords of the Docks," *American Mercury* 33: 132, December 1934.

Winter, Ella, "Stevedores on Strike," *New Republic* 79: June 13, 1934, 120.

Yellen, Samuel, *American Labor Struggles* (New York: Harcourt Brace & Co., 1936).

INDEX

Alameda County Central Labor Council, vote on general strike, 163
Alaska, feed and supply, 115
Alexander, Wallace M., 73
American-Hawaiian Steamship Company, 25; dividends, 71; wage rates, 100
American Shipmasters' Association, 159
American Society of Marine Engineers, 100, 159
Andersen, George, 23, 94, 217
Anti-radical detail, 200
April 3 agreement, 83–86
Ash, Robert S., 185
Atlas Trucking Company, 134, 223

Barker, B. H., 102
Barrows, Major General David Prescott, 152, 214
Barry, John D., 191
Belt Line Railroad, 96–97, 118, 147
Bennett, Dewey, 65
Bergoff, Pearl L., 200
Billings, Warren, 28
Black, Elaine, 94, 224–25, 232
Black, Senator Hugo L., 59
Bloody Thursday, 11, 13–15, 149–50
Blue Book union, 45–47, 57–58; dues sweep, 60–61
Bordoise, Nick, 12, 13, 14, 149
Boynton, Managing Director Albert E., 73, 147, 218
Brady, District Attorney Matthew, 216, 232

Brass check loans, 36
Brennan, Charles, 95
Bridges, Harry, 9, 10, 12, 108, 114, 139, 148, 150–53, 210, 218–19, 228, 234–35; and Blue Book, 45; on brass check loans, 36; calls for strike committee, 80; city relief, 54; at coroner's inquest, 14; and Darcy, 64; describes shape-up, 34; directions to union committee, 78; NLB presentation, 161; objects to negotiations, 86; on output, 43; proposes food depots, 177; protests violence, 151, 153; rise to leadership, 63; response to radicalism charge, 79; shape-up at Matson dock, 62; on speed-up, 40, 41; at Teamsters meeting, 164–65; union reestablished, 62; unopposed for strike committee chairman, 87
Brier, Royce, 15, 228
Broun, Heywood, 190
Brown, Donald Mackenzie, 148
Brown, Frank, 156
Bryan, Jack, 44, 67
Bulcke, Germain, 46, 54, 59, 144

Cahill, Utilities Manager Edward G., 184
Cameron, Frank, 107
Cameron, George, 175
Carr, James, 171
Carson, Portland Mayor Joseph, 128, 226
Casey, Michael, 9, 23–24, 33, 117–18, 126, 135, 146, 208, 223; and Industrial As-

sociation, 117; and sympathy strikes, 95; and Neylan, 174; July 8 meeting, 158; July 11 meeting, 164–65

Casual employment, 35–36

Chamber of Commerce, San Francisco, 23, 26–28, 63

Chandler, Harry, 74

City Front Federation, 23, 25

City Front Labor Council, 22

Clothing Workers, Amalgamated, 60

Coast Seamen's Union, 22; formed, 32, 98. *See also* Sailors' Union of the Pacific

Coldwell, Colbert, 73

Collins, Leo, 233

Columbia River Longshoremen's Association, 65

Committee of five hundred, 199, 227

Communist Party: "our strikes," 64; Bridges as member, 63; Darcy, 64; policy reversal, 59

Cook, C. W., 25

Council of Wharf and Wave Unions, 22

Counderakis, Nick, 11–14. *See also* Bordoise, Nick

Cox, Local 38-79 Secretary Ivan, 67

Creel, regional NRA director George, 61, 78, 81–82

Cross, Ira B., 55

Crum, Bartley, 174

Cummings, Attorney General Homer S., 178

Cushing, Oscar K., 138, 238

Daffron, Shelby, 157, 236

Darcy, Sam, 58, 64, 241

Deadline, March 7, 77; strike March 23, 80

Deal, Clyde W., 169

Decasualization schemes, 38

DeGuire, Captain Arthur, 105

Derry, Charles, 156, 222

Dietrich, Eugene "Dutch," 10, 94, 233

Dock work, reduced pay, 42

Dollar, Captain Robert, 25, 26, 29

Dollar Lines, subsidies, 71

Dore, Seattle Mayor John F., to open port, 115–16

Durein, Theodore, 90, 91

Eliel, Paul, 16, 114–15, 118, 120, 223; on blacklisting, 99; on Blue Book union, 29

Eliot, Harvard President Charles William, 92

Ellison, E. E., 55

Employers' Association (1901), 23–24

Employer Service Bureau, 99

Engle, James, 150–51

Farley, Postmaster General James, 228

Federal Laboratories, Inc., 102, 103

Fink, 138, 161

Fink books, 234

Finnegan, John J., 160

Foisie, Frank P., 35, 50, 53, 65, 86, 115

Forbes, Industrial Association president John, 137; accepts Mailliard request, 121

Funeral for Bloody Thursday victims, 11–13, 15–17, 160–61

Furuseth, Andrew, 24, 99, 140, 234

Gage, Governor Henry T. Gage, 24

Gallagher, Andrew, 106

General strike, 17; activity resumed, 222; confusion in press, 169–70; days given up, 236; early proposals, 133; eggs undelivered, 168; end voted, 221; first day, 182–91; goals, 132–33; impact, 212–13; legal status, 178–79; no danger of, 157; oil companies halt deliveries, 167; parcel post loaded, 168; preparations, 167; real start, 166; recedes rapidly, 226; Red raids, 192–203; settlement emerging, 208; shoppers rush stores, 168; spreads, 166–67; unaffected by red raids, 202; view of, 10

General Strike Committee, 168–69; Derry amendment, 222; ends strike, 221; forces end, 227; Kidwell resolution, 209–210, 218; Muni carmen, 184–185; oil embargo lifted, 212; opens restaurants, 209; opens restaurants, butcher shops, 212; second Kidwell resolution, 221–222; settlement emerges, 203; trade union goals, 203

General strike, East Bay: Key System halts, 185; National Guard, 185; ready to join, 170; return to jobs, 223; union permits, 177; unions act, 158; unions vote, 163; vote on return, 215

General strike, Portland: cargo-handling resumed, 225; fuel shortage, 186; Mayor Joseph Carson, 226; National Guard,

General strike, Portland (*cont.*)
225; shoppers flood stores, 186; unions consider, 157; Wagner due, 186; Wagner fired on, 215
General strike, Seattle; Reynolds on, 215–16
Goldblatt, Louis, 114
Grade books, 99. *See also* Fink books
Grady, Dean Henry F., 81
Great Depression, 11, 18, 53–56
Green, William, 55, 60, 163–64, 168, 214

Haggerty, Daniel P., 154
Hanna, Archbishop Edward J., 138, 139, 161, 175–76
Harmony Club, 29
Hazards, job, 41–42
Hearst, William Randolph, 187, 237
Hedley, George P., 15, 151, 161
Helland, Ole, 236
Hickok, Lorena, 74
Hinckley, Robert H., 177
Hiring: cannot be arbitrated, 155; casual employment, 35–36; Cushion-Foot Olsen, 34; Department of Labor study, 36; discrimination, 42; employers disclaim abuses, 37; hiring hall under April 3 agreement, 86; job-buying, 36; joint hall plan, 67; longshore, Seattle, Portland, San Pedro, 30; McGrady proposal, 116; Plant describes, 35; Portland employers' hall, 51; San Pedro hall, 51–52; Seattle employers' joint scheme, 50–51; shape-up, 34; under decasualization schemes, 38; under June 16 agreement, 125; under NLB award, 239
Hiring clause, 61
Holman, Lee, 61; appointed organizer, 57; barred from office, 84–85; leads reorganization, 49
Hopkins, Harry, 74
Howard, International Typographical Union President, 176
Hull, Secretary of State Cordell, 178

Ickes, Secretary of the Interior Harold, 115, 179
ILA, Pacific Coast District, 24, 25; convention, 1934, 77–80; convention called, 68; negotiating demands, 77; Stern plan rejected, 67; strike vote, 67
ILA, Portland, 24; attempts reorganization,

48; denies charges, 121; proposes settlement, 122; representation plan, 65; strike committee, 80
ILA, ports in Oregon, Washington, 25
ILA, San Francisco: Holman attempts reorganization, 49; Ralph Mallen protests Kidwell resolution, 219; protests police action, 105–6; reaffirms coastwide unit, 117; reaffirms demands, 110; Red Book union revived, 58–59, 64; rejects May 28 agreement, 112; replies to Mailliard attack, 107; strike end betrayal, 227
ILA, San Pedro, 24; effort, 65; and Marine Service Bureau, 66
ILA, Seattle: hostilities renewed, 225; reorganizes, 48; representation plan, 65; spasmodic clashes, 186
ILA Strike Bulletin, 230
ILA, Tacoma, 24; between 1922–1931, 52; leads reorganization attempts, 48
Industrial Association, 16, 63, 95; involvement, 119–20; open shop drive, 1921, 72–73; plans to open port, 134–37; port opening July 2, 142; reporter network, 171; undercover surveillance, 76
Industrial conference, President Wilson's, 31
Industrial Workers of the World, 18, 26
International Labor Defense, 94
International Longshoremen's & Warehousemen's Union, 228
International Longshoremen's Association, organized, 22
International Seamen's Union, 218

Jackson, Harry, 160
Job action, 237–38
Job conditions, 39
Job distribution, 37–39
Johnson, General Hugh S., 210; adopts Neylan strategy, 218; arrives San Francisco, 204–5; and General Strike Committee, 219; Greek Theater speech, 194; open shop ruling, 73, 79, 82; unwelcome intervention, 207
Johnson, U.S. Senator Hiram, 179
Joint Marine Journal, 227
Joint Marine Strike Committee (JMSC), 129, 130
Jones-White Act, 70
June 19 mass meeting, 131

June 16 agreement, 123–26; aftermath, 128; settlement blows up, 127; terms, 124–25

Kagel, Sam, 9, 100, 118, 159, 227
Kidwell, George, 9, 169, 156–57, 180–81, 210, 221–22
Kingsbury, Kenneth, 173
Knights of Pythias, 12
Knowland, Joseph, 74
Knudsen, John, 236
Koster, Frederick J., 26, 73

Labor Clarion, 15
Ladies Garment Workers Union, International, 60
LaFollette Committee, 76, 127
LaFollette Seamen's Act 1915, 99
Lake Erie Chemical Co., 103
Lapham, Roger, 44, 63, 74–75, 134, 148, 173, 176, 178, 180, 218; and acting governor, 121; calls Perkins, 178; phones McIntyre, Perkins, 173
Larrowe, Charles P., 18, 243
Larsen, "Pirate," 111, 172
Laski, Harold J., 189
Law and Order Committee, 26–28. *See also* Chamber of Commerce, San Francisco
Lawrence, David, 190
Lazarus, Judge Sylvain, 217, 231–32
Leland, Coroner T. B., 150
Leonard, J. L., 83
Lewis, William, 39, 81, 84, 87, 88
Lindgren, Bruce, 236
Lindner, Clarence, 187
Lippmann, Walter, 189
Longshoremen, black, 96
Longshoremen's Association of San Francisco and Bay District, 29. *See also* Blue Book union
Longshoremen's Council of California, 47
London Morning Post, 190
London Sunday Graphic, 188
Los Angeles Times, 74

Marine Cooks and Stewards (MCS), 101
Marine Engineers' Beneficial Association (MEBA), 100
Marine, Firemen, Oilers, Watertenders and Wipers (MFOW) Association, 101
Marine Service Bureau, 234
Marine Workers Industrial Union (MWIU),

57–58, 160, 224; abandoned, 65; barred in General Strike Committee, 169; organizing campaign San Francisco, 48–49; policy reversal, 59; turns to seamen, 101
Maritime industry, Pacific Coast, 69–71; subsidies, 70–71
Maritime unions, ask joint return to work, 110
Marsh, Federal Conciliator E. P., 62
Martial law, 221
Masters, Mates and Pilots, National Organization of (MM&P), 101
Matson Navigation Company, 97; firings, 62–63; "Old Captain" [William], 25; profits, 71; special board, 61; strikers reinstated, 62; walkout, 61
Maxwell, Milton S., 156
May 28 agreement: hiring halls, 111; Northwest strike committees reject, 112; recognition, 111; Ryan, Plant offer proposal, 110–12; San Francisco strike committee objects, 111; San Pedro rejects, 112
McAulilffe, Florence, 187
McBean, Atholl, 73
McCann-Erickson, Inc., 123, 127, 162–63
McCarty, Ignatius H., 150; protests Federal's bill, 103
McClung, Ray, 180–81
McGrady, Edward Francis, 106, 139; attempts mediation, 106–7; charges radicalism, 107; policy, 180–81; reports red scare, 107; returns to Washington, 116; wires Perkins, 158
McIntyre, Marvin, 107, 172; wires Roosevelt, 153
McLaughlin, John P., 118, 208
Mechanization: forklift, 40; in hold, 40; motorized jitneys, 39; slingboards, 39
Meherin, Elenore, Easy Bay opinion, 223–24
Meier, Governor Julius, telegraphs President, 226
Melnikow, Henry P., 9, 23, 48, 73, 75, 118, 180–81
Merihew, David, 195
Mittelstaedt, Col. R. E., 152
Moffett, James, 173
Mooney, Tom, 28
Municipal Railway, carmen, 184–85

National Guard, 152–53, 187, 214, 230
National Longshoremen's Board: appointed June 26, 137–39; asks arbitration, 143; asks ILA to arbitrate, 219; calls on shipowners to accept arbitration, 219; Johnson as spokesman, 218; July hearings, 158–60, 161–62; longshoremen's award, 238–39; opens arbitration hearings, 238; proposal collapses, 154; seamen's award, 239
National Recovery Administration, 59
National Recovery Administration regional office, 61; refuses to intercede, 62
National Youth Day, 113
Nelson, Bruce, 18, 243–44
Newman, William, 113
Neylan, John Francis, 74, 131, 174–75, 210, 227; and General Johnson, 205–7; and Casey, 208; ice-water lunch, 228–29

Oakland Tribune, 74
O'Connell, John A., 84, 164–65; and Blue Book union, 46
O'Grady, E. B., 100, 159
Olsen, Charles, 14, 149
O'Neal, Edward A., 55
Open the port, plans to, 134–37, 139–40

Pacific Coast Labor Bureau, 9, 10
Pacific Gas & Electric Co., 168
Pacific Steamship Company, 97
Paris Temps, 190
Parker, Dick, 104
Perkins, Secretary of Labor Frances, 74; and Lapham, 173, 178; legal status of general strike, 178–79; telegram to Roosevelt, 173–74; telegraphs proposal, 135
Petersen, A. H., 38, 39, 41, 66
Petroleum Emergency Committee, 167
Pettis, John A., 61
Phelan, Mayor James D., 23
Phleger, Herman, 37, 74, 145, 148, 180, 229
Pidgeon, Arthur, 147
Pier 18 clash, 104–5
Plant, Thomas G., 25, 53, 75, 76, 79, 83, 87, 88, 92, 148, 159; describes hiring, 35; NLB presentation, 161; on 1919 strike, 28; on aftermath, 240; on Blue Book union, 29–30; on deadlock, 134; on output, 43; response to JMSC, 130
Police Department, San Francisco, orders teargas, 103

Port opening, July 2, 141–53; July 3, 143–46; July 4, 146–47; July 5, 147–53; July 5 confrontation at Steuart Street, 149–50 (*see also* Bloody Thursday); July 6, 154
Preparedness Day bombing, 27–28
Pressel, Leonard, 114
Printers' union, negotiations, 176
Publishers, British general strike, 187; antired invective, 202; coordinated efforts, 187–89; editorial unison, 131; identical editorials, 175

Quigle, E. A., 49
Quinn, Chief of Police William J., 12, 87, 105, 134, 139, 151, 167, 177–78, 195, 201. *See also* Red raids

Rand, Jean, 113
Rank-and-file caucus, 63–64; Albion Hall caucus, 63–64; Committee of 500, 61–62; emerging group, 59; tactics, goals, 64
Red raids, 192–203; anti-radical detail, 200; Elaine Black, 224–25, 232; District Attorney Matthew Brady, 216; California, 197; *Call-Bulletin* apes *Chronicle*, 197–98; Robert Cantwell, 201; *Chronicle* finds raids funny, 196–97; conservative union labor, 198; Miriam Allen De Ford, 201; Ex-Service Men's League, 194; Finnish hall, 197; Superior Court Judge I. M. Golden, 232; Industrial Association, 199; Industrial Workers of the World, 218; International Labor Defense, 195, 224; Harry Jackson, 224, 232; Judge Lazarus, 217, 231–32; longshoremen's strike kitchen, 194; Mission Workers Neighborhood House, 195; MWIU, 192; National Guard, 192; Neylan, 199; Open Forum Club, 218; purpose, 193–94; John Rogers, 224; Rossi, 201; San Jose radicals, 197; secret Communist meeting, 224; Evelyn Seeley, 195; Judge George Steiger, 216, 224, 232; teamsters, 198; George P. West, 231; *Western Worker*, 194; Joseph Wilson, 224; Workers' Open forum, 196
Red scare, 241, 246 n.1, 252 n.20; Bridges, 243; Brody, 244; Darcy's claims, 241; employers and allies, 241; Larrowe,

243; MWIU, 242; Nelson, syndicalist action, 243; Quin, 242; revival of ILA, 242; *Waterfront Worker*, 242–43

Reichert, Rabbi Irving F., 61

Resner report on law enforcement, 91, 94, 95, 233

Reynolds, Judge Charles A., 83, 215

Ridley, E. L., Seattle hiring plan, 50

Riggers' and Stevedores' Association, 20, 30, 47; founding, 20

Roger, Will, 180

Rolph, Mayor James, 26

Rolstad, Oscar E., 159

Roosevelt, Eleanor, 190–91

Roosevelt, President Franklin Delano, 9, 79, 81, 83, 87, 219; Howe's estimate, 180; McIntyre report, 210; New Deal, 11; Perkins reports, 179; press opposition, 74; recovery bill, 59; signs Public Resolution No. 44, 137; victory, inauguration, 56

Rosenthal, Joe, 151

Rossi, Mayor Angelo, 15, 63, 106, 122, 135–37, 227 (*see also* Red raids); announces end of general strike, 222; broadens powers, 180; claims emergency powers, 172; seeks postponement, 142

Roth, Ed, 45

Roush, Joseph M., 103, 150

Rukeyser, Merryle S., 190

Ryan, Joseph P., 49, 58, 63, 66, 77, 78, 81, 84, 122, 129, 140, 214; arrives San Francisco May 24, 109; on maritime union settlement, 110; May 28 agreement, 111–12; offers proposal to northwest locals, 112

Sailors' Union of the Pacific (SUP), 101

San Francisco Chronicle, 74

San Francisco Labor Council, 9; anti-communist resolution, 132; Blue book union, 46; condemns Merriam, National Guard, 155; Strike Strategy Committee formed, 155

Scharrenberg, Paul, 48, 58, 101, 131, 158

Schlesinger, Arthur J., Jr., 55

Schmidt, Henry, 10, 12, 41, 58, 63, 81, 101, 111, 114, 117, 144, 148, 150; aftermath, 240; picket parade clash, 93; remembers Bryan, 44

Schrimpf, Henry, 113

Schwerin, R. P., 25

Seamen, harsh treatment of, 98

Section 7(a), 58, 60, 65, 73, 137

Shelley, John F., 170

Sherman, P. Tecumseh, 178

Ship clerks, 160

Shipowners' Association of the Pacific Coast, 100, 234

Shipping industry code, 73; hearings, 66

Shoemaker, John, 105

Shoup, Paul, 73

Sinclair, Upton, 31, 196

Singer, A. J., 51

Slobodek, Mitchell, 56–57

Smith, Seattle Mayor Charles, 121, 74, 175, 183

Speed-up, 40–41

Sperry, Howard S., 11, 13, 14, 149, 236

Spooner, Bill, 171

Steamship companies offer bargaining, 164

Steiger, Judge George, 216, 224, 229

Stern, Boris, 37, 50, 73, 76, 146, 209; joint hiring plan, 67

Storie, William, 73, 118, 134

Strikebreakers, Eliot on, 92; employers' rights, 92; Oakland strikers board Oregon Maru, 104; Portland Strikers face, 104; San Francisco, 88–90, 91; San Pedro, 89, 90–91; strikers' claim, 92; University of Washington, 91

Strike Strategy Committee, 155–57; proposes General Strike Committee, 168

Strike, longshoremen's, 1916, 24–27; 1919, 28–30; Portland, 27; Seattle, 27; Tacoma, 27; aftermath, 17–19; begins May 9, 88–98; convention-ordered strike vote March 7, 80; gentlemen's agreement, April 3, 83–87; June 16 agreement, 123–26; March 23 walkout postponed, 81; May 28 agreement, 110–12; May 28 agreement rejected, 112; plan to open ports: Portland, Tacoma, Seattle, Los Angeles, 128–29; response in San Francisco, Portland, San Pedro, 88; return to work, 234–35; settlement, 17; strike vote, 67; teamsters boycott docks, 96; teamsters refuse to handle cargo worked by strikebreakers, 118; unaffected by red raids, 202; vote on coastwide arbitration, 230; vote on strike, 86

Strike, maritime: dead, injured, 236; workdays given up, 236

Strike, Market Street Railway, 176, 184, 212–13, 223

Strike, seamen's, 11; 1921, 32, 99; aftermath, 17–19; asked redress 1933, 101; ends strike, 31, 235, 236; ISU votes strike, 101; MEBA joins strike, 102; MM&P joins strike, 102; representation election, 233; return to work, 234–35; settlement, 17; shipowners offer bargaining, 164; shipowners agree to arbitration, 229; shipping code hearings, 102

St. Sure, J. Paul, 170, 185, 229

Tacoma Central Labor Council, threatens general strike, 89

Teamsters: East Bay walk out, 165; July 11 meeting, 164–65; June 7 meeting, 118–19; May 13 meeting, 95; Oakland, Portland, Seattle, refuse to handle struck cargo, 89; refuse to work cargo handled by strikebreakers, 118; strike, 1901, 22–24; vote strike July 8, 157–58; vote to boycott docks, 96; vote to return, 229

Tear gas, 102–3

Thirty-hour week, 59

Thousand-dollar vagrants, 217, 232–33

Trade Union Unity League (TUUL), 57

United Licensed Officers, 88

United Mine Workers, 60

U.S. Shipping Board, 99

Vandeleur, Edward H., 154, 168–69, 180–81, 184, 191, 209, 210, 227

Vizzard, J. F., 229

Wage cut, 1932, 56–57

Wagner, U.S. Senator Robert F., 67, 186, 226

Walthers, Alex, 28, 160

Waterfront Employers Union: accepts arbitration, 164; agrees to meet union committee, 78; asks Industrial Association intervention, 120; Blue Book agreement, 61; cut restored, 67; employers' strike plan, 75; formation of, 25; in longshoremen's strike, 1916, 26–27; in longshoremen's strike, 1919, 29–30; pays for teargas, 101; Plant elected president, 75; police protection, 76; restates position, 80; signs agreements with Blue Book union, 45; strikebreaker recruiting office, 93; and strikebreakers, 88–90, 235

Waterfront Worker, 30, 34, 36, 40–41, 54, 56, 64, 242–43; MWIU help, 58; program, 57, 64; policy turnaround, 9, 63

Waterfront Workers Federation, 25

West, George, 199

Western Worker, 13

WEU in 1919 longshoremen's strike, 29–30

Wheeler, Charles, 194

Wobblies, 18. See also Industrial Workers of the World

Young Communist League, 113